UNDERSTANDING STUDENT LEARNING

Understanding Student Learning

NOEL J. ENTWISTLE and PAUL RAMSDEN

CROOM HELM
London & Canberra
NICHOLS PUBLISHING COMPANY
New York

© 1983 N.J. Entwistle and P. Ramsden
Croom Helm Ltd, Provident House, Burrell Row,
Beckenham, Kent
Croom Helm Australia, P.O. Box 391, Manuka,
ACT 2603 Australia

British Library Cataloguing in Publication Data

Entwistle, N.J.
    Understanding student learning.
    1. Learning, Psychology of
    I. Title   II. Ramsden, P.
    370.15'23   LB1051

    ISBN 0-7099-0921-7

First published in the United States of America 1982
by Nichols Publishing Company, Post Office Box 96, New York,
NY 10024

Library of Congress Cataloging in Publication Data

Entwistle, Noel.
    Understanding student learning.

    Includes bibliographical references and index.
    1. Learning. 2. Study, Method of. I. Ramsden, Paul.
II. Title.
LB1060.E55 1983   370.15'23   83-11443
ISBN 0-89397-171-5

Printed and bound in Great Britain
by Billing & Sons Limited, Worcester.

CONTENTS

FOREWORD

by William G. Perry Jr.
Professor of Education, Emeritus,
Harvard University

        The authors of this book invite you to accompany
them in the search for an understanding of how
college students learn.   Fifty years have proved
that this understanding will be complex and hard to
find.   Yet the goal is worthy of such heroic
strategies of search and subtle tactics of
divination as this book reports.   I share these
authors' conviction that success in this search may
enhance the quality of our civilization through the
improvement of advanced teaching.
        Professors of Arts and Sciences on both sides
of the Atlantic long shared a conviction that all
the arts are subject to intellectual analysis - all
the arts but one: that of teaching in higher
education.   This art was held sacred to the individual.   The good lecturer was one who knew his
subject and gave a clear exposition of it enlivened
by his own personal style.   Though many a con-
scientious lecturer wondered how so many students
managed not to learn what he explained so clearly,
he had little to comfort him but the thought that
students differ in their aptitude.   For shaping his
teaching, he had few resources to call upon beyond
his own experiences of having been taught.
        The recent economic necessity to attract
students and 'retain' them - especially competitive
in the United States - has forced the issues into
the open.   It is now legitimate to concede that
some college teaching may be susceptible of improvement - even perhaps one's own.   There has followed
a wave of 'Faculty Development Programs', the
assumption being that the way to improve teaching is
to get in there and improve it.   Much university
teaching has been so impoverished that even these
direct methods have brought some results and won the
gratitude of teachers who had worried in secret.

But in these programs the TV camera and the 'teaching hints' have commonly focused solely on the <u>teacher's presentation</u>. The students have then been allowed to evaluate the results with scales that ask 'Are the lectures well organized?'

Rarely does the evaluation form ask the student 'Did this course give you an opportunity to organize your thoughts about the subject?' The very form of the evaluation itself therefore confirms the students in a Lockean assumption about education in which their responsibility is to be passive recipients of the teacher's art. Such teachers' arts as clarity, organization and illustration are indeed open to analysis and improvement in their own right with only implicit reference to students. But I was once on the staff of a war-time course in celestial navigation in which every improvement in the lucidity of our exposition, beyond a certain point, was accompanied by a deterioration in most students' capacity to solve navigational problems. When we cleverly pretended befuddlement at critical moments and asked the students to bail us out, the result gave us confidence that it would be safe to go to sea with them.

The present authors assume boldly that the sole purpose of teaching is to facilitate learning. They assume that learning, well organized or not, is done by the student. They state openly their hope that once we understand more about how different students learn, we can help them to learn better. But who are 'we'? 'Study-counsellors' or 'educationists' like myself? The authors trust, as I do, that as professors of Arts and Sciences come to understand more about students' ways of learning, they will the better assist the learning; in short, they will teach better.

We are back to a prior question. Do we not know how students learn, or should learn, already? We once thought so. In 1942 I composed a manual of 'Effective Study Methods' for freshmen in a small college. Years later I discovered that my great-grandfather had composed in 1842 an identical manual for students in an academy in his parish. His language differed from mine in being quaint, but otherwise the handbooks were identical from their emphasis on principle to the inclusion of a ruled calendar on the back for the students' convenience in designing a schedule of their time. It is a commentary on the slow growth of knowledge in the field that both of these manuals were ahead of their own day - my ancestor's because he was original,

mine because I had at hand a decade of a movement
called 'Guided Study' or 'Supervised Study'.
What was radical in both manuals was that each contained one small concession to the realities of
student experience: we both acknowledged that life
seldom conformed to the boundaries of a rigid
schedule, making the schedule a source of such overwhelming guilt that moral survival required its
consignment to the waste-basket. We each suggested,
instead, that the student keep a log-book of reality
and we offered fictitious and only slightly idealized
examples of how such schedules-in-the-past-tense
might read.

Apart from this small comfort, our manuals were
probably as useful, useless, and disruptive, as any
others.   In the forties and fifties researchers made
the stunning discovery that the explication of
'principles and procedures of effective study' was
largely redundant: most students knew them in
advance; they simply did not follow them.   Such a
negative finding of mere research was of course not
enough to stop established practitioners of study-
coaching like myself.   Some students seemed to
benefit from our efforts.   ,

But we could not quiet our curiosity.   In
what ways did these 'some' students differ from other
students?   Did other students learn best in ways othe
than those outlined in our catechism of principles?
These simple, fateful questions then multiplied, burst
the boundaries of the field and went questing in all
directions at once.   Relevant variables revealed
themselves to researchers in individual differences
in personality, motivation, styles of perception and
cognition, and manners of 'information processing',
all qualitative differences well-nigh dissolving
the global notion of 'aptitude'.

These variations of mind and temperament obser-
vable in individual learners were found to interact
(as the folklore had always known) with the character
of the several disciplines: qualitative vs. quantitative, concrete vs. abstract, analytic vs. synthetic,
ambiguous vs. unambiguous, hierarchical vs. con-
tiguous and so on.   Viewed as characteristics of
the several disciplines, however, these variables
proved to be unstable.   Not only did they vary
from department to department and course to course
within a discipline but they varied, as the students
well knew, with the way a given course was taught.
The search now entered the social and institutional
context in which the learning was carried on.   Here
differences appeared in level of performance demanded,

procedures of assessment, fixedness and flexibility
in the guidelines for action, degrees and quality
of personal attention in the relation of teacher
and learner. These variables, in turn, were found
to reflect assumptions about the nature of knowledge-
ability defining the context of a classroom or
institution. Here the search has led into realms
of epistemology and the sociology of knowledge.

It is into the matrix of these variations of
learners, subjects and contexts that the present
authors take you. That they work successfully with
all three kinds of variables at once is enough to
put them at the forefront of the field; but their
trail opens fresh vistas through their creative
synthesis of disparate methods of inquiry.

First of all they have combined both quantitative and qualitative modes of inquiry. They
modestly claim only to have 'alternated' these modes,
but you will probably feel that they have made a
productive synthesis through interweaving of quantitative analysis of questionnaires with the qualitative
assessment of interviews. (The latter assessments,
contributed by the Gothenburg researchers, had been
subjected to strict quantifiable discipline. I
would urge you to accord these data a status of
'objectivity' of their own quite comparable to that
of factor analysis of questionnaires. This is a
claim the authors are almost, but not quite, ready
to make).

In their assessment of social contexts, also,
the authors have built on the phenomenological foundations of the Gothenburg group by focusing on
students' perceptions rather than on the observations
of outside researchers in which relevance has so long
been sacrificed to the assumption of objectivity.
Here, too the range in different students' perceptions
of the same context has led back fruitfully to
individual differences.

In keeping with these modes of inquiry the
authors have subordinated the conventional input-
output model of research to focus on the delineation
of process. The old preoccupation with students'
ultimate performance following different methods of
instruction has too often obscured the rich variety
of the intervening learning behaviours and the
influence on these behaviours of the learner's antici-
pation of the very means by which performance will be
assessed.

The authors synthesize these modes of inquiry
and foci of attention in a way that provides heuristic
power beyond the sum of the parts. I shall not

venture to summarize the steps of their search or
their findings. You may find it helpful, however, if
I raise certain questions that will doubtless rise
of themselves as you read. By having them in mind
in advance, you may be prepared to appreciate from
the outset the challenges the authors have faced
and the skill they have brought to their tasks.

First of all, about nomenclature. It is
inevitable in so complex a field, drawing on research
findings suddenly emerging in diverse sources, that
terms and concepts should be unstable. Consider
such terms as 'cognitive style', 'perceptual style',
'learning style', 'learning strategies', 'approach',
'orientation', 'study pattern', 'learning skill',
'learning process','strategic approach' or simply
'way'. I find little consensus among researchers
about the conceptual referents of such terms or
about the relationships among them. The authors
of this book cannot be immune to these difficulties.
Indeed you may find their struggles to keep any
one of these terms in one place as illuminating as
their frequent successes.

Let us suppose now that the authors succeed in
keeping such terms as 'meaning orientation', 'deep
approach', 'surface orientation', 'holistic approach'
etc. in stable reference to distinguishable processes
characterizing the ways different students learn.
If we then assume that such learner-characteristics
(singly or in constellations) tend to remain stable
over time in individuals we will find it appropriate
to speak of different 'types' of students. The
preponderance of research on 'learning styles' to date
can be taken to justify the assumption of stability
of a large number of learner traits. These findings
provide the foundations of a number of typologies
classifying learners by various constellations of
traits posited as stable over time. This evidence
commends us to think in terms of types of students,
each type characterized by abiding preferences for
proceeding in a certain way in address to learning
tasks, even though these tasks may differ. Indeed
some recent studies have reported that when college
students specialize in subject-matter congruent with
their preferred styles, they intensify their preference and narrow their variability in response to
differing tasks.

We now face a serious dilemma. If we accept
the evidence for stability, we should simply add the
new findings about learner types to our historic
efforts to identify students' strengths and steer
them toward the specialties most congenial to them.

We could do no more.

On the other hand the authors of this book explicitly state their hope that the understandings of research into students' styles will help us to teach students to learn the better <u>how to learn</u>. Presumably, since all students must learn in more than a single discipline, they should learn to vary their learning strategies in keeping with the nature of various tasks. How can we support such a hope? Are we to imagine that learner 'type', though stable, is not, somehow, immutable? Or are we to suppose that stability and flexibility occur at different levels and that we can help students develop variations <u>within</u> their preferred learning mode without violating its integrity?

The authors of this book did not intend to address this dilemma directly. They live with the question as a tension pervading the field, and they offer their advances as contributions toward a later resolution. As reader, however, you may find yourself pondering the issue. I want therefore to share some questions about the assumptions that create the question.

First, a small technical concern regarding the measures from which the finding of 'stability' of 'type' or 'style' derives. How much time is the respondent allowed on each test? A leading researcher recently told me "The differences in the means of the types in our population were small and we could only get them if we put the students under heavy time pressure, stop-watch and all". Could it be that, denied the opportunity to survey the nature of the tasks, the students are artifically limited to some most frequently used 'best bet' approach? If so, the test may in fact reveal a student's 'best bet' way of learning, but it cannot demonstrate that this way remains invariant when the student perceives differences in tasks. Such a bias of measurement may be compounded when analysis is limited to students scoring at the extremes of a trait dimension. May not flexibility of style be greatest in the students scoring nearer the mean? You will be grateful to the authors for letting you know just how they designed each inquiry.

On a broader scale, most striking is the authors' inclusion in their opening chapter of descriptions of the intellectual development of students in the college years. One of these descriptions starts with tripartite typology on a dimension of impulsivity and rationality. It then traces the convergence over time of students at the extremes

oward the balanced ideal type at the mean.   The
econd description of development traces the way
tudents evolve more complex forms of thought to
ccommodate their perception of increased complexity,
ncertainty and ambiguity.   In this evolution the
tudents sequentially revise their conceptions of
nowledge, their sense of their role as learners,
nd their expectations of teachers.   Both of
hese descriptions were derived from longitudinal
tudies of relatively small samples extending over
ears.

The authors point out that their own undertaking,
emarkable for its scope and depth, provides neither
unds nor time for longitudinal research.   Yet they
ere so generous as to give space to these descriptions
f student development, leaving it to the reader to
peculate on the relevance of such developmental
ssues to conceptualizations of student types.   As
he author of one of these descriptions of development,
 join them in hoping that you will indeed speculate.
he question is unavoidable: "Could a certain con-
tellation of learner-characteristics represent less
n enduring student-type and more a moment of
volution in a student's notion of what learning is
ll about?"

You will of course find more issues to ponder
han those I am sketching.   What fascinates me is
he way they all seem to converge at each marker
he authors establish in their quest.   I end with
he example.

In their search for traits distinguishing 'deep'
earners and 'surface' learners, the authors discovered
 type of studentswho seemed to be game-players.
hese seemed concerned first of all with out-guessing
he ultimate assessment, and they pumped their
nstructors in the service of this goal.   The point
f it all seemed to be, for them, the score.   The
uthors named this type 'strategic'.   I confess a
eservation regarding this use of the term to label
n address to social context since the authors also
se it in its usual sense to refer to approaches to
earning in address to subject matter.   In any case,
heir first overall analysis showed that students
vincing this 'strategic approach' were among the
surface' learners.   Characteristically, the authors
d not stop with this sensible observation but con-
nued to test it with the interplay of factor analysis
d ratings of interviews.   This analysis differentiated
 sizable minority of the 'strategic' group who emerged
s deep learners.

This fine discrimination involves the very

FOREWORD

foundations of education. Could it be that by
paying careful attention to what a good teacher has
on his mind some students can learn to read and learn
with deep comprehension? As teachers, this is our
only hope.
 We have been hoping it for centuries. We know
from our daily experience with 'some' students that
the hope is well founded. These authors bring us
to the very brink of the scientific confirmation of
the hope with modern research tools. But they are
doing far more than confirming what we feel we know
already. They are delineating the ways those 'some'
students learn and how they learn to learn. So
also, then, for those 'other' students. Only from
such delineations we can hope to expand 'some'
students to 'most'.
 Students sometimes speak for themselves about
this motion. In the later chapters of this book
the authors quote from students' interviews. In
these, some students report the excitement of
realization' - the discovery that learning can be
more than memorization, even meaningful. We can feel
how near the authors have come to the goal of their
search.
 They do not pretend to have found it. Indeed,
we may feel that they have been so dedicated in their
care for precise delineation of each clue in the
search that they have been reluctant to stand back,
as we can, to see how close they may have come to
the place where all the pieces will fall together.
 Such modesty is appropriate to the difficulties;
the ultimate synthesis must include identification
of: those strategies or styles of learning so inte-
gral to persons that to learn other ways would be
inefficient or violating; those styles or strategies
which seem readily learnable; those aspects of
development that provide or accompany such readiness;
those instruments which best reveal these variables;
and finally, those conditions of institutional and
teaching context - as the various students perceive
them - that best facilitate the students' learning
and their learning how to learn.
 When we thank these authors for advancing us so
far in this search, they will I am sure reiterate
their heavy debt to other researchers in Britain,
Sweden, Switzerland and North America. They offer
this book as an invitation to international collaboration in the search.

Watertown, Massachusetts
March 1983

PREFACE

This book is an abridged and less technical version of the Final Report on a five-year Social Science Research Council research programme begun in 1976. The full report on Research Grant HR 3881 has been lodged with the British Library at Boston Spa. The purpose of the research programme was to investigate students' approaches to learning, and to determine the extent to which these reflected the effects of teaching and assessment demands rather than representing relatively stable characteristics of the individual learners.

The research programme was directed by Noel Entwistle, then Professor of Educational Research at the University of Lancaster. The Senior Research Officer working full-time on the programme throughout its duration was Paul Ramsden. For the first two years, Maureen Hanley (nee Robertson) worked on the development of the questionnaire on reading academic articles and on the development of the inventory. For the next two years this post was filled by Sarah Morison (nee Burkinshaw). The programme also involved other members of the Institute for Post-Compulsory Education at Lancaster, and we are particularly grateful for the continuing discussions we had with Dai Hounsell about our emerging findings. We are also grateful for the interest and enthusiastic help given by Patrick Thomas of Brisbane College of Advanced Education who was visiting Research Fellow at Lancaster in 1978/79.

The qualitative analysis of the interview data, and the main survey of student approaches to learning and perceptions of courses, were carried out by Paul Ramsden. He has the main responsibility for chapters 7 8 and 9, which have been written up more fully as a doctoral thesis.

Sarah Morison undertook the experiments and

produced the draft reports which formed the basis of chapters 5 and 6.

The camera-ready copy from which this book has been produced was typed by Jane Moore. Our gratitude for her accuracy and fortitude in coping with this extensive task, in addition to her normal secretarial duties, can be well imagined. Her forbearance in dealing with our last minute amendments and additions is much appreciated.

ACKNOWLEDGEMENTS

We are grateful to John Wiley and Sons Ltd. for permission to reproduce extracts from 'Styles of Learning and Teaching' by N.J. Entwistle published in 1981.

Chapter One

STUDENT LEARNING IN ITS CONTEXT

Higher education is a large and expensive undertaking. Its effects are felt by all of us.
There are currently over half a million full-time
students in the British system of education which
builds on, and goes beyond, sixth-form studies and
their equivalent. A sizeable proportion of the
country's wealth flows into the sixty-seven
universities and polytechnics which dominate this
sector. Many of the students who graduate from
these institutions will eventually occupy some of
the most powerful and prestigious positions in our
society. Whatever contractions the system may face
in the 1980s, no-one would wish to argue that an
understanding of what goes on in higher education
is unimportant.
    It comes as something of a surprise to realise
that, as recently as twenty years ago, there was
hardly any research into higher education in
Britain. Writing in 1972, the editors of a
symposium of articles on research in this field
could say that

    a decade ago, the universities and colleges of
    Britain were open to the accusation that they
    did research on almost every topic but them-
    selves ... If they were aware of the need for
    a better understanding both of fundamental
    principles in teaching and learning and of
    human relationships in the quadrangle, they
    did singularly little about it. Ten years
    ago a book of this kind would necessarily have
    been very thin. (Butcher and Rudd, 1972).

    Research into higher education has since
established itself in this country, as the founding

1

of new journals and periodicals (such as The Times
Higher Education Supplement and Studies in Higher
Education) demonstrates. It is interesting to examine Butcher and Rudd's selection of papers; they
give a flavour of the developing pattern of research.
There are papers on the objectives and administration of higher education, including the academic
profession and its role; discussions of economic
and planning issues; articles on student protest;
papers concerned with development and change in the
student (including, for example, the effects of
counselling); articles on experiment and change in
teaching methods; and there is a section on the
selection and academic performance of students.
With the possible exception of the chapter on
student protest, this list gives a good summary of
the kinds of research which have taken place since,
as well as before, 1972.

At the heart of higher education is the three-
way transaction between the student, his teacher,and
the material being studied. Students in higher
education are expected to learn complex subject-
matter and develop independence of judgment in the
course of a dialogue with their teachers. But
little direct attention has been given by researchers to the process of student learning and the
effects of teaching on it. Although student performance - measured in terms of degree results - and
student wastage have been examined, how the student
learns has not, at least until very recently.
Although research into teaching methods is well represented - and has expanded greatly since 1972 -
inquiries relating the teaching to students' learning
are much less common. The research tradition in
the field of higher education has touched on its
central triangle but has barely begun to enter it.

How are we to explain this lack of interest?
One of the reasons may be the dominant view of
lecturers in higher education that success and failure is the responsibility of the individual student.
Up to a point, this idea is a very reasonable one.
It stems partly from the concern for the individual
which distinguishes the British higher education
system from its counterparts in other countries. It
also has its roots in the experiences of the lecturers themselves when they were undergraduates. They
were, by definition, very successful students. The
general view seems to be that there are few "good"
students - students able to become deeply involved
in a subject and evaluate it critically - and many
weak or mediocre ones (see Entwistle and Percy,1974,

for evidence of this view). Lecturers tend to
think that the context or environment of student
learning is not of great importance: they attribute
success or failure to the characteristics of the
student, not to their teaching.

As a consequence we know remarkably little
about the effects of lecturers' teaching, assessment,
and course organization on student learning.
Students in British universities and polytechnics
spend a good deal of their time in one or two
academic departments; it seems quite possible that
the way students approach studying is influenced by
the way the departments are run. What are the
differing demands made on the students by learning
tasks in both arts and science departments, and how
do students respond to these demands? What makes
one department a "better" place to learn than
another? Students themselves are clearly aware
that departments differ in their attitudes to them,
just as they recognize that some lecturers are more
effective at putting over their subject than others.
Is student learning genuinely not a function of how
well lecturers teach? (If not, the implications
require at least some thought.)

The emphasis on individual attributes of students in the explanation of academic success and
failure has been complemented by the research designs
which have typically been used. A rather simple input-output model of students entering university
with a bundle of characteristics and leaving it with
or without a good degree has been adopted. The
results of attempts to predict academic success by
this method cannot be said to be unequivocal.
Correlations between performance and student characteristics - personality traits, previous evidence of
ability, scores in intelligence tests - are often
disappointingly low. It seems that something
happens during the period of the student's university
experience which traditional research has not examined.

All this does not mean, of course, that individual differences between students should be ignored.
Students enter higher education with different
interests, expectations, motivations, and personalities. It would be surprising if the ways they
study were not related to their individual preferences. But it is quite another thing to argue that
there is one best combination of individual characteristics which leads to success, or that "good" and
"weak" students remain unchanged by the teaching and
courses they encounter. Individual differences and

the university environment interact subtly and con-
tinuously, and a proper understanding of student
learning needs to take both things into account.
   This book contains the findings of the largest
programme of research into student learning ever
carried out in Britain, in a form which we hope will
be accessible to students, lecturers, and all who
have an interest in higher education.   We hope it
will be seen partly as a contribution towards a
changing emphasis in research into higher education.
Our focus is on the process of student learning itself, and on the way it is influenced for better or
worse by the environment in which it takes place.
The approach derives much of its impetus from the
seminal work of a group of researchers at Gothenburg
University in Sweden, whose research will be described in the next Chapter.   Qualitative methods,
such as semi-structured interviews, are one of the
hallmarks of this perspective.   More traditional
quantitative techniques can, as we shall see, also
be incorporated without losing sight of the main
strengths of the approach;   indeed, they can enrich
it.   This perspective cuts across disciplines: insights from sociology and anthropology complement
psychological viewpoints.   The interest is not so
much in the conventional outcomes of higher education - degree performance and numbers of students
as a proportion of resources invested - as in what
learning means to the students.   This kind of research examines different conceptions of subject-
matter and differences in how students tackle learning tasks, and looks at how these differences arise
and how they are related to the level of understanding reached.   How do students approach every day
academic tasks like reading, problem solving, and
assessment?   Why do they seem to prefer very
different approaches?   How do students' ways of
learning in different subjects differ?   How is their
learning influenced by personal preferences and the
tasks and teaching they encounter?   Which ways of
studying are most likely to bring success and satisfaction?
   Many of these questions start from the point of
view of the student, rather than that of the teacher
or researcher.   We shall argue that they offer an
understanding of the reality of student learning
which other perspectives cannot.   The answers to
these issues also have some far-reaching practical
implications.   Many of the findings of this research have immediate relevance to lecturers who
wish to improve their teaching, and for students who

want to improve how they study.   There are also
important implications for increasing the efficiency
of learning in the costly business of higher
education.

Chapter Two

INTELLECTUAL DEVELOPMENT AND APPROACHES TO STUDYING

The research programme at Lancaster grew out of
previous work there which had been funded by the
Joseph Rowntree Memorial Trust. The main purpose
of that six-year study, which began in 1968, was to
examine the objectives of lecturers in higher
education in relation to students' academic performance. The research on students divided into two
parts. One was a longitudinal survey designed to
identify student attributes which might predict
their subsequent degree performances. The other
was an interview study intended to explore students'
reasons for entering higher education and their experiences of it. The experience gained in this
study substantially influenced the planning of the
new research programme. On the one hand, it had
shown the importance of trying to marry qualitative
and quantitative methods of educational research.
On the other, it had shown clearly the limitations
of the input-output model in thinking about higher
education. Relatively stable psychological
characteristics of students proved to be only weakly
related to levels of academic performance. It became clear that greater attention would have to be
placed on study processes and on the context, or
academic environment, within which students learn.
These two directions of research have been
developed out of quite separate sets of literature.
In presenting this report, therefore, the conceptual
basis for the research is also presented separately.
In this chapter the literature relating to intellectual development and approaches to studying is discussed, while research into the academic context of
learning in higher education is introduced in
chapter 7.
The studies which have influenced the work of
the programme are presented largely in historical

6

order, although at least one of these studies was not in fact 'discovered' until quite recently.

LECTURERS' EXPECTATIONS*

Part of the previous work at Lancaster was concerned with lecturers' aims and objectives and with students' experiences of higher education. Lecturers in various academic departments were asked questions about what they expected from 'good' students and what they saw as the characteristics of weaker students. Although there were, of course, great differences in the specific comments of lecturers in contrasting departments, there was an important common thread running through most of the replies. While knowledge and technical skills were expected, students had to be able to use these effectively - to combine and interrelate ideas. Short extracts from the comments of three of the lecturers provide an impression of what, in one way or another, most lecturers were demanding. An English lecturer, for example, said:

"I would be expecting a kind of alertness and openness - that may sound very general. Alert to what? Alert to all the signs of interest or significance in passages of literature. We try to develop their evaluative skills ... to develop the sense of what is the first hand piece of writing and what is purely derivative. .. the prime moral outcome of a literature course (should be the) ability to enter into different individual and social conditions ... to be able to realise what it is like to be somebody else, so that we can properly interact with other people and not always expect them to be mutations of oneself or of one's own culture."**

---

* This section, and parts of other sections, have been taken from Entwistle (1981) <u>Styles of Learning and Teaching</u>, published by Wiley, which contains fuller descriptions of previous research, together with discussions of its psychological bases.

** These interviews were carried out by Keith Percy and have been reported in more detail elsewhere (Entwistle and Percy, 1971; 1974).

A history lecturer saw the need for using evidence effectively, again combined with a form of social awareness.

"History, typically, does involve the assembly of evidence, coming to conclusions about certain problems ... (you tend) to consider (an idea) from all angles with a critical eye. Basically if you're treating it non-academically you tend merely to accept it and then to file it ... (but) then there's going to be no progress or change. Things are not going to move if you merely accept. You've got to scrutinize what you're doing (to see) if the thing cannot be done better."

In the science departments there was, of course, more emphasis on knowledge of facts, but even so there was also a recognition that factual information, in itself, is a rapidly diminishing asset. 'Knowledge' has to be reinterpreted to include

"techniques of analysis, rather than knowledge of facts; knowledge of techniques for finding facts, rather than the facts themselves."

The unifying theme both in the interviews and in the general literature on the aims of university education is that of 'critical thinking', or as Ashby has described it - 'post-conventional thinking'.

"The student (moves) from the uncritical acceptance of orthodoxy to creative dissent over the values and standards of society... (In higher education) there must be opportunities for the intellect to be stretched to its capacity, the critical faculty sharpened to the point where it can change ideas" (Ashby, 1973, pages 147-9).

What evidence is there that students do develop towards the intellectual goal described by lecturers?

RELATIVISTIC REASONING AND THE "REASONABLE ADVENTURER"

Two American interview studies shed light on this question. William Perry (1970) interviewed students once in each of their four years at Harvard or Radcliffe. Through all the transcripts of the interviews there seemed to run a dimension describing the progress students made from dualistic thinking to "contextual relativistic reasoning". Initially some students expected simple 'black and white' explanations in both their courses and their everyday life. Their experience of higher education was in conflict with this expectation; they found inconclusive evidence, alternative theories, and competing value systems. The enormity of this uncertainty challenges fundamental beliefs and values and can be a traumatic shock for some students.

Perry was able to identify nine positions along the dimension of intellectual and ethical development. Independent judges checked his categorizations. His summary of the nine positions is given below.

Position 1: The student sees the world in polar terms of we-right-good vs. other-wrong-bad. Right Answers for everything exist in the Absolute, known to Authority whose role is to mediate (teach) them. Knowledge and goodness are perceived as quantitative accretions of discrete rightnesses to be collected by hard work and obedience (paradigm: a spelling test).

Position 2: The student perceives diversity of opinion, and uncertainty, and accounts for them as unwarranted confusion in poorly qualified Authorities or as mere exercises set by Authority 'so we can learn to find The Answer for ourselves'.

Position 3: The student accepts diversity and uncertainty as legitimate but still temporary in areas where Authority 'hasn't found the Answer yet'. He supposes Authority grades him in these areas on 'good expression' but remains puzzled as to standards.

Position 4: (a) The student perceives legitimate uncertainty (and therefore diversity of opinion) to be extensive and raises it to the status of an unstructured epistemological realm of its own in which 'anyone has a right to his own opinion', a realm which he sets over against Authority's realm where right-wrong still prevails, or (b) the student discovers qualitative contextual relativistic reasoning as a special case of 'what They want' within Authority's realm.

Position 5: The student perceives all knowledge

and values (including authority's) as contextual and relativistic and subordinates dualistic right-wrong functions to the status of a special case, in context.

Position 6: The student apprehends the necessity of orienting himself in a relativistic world through some form of personal Commitment (as distinct from unquestioned or unconsidered commitment to simple belief in certainty).

Position 7: The student makes an initial Commitment in some area.

Position 8: The student experiences the implications of Commitment, and explores the subjective and stylistic issues of responsibility.

Position 9: The student experiences the affirmation of identity among multiple responsibilities and realizes Commitment as an ongoing, unfolding, activity through which he expresses his life style."
(Perry, 1970, pages 9 - 10).

Perry (1978) provides a humorous interpretation of his carefully articulated scheme, in terms of four 'discoveries of the obvious'.

"When we first come into this world, it is obvious that there are authorities and that they know what they are doing, or at least so it seems. They tell us what to do and what not to do, and so they know what they are doing. That is discovery 1.
Discovery 2 is that they do not know what they are doing after all. And since they do not seem to know what they are doing and do not have all the answers, we think, 'Hurray! As soon as I can get out from under their tyranny I'm free, and any opinion is as good as any other, mine included.'
Discovery 3 is that when I get out from under their tyranny I walk smack into a plate-glass wall and find that I am still subject to a tyranny, not of they but of fact. And in that tyranny of reality I discover that, although there are a lot of differences of opinion among reasonable people, not every opinion is as good as any other, including some which I have that are no good at all. And then I have to get to work and start thinking about

all these things ...
  Then I make one more discovery, another
obvious one, that I am faced with the challenge
of affirming myself and my life as a person.
Given so many differences of opinion among
reasonable people, differences which reason
alone cannot resolve, I see that I can never be
sure I am making the 'right' decisions in life.
And yet I must decide. Oh, I have been told
never to make a wrong decision lest I regret it
all my life, but now I see I have no protection
against regret. Unless I am going to weasel
out of really living, I must choose what I believe in and own the consequences, and never
know what lay down the roads I did not take.
I have discovered ... what it means to commit."
(pages 267-8).

  Perry is stressing how students move from the
simplistic acceptance of facts presented by authority, through a period of confusion about the nature
of knowledge and belief, to a recognition that we
need to establish a personal philosophy of life
which is built out of our own interpretation of
relevant evidence, but which recognizes, and is
tolerant of, other people's alternative, even con-
flicting, interpretations of 'reality'.
  A very similar dimension of intellectual development emerged from Roy Heath's (1964) interviews at
Princeton. But he defined it in terms of an ideal
type - the 'reasonable adventurer' - and three distinctive personality types 'the non-committer', 'the
hustler', and 'the plunger'. The contrasting personalities moved along different paths towards the
intellectual pinnacle already scaled by the reasonable adventurer. These personalities were limited
both in their personal relationships and in their
thinking. For example, the non-committer is over-
cautious, while the plunger's "thoughts zip from one
idea to another without apparent connection". The
reasonable adventurer manges to integrate these
apparently contradictory attributes showing

  "the combination of two mental attitudes: the
  curious and the critical. They do not occur
  simultaneously but in alternation. (The
  reasonable adventurer) at times is a 'believer'
  but at other times he is a 'skeptic'. The less
  effective personalities may show tendencies toward one attitude or the other but may not experience the full reach of either". (page 31)

In a moment we shall meet again this description of thinking which brings together competing tendencies to create a whole which is more than the sum of parts.

THEMATIZATION AND CUE CONSCIOUSNESS

One limitation in both Heath's and Perry's research is the lack of any systematic exploration of the ways in which their more intellectually mature students approach everyday learning tasks. The questions asked are general; both Perry and Heath were interested in a whole range of students' experiences, both personal and academic. In contrast a series of studies, carried out mainly at Gothenburg University in Sweden, has examined conceptions of learning and the way students tackle an academic task of central importance in higher education - reading an academic article. The first two investigations demonstrate a connection between approaches to learning and intellectual development.

Saljo (1979) conducted interviews with adults who had differing lengths of formal education. He was interested in their conceptions of learning. One of the main characteristics of people who had either had an extended education, or had taken up studying again in adulthood, was the recognition that there are different types of learning appropriate for different sorts of tasks. For the majority of unsophisticated learners in the sample, learning was 'taken for granted' as involving rote memorization. For those who had experience of higher education, learning had become <u>thematized</u>.

"Learning is something that can be explicitly talked about and discussed and can be the object of conscious planning and analysis. In learning, these people realize that there are, for instance, alternative strategies or approaches which may be useful or suitable in various situations depending on, for example, time available, interest, demands of teachers and anticipated tests." (page 446).

The main distinctions drawn by these more sophisticated learners, besides the importance of context on the approach adopted, were between learning for real life and learning in school or between learning and understanding.

The 'awareness' that these learners show about

the selection of appropriate strategies is similar to the 'cue-consciousness' described by Miller and Parlett (1974) in relation to students' preparation for examinations.

"One group of students talked about the need to be perceptive and receptive to 'cues' sent out by staff - things like picking up hints about exam topics, noticing which aspects of the subject the staff favoured, noticing whether they were making a good impression in a tutorial and so on".   (page 52).

The artificiality of the examination situation, and its effects on learning strategies, is seen clearly by one of the students interviewed in this study.

"What is the purpose of the examination game? It becomes purposeless except for you, because you know you want to get a certain class of degree within the system, but as far as assimilating knowledge properly is concerned, it just doesn't work, because if you play the game properly you're choosing all the time, and not getting an overview because you know there will be a certain question you have to answer" (page 61).

The authors of the study identified two more groups of students. The "cue-deaf" were less sophisticated strategists, not believing that the impression made on staff could affect their results and not picking up hints. The "cue-seekers" were cue conscious in a very active fashion - they went out of their way to make a favourable impression on their lecturers and to buttonhole staff about the exam questions. Miller and Parlett argue that the three groups of students mirror Perry's three main stages of intellectual development (dualistic, rela- tivistic, personal commitment to relativistic reasoning).

READING ACADEMIC ARTICLES

The main series of investigations at Gothenburg, led by Ference Marton, has looked in detail at one of the main types of learning demanded of students - reading, and understanding, academic articles. Marton criticises previous research on prose learn- ing as being so preoccupied with the quantitative

outcome of learning (how many facts and ideas have been remembered), that qualitative aspects of students' understanding of what they have read have been ignored, in spite of the pioneering research of Bartlett (1932). The prose passages have also been trivial in content, short or artificially contrived to facilitate experimental control. Marton examines students' approaches to reading relatively long (1500 words) passages from actual academic articles. These passages are chosen to be intelligible without prior technical knowledge of the subject areas, and to contain a tight logical argument based on the use of detailed supportive evidence. Students are invited, individually, to read the article at their own pace, and in the way they do normally while studying,but they are told that questions about it will be asked afterwards. When students have finished reading, they are interviewed to discover what they have learned and how they approached the task.
   During the interview, the students are first asked a general question of the form, "Well now, perhaps you can tell me about what you've been reading". Students are encouraged, through neutral questioning, to elaborate what they have remembered. They are then asked more specific questions about sections of the text, followed by another general question, with probes, to discover how they had interpreted the instruction to read the article,what their intention was in approaching the task (what they expected to get from the article), and how the experimental situation had affected them (whether they were anxious, for example). Finally, in some of the studies, questions were asked about their normal approach to studying.
   The interviews were tape-recorded and transcribed. Analysis of the lengthy transcripts was difficult and time-consuming. The interviews were initially read through as a whole and then responses to separate questions were examined carefully. In a sense the approach to analysis is similar to the development of 'grounded theory' (Glaser and Strauss, 1967). No explicit theoretical framework is imposed on the data. The responses are examined looking for important consistencies within each transcript on its own, then patterns of response recurring across the interviews are identified (Svensson, 1976). Finally explanatory constructs are hypothetized to facilitate understanding of the students' approaches to learning and levels of outcome (what they remembered).
   This method of analysis puts an enormous

responsibility on the research worker to be guided
by the data without imposing preconceived interpretations. It is, of course, crucial to check
that similar constructs are identified by independent judges. It is extremely unlikely, faced with
a relatively unstructured set of free responses,that
different judges will identify identical explanatory
constructs. In this research, however, there was a
high level of agreement on the categories which were
chosen to describe both the levels of outcome and
the approaches to learning (Svensson, 1977).

There is also great difficulty in communicating
the findings of this type of research. In most
analyses of interview transcripts, the main categories which best describe recurring types of answer
are reported with choice quotes to illustrate them
(as in Perry's study). What Marton and his
colleagues have done is to extend the process of
qualitative analysis much further. Students'
comments are examined more intensively to consider
the implications of consistencies and variabilities
within an individual transcript, as well as between
transcripts. The categories within each explanatory
construct that emerges are then delimited - the
boundary of meaning surrounding each category is explored in terms of the differing emphases or aspects
mentioned by individual students. The quotations
included are thus very carefully selected to provide
a definition of the various categories within each
explanatory construct. The instances used to de-
limit the categories can then form the basis on
which independent judges can assign transcripts to
response categories (Marton, 1975). Of course,
when it comes to publishing findings from such
studies, there is rarely sufficient space available
to make fully clear the detailed way in which categories are delimited, and there is a danger that the
results will be treated as little more than impressionistic. In fact this form of qualitative analysis now has its own checks and balances, its own
systematic procedures, to produce findings which have
their own rigour and their own form of scientific
objectivity.

Following this analytic procedure Marton and
his colleagues were able to describe important
regularities both in the qualitatively different
outcomes of learning (what students were able to recall about the articles) and in their approaches to
learning.

LEVELS OF UNDERSTANDING

The problem with categorizing the outcome of learning is that it necessarily depends on the particular article read. But as long as the article is appropriately difficult and presents a clear argument supported by evidence, it is possible to use a general classificatory scheme for describing differences in the levels of understanding reached by students in these experiments. It is usually possible to identify four types of response (Fransson, 1977; Säljö, 1975).

A. Conclusion-orientated, detailed

The student summarizes the author's main argument, shows how evidence is used to support the argument, and explains the thoughts and reflections used to reach personal understanding of that argument.

B. Conclusion-orientated, mentioning

Again there is an adequate summary of the main argument, but the use of evidence or personal experience to support that argument is not made clear.

C. Description, detailed

The student gives an adequate list of the main points presented in the article, but fails to show how these are developed into an argument.

D. Description, mentioning

A few isolated points are made, some relevant, others irrelevant. At the bottom end of this category an impression of confusion and misunderstanding is given by the student's comments.

When students talked about their approach to, and process of, reading the article, again a simple distinction occurred. Some students adopted a deep approach. They started with the intention of understanding the meaning of the article, interacted actively with the author's arguments (relating them to previous knowledge and their own experience) and tried to see to what extent the author's conclusions were justified by the evidence presented. Other students seemed to rely almost exclusively on a surface approach. Their intent was to memorize the

16

parts of the information they considered to be important, guided by the type of questions they anticipated being asked subsequently. These students were thus constrained by the specific task requirements, and anxious about that constraint. While these descriptions are clearly ideal types and few students will show all the characteristics attributed to either type, when students were assigned to one or other category on the basis of one of the main defining features it proved possible to make such an allocation with high inter-rater reliability for most, and sometimes for all, students. This distinction between deep and surface approaches to learning thus appears to be a powerful form of categorization for differences in learning strategies. Svensson (1975) independently read the transcripts and although his categorization coincided closely with that of Marton, there were differences in emphasis and terminology which are worth noting. His categories were 'holistic' and 'atomistic' which represented different ways in which students organized or structured their responses in describing what they remembered. The 'holistic' approach involves integrating the main parts into a structured whole. The 'atomistic' approach concentrates on aggregating the parts without interrelating or integrating them. These initial categorizations allowed the relationships between approach and learning to be investigated. Marton used what he calls a disjunctive method of assigning students' responses to categories. He classified the approaches used by students as deep or surface if they showed at least one clear indication of either of these approaches. Where the approach was unclear a third category was used. The relationship Marton established can be seen in Table 2.1.

Table 2.1 RELATIONSHIP BETWEEN LEVEL OF OUTCOME AND APPROACH TO LEARNING (from Marton and Säljö, 1976a)

Level of Understanding	Approach to Learning		
	Deep	Not Clear	Surface
High	9	6	1
Low	0	1	13

A deep approach is thus, at least in this small sample, clearly related to a deep level of understanding. Marton also found that the deep approach was associated with better recall of detail, particularly after a five week interval. Svensson (1977) has argued that this relationship should be thought of not simply as statistically significant, but as to some extent inevitable. While it is possible for a student adopting a deep approach to fail to reach a deep level of understanding through lack of previous knowledge or lack of attention or effort, it is impossible for a student adopting a surface approach ever to reach a deep level of understanding, as long as he persists with that approach. If deep understanding depends on being able to relate evidence and conclusion, a student's approach must necessarily have included this activity if deep understanding has been reached.

FACTORS AFFECTING THE APPROACH TO STUDYING

The next step in the Gothenburg studies was to examine the link between a student's approach to learning in the experiment and the normal approach to studying, based on the final question in the interview. Svensson (1977) was able to detect deep and surface approaches to normal studying and to compare these both with the experiment and with the examination performance of the students at the end of their first year. Table 2.2 shows that there were close relationships in both these ways. 23 out of 30 students were categorized as taking the same approach in the experiment and in normal studying. Of the students classified as being deep in both, 90 per cent had passed in all their examinations, while only 23 per cent of the doubly 'surface' students had this level of success.

Table 2.2   RELATIONSHIP BETWEEN APPROACHES TO LEARNING
AND STUDYING, AND EXAMINATION PERFORMANCE
(FROM SVENSSON, 1977)

Cognitive Approach		Examination Performance		Total
Experiment	Normal Studies	Passed All	Some Failure	
Surface	Surface	3	10	13
Deep	Deep	9	1	10
Deep	Surface	4	2	6
Surface	Deep	1	0	1

Svensson went on to show that students adopting a deep approach also tended to spend longer in
studying.   Again this relationship is almost inevitable.   Students who study their subjects deeply
are likely to find the material more interesting and
easier to understand.   Long hours of work become no
hardship then.   Students who adopt a surface
approach are concentrating on an inappropriate
technique of learning - rote memorization.   It takes
a long time to cover books in this way, and it is a
tedious and unrewarding activity.   Thus, eventually,
students who persist with the surface approach are
likely to do less and less work and eventually fail
their examinations.   Svensson (1977) reported the
results of one examination in which 9 out of 11
students adopting a deep approach to normal studying
also did three or more hours' independent work a day.
All 9 passed the examination.   Nineteen students
adopted a surface approach and 8 of them, even in
the first year, admitted to working less than three
hours a day.   All 8 failed the examination.
In another study Säljö was interested in
whether students' approaches to studying were affected by the type of questions they were given in tests
(Marton and Säljö, 1976b).   He used two comparable
groups of students and three separate passages of
prose.   The students were asked to read each of
these passages, and after each passage they were
asked a series of questions.   After each of the

first two passages one group was given questions
designed to encourage a deep approach - attention to
the underlying meaning. The other group was given
specific factual questions, intended to induce a
surface approach. After the third passage both
groups of students were given the same set of
questions containing both 'deep' and 'surface'
questions. Säljö found that students in the
'surface' group who had initially adopted a deep
approach tended to have shifted to a surface
approach by the time they read the third passage.
Although there was an effect on students in the
'deep' group, most of the students who had initially
adopted a surface approach apparently found it
difficult to move fully to a deep approach.
Instead they adopted what Säljö called a 'deep
technified' approach. These students were content
with summarizing the author's argument without
examining it actively or in detail. Säljö's conclusion that it is much easier to induce a surface
approach than a deep one could be important. We
shall refer back to it in subsequent chapters.

   Another of Marton's colleagues examined the
level of understanding of basic concepts reached by
first-year students of economics. Dahlgren (1978,
Dahlgren and Marton, 1978) paid particular attention
to the naive concepts, such as that of 'price',
which students had at the beginning of the course
and to the technical meanings they should have
understood by the end. The layman's idea of price,
for example, can be expressed as what an article is
worth - what its value is. This implies that
'price' is a fixed attribute. The economist's concept of price brings in the idea of supply and
demand. The price of an article depends not just
on the production costs and raw materials, but also
on its popularity in relation to its availability.
Dahlgren was able to show that although the results
of a first-year examination implied that students
should have developed an understanding of the technical meaning of such basic concepts, in fact:

   "If a more thorough understanding is required
   in order to answer a question, the number of
   acceptable answers is very low ... In many
   cases ... it appeared that only a minority of
   students had apprehended basic concepts in
   economics in the way intended by teachers and
   text-book authors. Complex problems seem to
   be solved by application of memorized algo-
   rithmic procedures ... In order to cope with

20

overwhelming curricula, the students probably
have to abandon their ambitions to understand
what they read about and instead direct efforts
towards passing the examinations ... (which reflect) the view that knowledge is a quantity,
and that the higher the level of the educational system, the more pieces of knowledge should
be taught per time unit" (Dahlgren, 1978, pages
1, 11, 12).

Putting together Säljö's findings and
Dahlgren's comments we see that the type of question
given in a test can induce a surface approach to
studying and that the factual overburdening of
syllabuses and examinations may be responsible for
the low level of understanding exhibited by students
when prevented from reproducing answers by well-
rehearsed methods.

In many of the reports produced by the Gothenburg research group there is a repeated emphasis
on the importance of both <u>content</u> and <u>context</u> in
affecting a student's approach to learning.   Thus
it is not possible to characterize a <u>student</u> as
'deep', only an <u>approach</u> to a particular academic
task.   The effect of content and context is shown
elegantly in the last of these studies.   Fransson
(1977) examined how levels of interest and anxiety
affected students' approaches to learning.   Level
of interest was controlled by selecting an article
concerning examination procedures in the education
department.   One group of students were in that
department;   another group, from a different department, were expected to have much less interest in
the article.   Two situations, or contexts for
learning, were created.   In one condition students
were told that after reading the article, one
student would be chosen to explain out loud what he
had learnt.   The explanation would be tape-recorded
for subsequent detailed analysis.   A large tape-
recorder placed in a prominent position reinforced
what was intended to be an anxiety-provoking
situation.   In the contrasting situation, attempts
were made to create a relaxed friendly atmosphere.

It was clear from the results that both interest
and anxiety did affect the students' approaches to
learning, but not in a simple way.   It was not so
much that anxiety-provoking <u>situations</u> induced a
surface approach to learning, but that students who
<u>felt</u> the situation to be threatening, whether that
was intended or not, were more likely to adopt a
surface approach.   Lack of interest or perceived

21

relevance also tended to evoke this mechanical rote-learning approach. Thus where a student feels threatened, or under pressure to respond to examination demands or syllabuses which have little personal relevance, it is less likely that a deep approach will be adopted.

HOLIST AND SERIALIST STRATEGIES OF LEARNING

Pask and his colleagues have carried out several series of experiments in trying to discover important differences between students in their learning strategies. Marton deliberately left his instructions about reading the article vague. The students had to decide for themselves whether reading for understanding or rote memorization would be the best way of answering the subsequent questions about the article. Through this ambiguity it was possible to demonstrate the contrasting approaches to learning that students considered appropriate for this academic task. In most of Pask's experiments, however, the students are required to reach a deep level of understanding, and Pask is interested in the strategies they use in trying to carry out this instruction.

In the first series of experiments reported by Pask (Pask and Scott, 1972) he asked students to try to establish for themselves the principles of classification underlying the division of two imaginary species of Martian animals - the Clobbits and the Gandlemullers - into a series of sub-species. In the first experiments, information about Clobbits was provided in the form of 50 cards. These were placed face down in ten columns (each column representing a separate subspecies). The five rows contained separate categories of information about the ten subspecies (e.g. habitat, physical characteristics, drawings of animals, etc.). Students could also write their own information cards if they found this helpful.

Students were asked to turn over the cards to obtain the information they wanted. They were told to turn the cards over one at a time and to give a reason for the particular card they had chosen. Each reason amounted to a hypothesis about the nature of the classification system which the information on the card was expected to test. A record was kept of the order in which the cards were used and also of the hypothesis given at each step. Finally students were required to 'teach back' to the experimenter what they had learned about these

Martian animals.

Pask discovered interesting differences both in the types of hypothesis used by students and in the ways in which they explained the classification schemes. Some students concentrated on a step-by-step strategy in which they used simple hypotheses about, say, a single property of the animals

"Do Gandlemullers have sprongs?"

This strategy was described as <u>serialist</u>, indicating the linear progression from one hypothesis to the next. Other students used more complex hypotheses which combined several properties simultaneously.

"Are there more kinds of Gandlers with mounds (dorsal or cranial) than Plongers?"

This strategy was described as <u>holist</u>, (not to be confused with Svensson's different use of the same term), which indicates a more global approach to problem solving. Pask also identified an additional type of holist, <u>the</u> <u>redundant</u> <u>holist</u>, who depended on individualistic ways of discriminating between the sub-species.

"The ones that were discovered first are gentle; the other kinds, the aggressive beasts that were found later, well they are the ones with less mounds."

The important aspect of the redundant holist is that imaginary descriptive terms are used. In the above example, there was nothing in the information given to the student to suggest either an order of discovery or 'temperamental' differences between the sub-species. What seems to happen is that the redundant holist personalizes learning. The order of discovery is probably the order in which he turned up the cards, while an impression of gentleness or aggressiveness was perhaps created by the drawings. In the end the redundant holists understood the principles of classification just as well as the holists or serialists, but they relied on personal (redundant) 'props' to aid that understanding.

When students were asked to 'teach back' what they had learned, very similar differences were found between the two main types. The serialists described the principles of classification in a straightforward logical manner keeping to the bare essentials. For example:

> "Zoologists have classified the Gandlemuller on the basis of physical characteristics. The three main types are Gandlers, Plongers and Gandleplongers. Gandlers have no sprongs. Plongers have two sprongs. Gandleplongers have one sprong. There are four subspecies of Gandler: M1, M2, B1 and B2. The M's have one body, the B's have two bodies. The M1 and B1 have a single cranial mound. The M2 and B2 have a double cranial mound ..."etc.

In contrast a redundant holist set about the description in a very different way:

> "I want to tell you about a funny Martian animal which has been recently discovered and classified by scientists conducting surveys. They are funny sluglike things with various protruberances. These animals are called Gandlemullers, because they churn about in the swamps near the Equator and Gandle is the Martian for swampmud, hence the swampmudmiller (Muller is German for miller). These things churn through the mud eating it by some curious process which means they eat and excrete at the same time."

Only after a great deal of redundant elaboration does this holist describe the essential properties of the various sub-species, and even then they are presented in an idiosyncratic order. It is perhaps unfair to describe the holist as illogical; it may be that the order follows a different set of rules. There may well be understandable principles in his ordering of the information; if so, they seem to be more like those used by novelists or journalists than by scientists. The holist starts with what seems to be the most interesting or striking point and includes a good deal of human or personal interest. The holist thrives on anecdote, illustration, and analogy, while the serialist uses these sparingly, if at all.

In later series of experiments Pask and his colleagues have been able to extend the descriptions of holists and serialists. For example, holists tend to look further ahead when asked to work their way through a hierarchy of sub-topics towards an understanding of the topic as a whole (Pask, 1976b).

They also have a wide focus of attention, bringing together several sub-topics, right from the start (Robertson, 1977).   Where students are given a choice between a series of abstract topics and an exactly parallel series of topics which are drawn from the 'real world', serialists work their way step-by-step through either the abstract topics or the real world topics, bringing them together only when forced to do so to achieve overall understanding of the main topic.   The holists in contrast move from real world to abstract and back again, examining the analogies between the two sets of topics as well.   In the end both groups of students can reach the same level of understanding, but their ways of reaching that understanding are very different.   The serialists apparently put much more emphasis on the separate topics and the logical sequences connecting them, forming an overall picture of what is being learned only rather late in the process.   The holists try to build up that overall picture, as a guide to learning, right from the start and see where the details fit into that picture much later on.

PATHOLOGIES OF LEARNING

Pask (1976a) has developed what he calls a conversational theory of learning which describes how a student works his way towards a full understanding of a topic by questioning, or trying out his ideas on, either a teacher or an 'alter-ego', another part of the mind which monitors and interacts with the learning process.   Pask argues that a full understanding occurs only when the student can explain the topic by reconstructing it, and can also demonstrate that understanding by applying the principles learned to an entirely new situation.   The theory also indicates that appropriate analogies are as important a part of understanding a 'teach-back' as the recognition of the logical steps and processes through which an understanding of the topic is built up.   Pask argues that the two major pathologies commonly found in learning are the failure to examine the logical structure or the evidence in sufficient detail, and the failure to make use of appropriate analogies.   The link between the holist and serialist strategies and learning pathologies, at least within Pask's theory, should now become clear.

The holist strategy involves looking at the whole area being learned, taking a broad perspective seeking interconnection with other topics and making use of personal and idiosyncratic analogies. The examination of the logical structure and of the supporting evidence comes later when understanding is demanded, but left to himself the holist is likely to put off what he may see as the more boring parts of learning. Heath describes his category of 'plunger' in similar terms:

> "His thoughts zip from one idea to another without apparent connection; ... characteristically (he) fails to clothe his ideas in a framework that would make sense to others ... He may beg permission to go ahead with a project ... only to lose interest later, particularly if hard uninteresting work looms ..."

Pask describes as <u>globetrotting</u> the tendency of the holist to make inappropriate or vacuous analogies. This pathology might also take the form of an over-readiness to generalize from insufficient evidence to form hasty, personal judgements.

The serialist falls into the opposite trap. He fails to make use of valid and important analogies and may not build up for himself any overall map to see how the various elements of the topic interrelate and how the topic fits into the subject area in general. Pask calls this pathology <u>improvidence</u>.

STYLES OF LEARNING

The strategies of learning described so far might be no more than reactions to a single task (the Clobbits) or to a particular piece of apparatus which controls learning in a somewhat atypical way. Pask accepts that his early experiments did artificially accentuate differences between students, but he argues that the holist and serialist strategies are manifestations of important underlying differences in the way people think and tackle problems. He argues that some students are disposed to act 'like holists' whenever they are given that opportunity, whereas others behave 'like serialists'. The <u>general tendency</u> to adopt a particular strategy is referred to as a <u>learning style</u>. The 'holist like' style is called <u>comprehension learning</u> which involves 'building descriptions of what is known'. The 'serialist like' style is called <u>operation learning</u>, which is 'the facet of the learning process concerned with mastering procedural details'.

Pask (personal communication) has likened these two aspects of thinking to the way an architect designs a building. He has to build up the overall plan (description building) and also to work out the detailed processes, and the logistics of those processes, (operation and procedure building) whereby the plan can be converted into an actual building. Any weakness either in the plan, or in the description of that plan, will prevent the building being satisfactorily completed (understanding being reached). Students who show sufficient consistent bias in their learning strategies to be described as 'comprehension learners' or 'operation learners' are likely to show equally consistent pathologies of learning. But there are other students who are readily able to adapt their learning strategy to the requirements of the particular task, emphasizing either comprehension learning or operation learning as appropriate, and using both in tandem wherever possible. Pask describes these students as having a 'versatile' style of learning.

> "A student who is versatile is not prone to vacuous globetrotting; he does indeed build up descriptions of what may be known by a rich use of analogical reasoning, but subjects the hypotheses to test and operationally verifies the validity of an analogy and the limits of its applicability" (Pask et al., 1977, page 68).

Pask's description seems to echo Heath's ideal type - the reasonable adventurer. Versatility is also descriptively related to "cue-consciousness" (Miller and Parlett, 1974) and to "thematization" in learning.

MATCHING STYLES OF LEARNING AND TEACHING

Perhaps one of the most important of Pask's experiments was his investigation of the effects of matching and mismatching learning materials with students' learning strategies. On the basis of the Clobbit experiment students were identified as having adopted holist or serialist strategies. Pask then asked the students to work through a set of programmed learning materials and take a test to discover how much they had learned. There were two versions of this material. One version was designed to suit the comprehension learner, being rich in analogy and illustration. The other was

presented in a logical, step-by-step sequence without 'enrichment'. Students were assigned either to
a matched or a mismatched condition (holist with
holist material; holist with serialist material;
etc). The results were dramatic, although based on
small samples; there was little overlap in the
scores of the matched and mismatched groups. The
students in the matched conditions were able to
answer most of the questions about what they had
learned, whereas the other students generally fell
below half marks.

Pask's descriptions of styles and pathologies
of learning seem to overlap, in places, with Marton's
ideas about deep and surface approaches to learning.
It was the intriguing possibilities raised by these
apparent connections which provided some of the
initial impetus for our own research programme. But
our approach was deliberately different. Our main
concern was to use both quantitative and qualitative
methods of collecting and analysing data, as a progression from the earlier research at Lancaster, and
to explore the effects of natural contextual differences - differences between academic departments -
in their effects on approaches to learning.

This chapter has described the work of both
Marton and Pask in detail as it is their concepts
which form the main theoretical basis for our own
work, and a full understanding of those concepts
seems to be an essential prerequisite to the description of our research design and findings which
follows.

Chapter Three

THE PROGRAMME OF RESEARCH

The main purpose in carrying out this programme of research was to extend, conceptually and empirically, the work of Marton and Pask described in the previous chapter, in relation to the previous research on students carried out at Lancaster. There were six main areas within the programme:

1.   The measurement of approaches to and styles of studying, using an inventory.
2.   The exploration of the cognitive skills, cognitive styles, and personality characteristics underlying different approaches to studying.
3.   The extension of Marton's work on reading academic articles, using a questionnaire.
4.   The identification, by questionnaire, of students' perceptions of the academic 'climate' of departments.
5.   The use of interviews to investigate students' strategies in carrying out particular types of academic task.
6.   An investigation of how contrasting academic contexts appear to affect the approaches to studying adopted by students in those departments.

Marton had limited his research methodology to qualitative analyses of small samples of mainly social science students. Pask had used lengthy experimental learning tasks, again restricted to small opportunity samples. The intention in this research programme was to obtain firmer evidence of the existence of contrasting learning styles or approaches to studying from a wider range of disciplines, and to explore the extent to which these approaches represented relatively stable characteristics of students, rooted in their abilities and personality, or in contrast were specific reactions

29

to the nature of particular academic tasks or learning contexts.

Methodologically there was a deliberate attempt to capitalise on the strengths of different approaches to research. Thus interviews with students were used both as a source of items for the development of inventories and questionnaires, and as the raw data for qualitative analyses. Data from inventories were exposed to repeated, complex statistical analyses to explore the nature of the relationships both between the various dimensions of approaches to studying, and between approaches to studying and students' perceptions of academic departments. The patterns of relationships emerging from these quantitative analyses were reassessed in the light of students' comments in the interviews, and new items or sub-scales were then produced for the inventories. Over a period of four years it was thus possible to make substantial advances in understanding students' approaches to learning and to produce carefully constructed instruments for further research or evaluation studies in higher education.

The general work on the programme can be described in three phases. In the first phase there was exploratory work on five fronts. A questionnaire variant of Marton's interview procedure on reading academic articles was given to three separate samples. Results from two pilot studies enabled improvements to be embodied in a questionnaire given to 248 first-year students. Secondly, a pilot version of an inventory to identify distinctive approaches to studying was developed from an existing Lancaster inventory supplemented with items suggested by the ideas of Perry, Marton and Pask. Thirdly, exploratory interviews were held in which students were asked to describe their approaches to specific academic tasks, and more generally to discuss their experiences of studying and their perceptions of the courses and the teaching they had encountered. Fourthly, interviews with staff were carried out to explore the possibility of defining 'academic climate' through lecturers' perceptions of the departments in which they worked. This last approach was not pursued, as a focus on students' perceptions seemed to be more fruitful with the limited time and resources available. Thus the final activity in this phase of the programme was the development from the interview data of a questionnaire to assess quantitatively students' perceptions of their courses and their main academic department.

In the second phase of the programme, the inventory of approaches to studying and the course perceptions questionnaire were given to 767 first-year students. Analyses of these data led to final research versions of the inventory and questionnaire being produced. From students' responses to the inventory it was possible to identify a group of 60 students with extreme scores on approaches to studying who agreed to spend some ten hours, spread over a period of over a year, taking tests of convergent and divergent thinking, cognitive and learning styles, and personality, and also taking part in a learning experiment involving the reading of three short articles. The main round of interviews with students from six contrasting departments was also carried out during this phase.

The final phase of the programme involved qualitative analysis of the interview data, which proved a formidable task. Statistical analyses were also carried out on the test scores of the 60 volunteers. Finally there was a major survey of 66 university and polytechnic departments throughout Britain. 2208 students completed the approaches to studying inventory and the course perceptions questionnaire, from which it was possible, in conjunction with the interview data, to assess the effects of academic departments on students' approaches to learning.

Details of each of these areas of research are presented in the following chapters. First there is a report on identifying distinctive approaches to studying through the development of the inventory. Chapter 5 describes the extent to which it was possible to find underlying differences in ability, cognitive style or personality between students with contrasting scores on the inventory. In Chapter 6 results of a series of learning experiments are presented in which students were asked to read academic articles, recall what they had learned, and comment on their reading and learning strategies.

Chapter 7 begins the exploration into the effects of academic context or environment on how students learn, with a description of the course perceptions questionnaire. Chapter 8 is a report on students' experiences of learning and studying in higher education, while Chapter 9 presents the results of bringing together the approaches to studying inventory with the course perceptions questionnaire. The final chapter is an attempt to take stock of the progress made during the programme in trying to understand how students learn. It

The Programme of Research

also presents indications of the practical utility
of the research in relation to teaching and learning
in higher education.

Chapter Four

IDENTIFYING DISTINCTIVE APPROACHES TO STUDYING*

EARLIER RESEARCH AT LANCASTER

In earlier research at Lancaster (Entwistle and
Wilson, 1970; Entwistle and Entwistle, 1970;
Entwistle, Thompson and Wilson, 1974; Entwistle
and Wilson, 1977) a series of inventories had been
developed, initially for the specific purpose of pre-
dicting subsequent levels of academic performance.
In the main study an inventory with two scales was
used - motivation and study methods.   1087 first-
year students from seven English universities completed these scales and correlations with subsequent
degree class were calculated.   The highest correlation reported was 0.39 (study methods in engineering), but overall levels were around 0.20.   Although
these values seem low, it must be remembered that
they are about the same as correlations between 'A'
levels and degree class.

One of the versions of the inventory contained
items indicative of extraversion and neuroticism
(Eysenck, 1970).   In higher education it has been
consistently found that introverts in most subject
areas tend to be more successful than extraverts,
but an interesting study by Wilson, (1969; Entwistle
and Wilson, 1977) showed that extraverts who had
high scores on motivation and study methods were
equally successful as introverts with comparable
scores.   However few extraverts, compared with introverts, had high motivation or good study methods -

---

* Much of the work on the first two versions of the
inventory was carried out by Maureen Hanley (née Robin-
son).   Later versions were developed in association
with Sarah Morison (née Burkinshaw), Dai Hounsell and
Patrick Thomas.

hence the overall relationship between introversion
and degree class. Although this earlier work was
not designed to examine study processes, nevertheless it did indicate that students of differing
personality types might approach studying in contrasting ways. This possibility was explored
further by the use of cluster analysis, which
identifies students with similar profiles of scores.

This method was used to define groups of
successful students who seemed to have followed
different paths to success. Three successful
groups and one which was unsuccessful were described
(Entwistle and Wilson, 1977). The first group was
outstandingly successful and was apparently motivated
by ambition or 'hope for success' (Atkinson and
Feather, 1966).

"Cluster 1 contained students with high 'A'
level grades who were satisfied with their
courses. These students had not had a particularly active social or sporting life, nor had
they concentrated on developing aesthetic
interests ... They were highly motivated and had
good study methods. In personality they were
emotionally stable and had high scores on
theoretical and economic values, linked with a
tendency towards toughminded conservatism.
This combination of characteristics suggests a
rather cold and ruthless individual, governed
by rationality and spurred on by competition to
repeated demonstrations of intellectual mastery.'

The second group was in many ways the opposite
of the first, yet students still obtained fairly
good degree results.

"The main defining features ... were high scores
on neuroticism and syllabus-boundness, and low
scores on both extraversion, (study methods),
and motivation. Their self-ratings were uni-
formly negative. They saw themselves as
neither likeable nor self-confident. They had
no active social life and few aesthetic
interests; (they worked long hours) ... It is
tempting to see these students as motivated by
'fear of failure' (Birney, Burdick, and Teevan,
1969)... The possibility that neurotic introverts with low motivation and poor study methods
might (still) be almost as successful as highly
motivated students was noted in a preliminary
analysis of the interview data. (Entwistle,

Thompson, and Wilson, 1974)" (op. cit, page 130).

The third group of students was also successful.   It contained mainly arts and humanities
students with high aesthetic and low economic
values who espoused radical ideals.   They were
highly motivated, had good study methods, worked
long hours, but were distinctly syllabus-free in
their attitudes to studying.

The final group contained the least successful
students.   This group had active social or sporting
interests combined with very low motivation, poor
study methods, and few hours spent studying.   Some,
but by no means all of the students, came to
university with poor 'A' level grades and had low
scores on a verbal aptitude test.

Another way of drawing attention to differing
attitudes to studying was to use factor analyses to
identify groups of items which were closely interrelated.   In this way the initial two dimensions
of motivation and study methods were broken down into
five sub-scales which paralleled the cluster analyses,
but produced two factors associated with poor degree
results.   The five factors were labelled competitive
and efficient, fear of failure, syllabus-free,
cynical and disenchanted, and disorganized and
dilatory.   The four most distinctive items from each
factor are shown in Table 4.1, and these items formed
the first part of the pool of items used to develop
the 'Approaches to Studying Inventory' for this
research programme.

DEVELOPMENT OF PILOT INVENTORIES

The purpose in developing a new inventory was
not to improve levels of prediction of academic
success;   it was instead an attempt to understand
students' approaches to learning.   In particular,
the intention was to measure, and to investigate the
inter-relationships between, the explanatory concepts identified by Marton and Pask.   Thus
additional items were written which were based on
Marton's descriptions of 'deep' and 'surface' processing and on Pask's indications of the varying
learning strategies used by 'holists' and 'serialists'.
In addition the ideas of Miller and Parlett (1974) on
'cue consciousness', as modified by Ramsden (1979)
into a more general dimension of 'strategic
approach to assessment', created an additional set of
items.

As the interviews with students progressed

(see Chapter 8) additional items were suggested. Eventually a pool of 120 items was used in the first pilot inventory. Alpha factor analysis with rotation to oblique simple structure (Nie et al, 1975) was used to identify groups of items which were consistently linked together. The items were also subjected to conceptual analysis in relation to the constructs found in the literature. It was soon clear that the 'deep approach to studying' and 'organized, motivated study methods' were major dimensions, and that a third factor brought together surface processing with fear of failure and syllabus-boundness.

Table 4.1   STUDENTS' ATTITUDES TO STUDYING

DISORGANIZED AND DILATORY   (Poor degree results)

My habit of putting off work leaves me with far too much to do at the end of term.

I'm rather slow at starting work in the evening.

It's rather difficult for me to organise my study time: at school this was done for me.

It is unusual for me to be late handing in work (Disagree).

CYNICAL AND DISENCHANTED   (Poor degree results)

I can't see any relevance to most of the work we do here.

There seems to be little point in following up the references we are given in lectures.

There are very few of the recommended text-books which are really worth buying.

I sometimes wish I had gone straight into work after school.

SYLLABUS-FREE   (Above average degree results)

I tend to learn more effectively by studying along my own lines than through set work.

I am often involved in following up my own ideas when I am supposed to be doing set work.

Often I try to think of a better way of doing something than is described in a lecture or book.

I should prefer the set work to be less structured and organised.

Table 4.1   STUDENTS' ATTITUDES TO STUDYING (continued)

FEAR OF FAILURE   (Above average degree results)

My friends always seem to be able to do things better than me.

Worrying about an exam or about work which is overdue often
   prevents me from sleeping.

I get very concerned about work which is overdue.

I don't often join in tutorial discussions: I prefer to
   listen.

COMPETITIVE AND EFFICIENT   (Very good degree results)

I play any game to win, not just for the fun of it.

I hate admitting defeat, even in trivial matters.

It's important for me to do really well in the courses here.

I consider the best possible way of learning is by completing
   the set work and doing the required reading.

At this stage it was possible to discuss our
factor analyses with John Biggs of Newcastle,
Australia.   He had been developing a Study Behaviour
Questionnaire (Biggs, 1976) which contained the ten
sub-scales shown below.

Academic aspiration	Pragmatic, grade-orientated, university as means.
Academic interest	Intrinsically motivated, study as end.
Academic neuroticism	Confused, overwhelmed by demands of course work.
Internality	Sees 'truth' coming from within, not (from) external authority.
Study skills and organisation	Works consistently, reviews regularly, schedules work.
Fact-rote strategy	Centres on facts, details, rote learns.
Dependence	Rarely questions instructors, tests; needs support.
Meaning Assimilation	Reads widely, relates to known, meaning orientated.

Test anxiety   Very concerned about tests,
                                exams, fear of failure.

Openness   (Believes) university (is) a
                                place where values are question-
                                ed.

                    (Biggs, 1976, page 72).

    The similarity between these scales and several
of the dimensions described by our own inventory was
striking; even the wording of many of the items
was similar.   Biggs indicated that his most recent
work strongly suggested the existence of three main
factors - utilizing, internalizing, and achieving -
each of which contained both a cognitive and a
motivational component as follows.   (Subsequently
described in Biggs, 1979):

Factor	Cognitive	Motivational
Utilizing	Fact-rote strategy	Extrinsic, fear of failure
Internalizing	Meaning assimilation	Intrinsic
Achieving	Study skills and organisation	Need for achievement

    The descriptions of these three factors were
similar to the ones emerging from the pilot version
of our inventory.   It was therefore decided to
bring the inventories even closer together by introducing additional items covering scales used by
Biggs, but not parelled in our inventory - intrinsic
motivation, extrinsic motivation, internality and
openness.   The second pilot inventory contained the
82 items from the first inventory most clearly
related to established factors, together with 24
items rewritten from the four scales developed by
Biggs.
    Table 4.2 lists the fifteen sub-scales included
in this version of the inventory, and the four
factors which emerged from the analysis.   Factor
analysis allows us to group variables together which
have elements of similarity in their inter-relationships.   Thus factors are 'global' dimensions
summarizing the individual scales which hang

together most closely.   The meaning of a factor can be deduced from the defining items of the scales which have the highest factor loadings on that factor. A negative sign indicates that the direction has to be reversed (for example, Factor I is associated with the reverse of syllabus boundness, which is syllabus freedom).

Table 4.2   FACTOR LOADINGS OF STUDY STRATEGY SCALES

Sub-scales	I	II	III	IV
Deep approach	62		33	
Comprehension learning	73			
Intrinsic motivation	54		47	
Internality	61			
Openness	50			
Surface approach		67		
Operation learning		67		
Extrinsic motivation		61		
Fear of failure		36		-32
Syllabus bound	-41	50		
Strategic approach		41		
Organized study methods			64	
Achievement motivation		36	45	
Disillusioned attitudes			-55	
Sociability				58

The second pilot inventory was given to 767 first year (second term) students from nine departments in two universities.   The disciplines covered were english, history, psychology, physics, and engineering.   Principal component factor analyses, with rotation to oblique simple structure, were used to investigate the inter-relationships between the sub-scales.   Four factors had eigen-values above unity and these explained 56% of the overall variance in the correlational matrix. Factor loadings are shown in Table 4.2.
The four factors can be described as follows.

I DEEP APPROACH/COMPREHENSION LEARNING OR MEANING
ORIENTATION

This factor is very close to Biggs' 'internalizing'. It carries the same emphasis on intrinsic
motivation and active search for personal meaning,
but it contains its highest loading on comprehension
learning. This factor may thus be considered to
contain a stylistic component in addition to those
elements identified by Biggs.

II SURFACE APPROACH/OPERATION LEARNING OR REPRO-
DUCING ORIENTATION

This shows a close similarity to the 'utilizing'
factor. It shows high loadings on surface level
approach and also on extrinsic motivation, syllabus-
boundness and fear of failure. But again the high
loading on operation learning could imply an
additional stylistic component.

III ORGANIZED STUDY METHODS AND ACHIEVING ORIENTATION

This is the 'achieving' factor, with high
positive loadings on organized study methods and
achievement motivation, and a high negative loading
on disillusioned attitudes. There are also significant loadings on both deep approach and intrinsic
motivation without any hint of a stylistic component
in this case.

IV STABLE EXTRAVERSION

The final factor appears to be a combination of
the two most basic personality traits described by
Eysenck (1970). A similar factor was reported
earlier in work on primary school children where
scales of both motivation and personality were
included (Entwistle and Bennett, 1973). It is
essentially stable extraversion.

This analysis appeared to support the claim by
Biggs that three second-order factors "seem to offer
a parsimonious and theoretically coherent model for
conceptualizing the more important ways in which
students may feel about, and behave towards, their
study" (Biggs, 1979, p. 383).

As the subscales of internality and openness
seemed to add little to the definition of the first
factor, they were dropped from subsequent versions of

the inventory. The isolated personality dimension
of sociability was also dropped. In their place,
it was decided to introduce sub-components of the
main explanatory concepts being investigated. In
the third pilot version of the inventory a distinction was made within approach to studying between the
intention, the process, and the outcome. Also the
styles of learning, comprehension learning and
operation learning, both of which Pask considers to
be essential in reaching understanding, were distinguished from their corresponding pathologies -
globetrotting and improvidence. Holists are likely
to exhibit both comprehension learning and globetrotting; serialists should score highly on
operation learning and improvidence. But students
adopting a deep approach, although being able to use
both comprehension and operation learning in a versatile manner, would not be expected to exhibit the
pathologies of learning.

One of the problems in developing the inventory
has been that the main theoretical constructs
identified by Marton and Pask have been evolving
during the life of the programme, partly through
new publications by the originators, partly through
seminars at which the ideas have been discussed with
other researchers, and partly through the findings
from our own inventories and interviews. Thus the
third pilot inventory had a short life. Shortly
after it had been used, an article based on the
previous version of the inventory was written
(Entwistle, Hanley, and Hounsell, 1979). In this
article a model of student learning was developed
which attempted to distinguish between deep/surface
approaches and comprehension/operation learning.
This model also distinguished two stages of both comprehension and operation learning in the way shown
in Figure 4.1.

In the final research version of the inventory
it was thus decided to restrict 'deep approach' to
the intention to understand and an active, critical
approach to learning, and to add as separate sub-
scale two of the components essential to a deep-
level outcome, but not previously covered in the
inventory. These sub-scales were labelled
'relating ideas' and 'use of evidence'.

FINAL RESEARCH VERSION OF THE INVENTORY

In deciding the items to be included in the
final research version of the inventory, all the
previous inventories were reviewed to identify items

Figure 4.1   A MODEL OF STYLES AND APPROACHES TO LEARNING

Approach or Style	Process		Outcome
	Stage I	Stage II	
Deep approach/ versatile	All four processes below used appropriately to reach understanding		Deep level of understanding
Comprehension learning	Building overal description of content area	Reorganizing incoming information to relate to previous knowledge or experience and establishing personal meaning	Incomplete understanding attributable to globetrotting
Operation. learning	Detailed attention to evidence and steps in the argument	Relating evidence to conclusion and maintaining a critical, objective stance	Incomplete understanding attributable to improvidence
Surface approach	Memorization	Overlearning	Surface level of understanding

which had worked well at some stage within one or
other of the sub-scales now to be formed.   Each
sub-scale, with the exception of surface approach
which had proved the most difficult to define, was
limited to a maximum of four items to ensure a
manageable overall length on the basis of the highest correlations between item and sub-scale total,
consistent with retaining the conceptual definition
of the sub-scales.   A list of sub-scales and
defining items is shown in Table A1 (Appendix)
together with the coefficients of internal consistency (Cronbach alpha).   The coefficients for the
main domains were as follows: meaning orientation
(16 items α =0.79);   reproducing orientation (16
items α=0.73);   achieving orientation (16 items
=0.70);   styles and pathologies (16 items α=0.59).
Although the levels of internal consistency are
rather low in some of the sub-scales, the reliability
estimates for three of the four domains are satisfactory.   And there is a good reason for the lower
reliability in the fourth domain.   It is unlikely
that styles and pathologies can be viewed as a single
domain.   The sub-scales could well be put together
in different ways for different purposes.   The total
score (with one style and pathology reversed) may
indicate an extreme 'redundant holist' say, but it
may be more meaningful to use comprehension learning
and globetrotting together to indicate a holist
style;   operation learning and improvidence together
to indicate a serialist style;   comprehension and
operation learning together to indicate versatility;
and globetrotting and improvidence to indicate
pathologies of learning.

MAIN STUDY

The inventory was presented to students as part
of a questionnaire in three sections.   The first
section asked for background information about
school examination results and honours specialism(s),
and also contained a self-rating question in which
students were asked to assess their own academic
progress to date (How well do you think you are doing
so far on this subject/course, compared with other
students?).   A similar approach to self-assessment
of mathematical aptitude proved successful in an
earlier study (Entwistle and Wilson, 1977), with a

correlation between self-rating and objective test score of +0.65. The second section contained the inventory of approaches to studying, while the final section was the Course Perceptions Questionnaire, the development of which is described in Chapter 7. A letter describing the purpose of the investigation was sent to 171 departments in 54 universities and polytechnics in England, Wales, Scotland and Northern Ireland. Ninety-five departments agreed in principle to cooperate, and an adequate proportion of completed questionnaires for anlaysis was eventually obtained from 66 of them.

The target population was second-year under-graduates (third-year in Scotland) taking honours degrees in departments of English, history, economics psychology, physics or engineering. The six disciplines were chosen to provide a range of special-isms: five of them had been used previously in the interview study (Ramsden, 1979).

Completed questionnaires were obtained from 2208 students, an estimated response rate of 73 per cent. (Returns from departments showed the class size, but it was not always possible to be sure exactly how many of the class had received the questionnaire). Students were asked to give their names (to allow degree results to be obtained sub-sequently), but they returned the questionnaires to the investigators in sealed envelopes, with a guarantee that departmental staff would not see their responses. The final sample contained 16 arts departments (491 students), 26 in the social sciences (852), and 24 in the pure and applied sciences (865).

RELATIONSHIPS BETWEEN APPROACHES TO STUDYING AND ACADEMIC PROGRESS

Although the current inventory was not designed primarily to predict academic performance, it is still of interest to examine the relationships between approaches to studying and academic progress. In this study it was only possible to investigate correlations between the inventory sub-scales and the self-rating of academic progress in the second year, but results using the second pilot inventory are available in relation to formal first-year assessment grades. It has also been possible to compare our self-rating correlations with samples of Australian first-year students who had been

given the final research version of the inventory.*
Table 4.3 presents correlations for the British and
Australian samples.

The correlations with the British students'
self-rating of academic progress by subject area,
in Table 4.3, showed consistent relationships in the
expected directions.   The closest overall relationships with academic progress were found with
organized study methods and positive attitudes to
studying, followed by intrinsic motivation, deep
approach, and syllabus-freedom (changing the names to
indicate the direction of relationship).   Subject
area differences show academic progress in arts to be
more closely related positively to deep approach and
comprehension learning, and negatively to all the sub-
scales within the reproducing orientation and to
operation learning and improvidence.   In social
science, higher positive correlations are found with
relating ideas, intrinsic motivation, and higher
negative correlations with disorganized study methods
and negative attitudes.   Social scientists appear to
be less heavily penalized for the pathologies' of
learning or adopting a surface approach.   The
relationships in science follow the overall values
fairly closely with the exception of strategic
approach and disorganized study methods which show
closer relationships with progress, and operation
learning which seems to be more of a benefit in the
sciences.

The Australian samples showed lower levels of
correlation overall, which could be explained either
by the objectivity of the index of academic performance (thus avoiding the possible circularity in
comparing two sets of self-ratings), or by the
difference between first and second-year students.
The pattern of relationships was, however, very
similar, the only exceptions being that the
Australian scientists showed a negative relationship
with operation learning, and that improvidence was
more heavily penalized in sciences than in the arts.

A useful way of determining which sub-scales
predict academic progress most effectively is discriminant function analysis.   In this statistical
technique, groups are formed on the basis of a
criterion (here academic performance).   The
analysis then identifies a discriminant function

---

* We are grateful to David Watkins of the Australian
National University in Canberra for allowing us to
present his findings.

Table 4.3 CORRELATIONS BETWEEN APPROACHES TO STUDYING AND INDICES OF ACADEMIC PROGRESS IN BRITAIN AND AUSTRALIA

	Arts		Social Sci.		Science		British
	Brit (N=491)	Aus (295)	Brit (852)	Aus (89)	Brit (865)	Aus (156)	Total (2208)
'A' level Grades	15	—	10	—	24	—	
Meaning Orientation							
Deep Approach	30	11	23	11	21	15	24
Relating Ideas	07	07	19	12	10	-08	12
Use of Evidence	16	07	17	12	13	02	15
Intrinsic Motivation	26	21	31	16	24	13	26
Reproducing Orientation							
Surface Approach	-27	-22	-13	-27	-20	-23	-19
Syllabus-boundness	-34	-17	-24	-06	-14	-07	-22
Fear of Failure	-25	-10	-15	-14	-15	-12	-18
Extrinsic Motivation	-13	-22	-09	-07	-06	-04	-09
Achieving Orientation							
Strategic Approach	09	02	20	09	27	00	19
Disorganized Study Methods	-22	-18	-34	-27	-37	-34	-32
Negative Attitudes to Studying	-26	-25	-33	-23	-30	-30	-29
Achievement Motivation	16	04	25	18	20	28	20
Styles and Pathologies							
Comprehension Learning	15	03	08	16	05	00	08
Globetrotting	-18	-25	-11	-03	-19	-19	-16
Operation Learning	-16	-09	-03	-03	06	-12	-04
Improvidence	-23	-10	-06	-18	-17	-27	-15
Significant for r >	.12	.15	.09	.27	.09	.21	.06
Multiple Correlation	—	.41	—	.47	—	.54	—

which shows which combination of the predictive variables (sub-scales of the inventory) most clearly differentiates between the different criterion groups. Using this technique on data from the second pilot study (N= 767 first-years with a criterion of assessment grades), the differences between the contrasting achievement groups were associated most closely with globetrotting, disorganized studying, extrinsic and intrinsic motivation, and to a lesser extent improvidence (Entwistle, Hanley and Hounsell, 1979).

In the main study (Ramsden and Entwistle, 1981), two extreme groups were formed in terms of students who said they were doing 'very well' in their courses (N=58) and those who said they were performing 'badly' (N=43). The sub-scales which defined the discriminant function most clearly were organized study methods, positive attitudes to studying, a strategic approach, and (to a lesser extent) high scores on achievement motivation and deep approach, combined with low scores on surface approach and globetrotting. This function places students correctly in their achievement category in 90% of instances. Of course, this level of prediction is likely to be an overestimate, due to the circularity involved in using self-ratings of both progress and approaches to studying. In the pilot study, with an objective criterion but a first-year sample, the level of correct prediction was 83% in the low group and 75% in the high group.

RELATIONSHIPS BETWEEN APPROACHES TO STUDYING

One of the main purposes of this part of the programme was to investigate the inter-relationships between the explanatory constructs measured by the inventory. (The correlations between the sub-scales can be found in Appendix Table A2). The inter-relationships between the sub-scales of the inventory follow the patterns anticipated. Each of the three main domains showsfairly close inter-relationships between the sub-scales. Even the fourth dimension, styles and pathologies, shows a reasonable consistency - five out of the six correlations are positive in the holist direction. The only exception was mentioned earlier. There is a positive relationship between globetrotting and improvidence, indicating that these pathologies are more closely linked with each other than with the stylistic component, which would have produced a negative correlation. Although it may be difficult at first sight to

47

understand how apparently opposite pathologies
could be associated in this way, interview comments
from some of the weaker students showed how this
might occur. For example, one student said:

> "I think it tends to be the case that I get
> bogged down in detail. I'm sure that's the
> case - I mean it explains why I'm so long-
> winded about any work that I do. I really
> don't find it easy to pick out the skeletal
> argument and just be satisfied with that ...
> When I'm reading to find out about a particular
> topic I tend to be a bit specific initially,
> but I do find that I get misled very easily
> and as soon as another area comes up which is
> perhaps not quite to do with the topic ...
> but has interesting connections, then I go off
> on tangents. Very regularly I end up sort of
> (laughs)miles away from where I originally
> started".

Meaning orientation was consistently related
positively to the sub-scales of achieving orientation
It was also related strongly to comprehension learning (as in previous analyses), but not to globetrotting, hence justifying the separation of style
from pathology in the inventory. Reproducing
orientation was positively related to serialist style
and pathology and also to both disorganized study
methods and negative attitudes. In this domain,
however, individual sub-scales behave less coherently
For example, surface approach and fear of failure
show higher relationships with the pathologies of
learning, while surface approach and extrinsic motivation are positively related to both strategic
approach and achievement motivation.

Factor analysis allows overall patterns of
relationships to be seen more clearly. Thus, the
SPSS program was used to carry out principal factor
analyses, followed by rotation to oblique simple
structure. Four factors had eigenvalues greater
than one and they accounted for 55 per cent of the
variance. The factor loadings are shown in Table 4.

The first two factors were almost identical to
those previously described as meaning orientation and
reproducing orientation. Again both factors showed
a strong stylistic component. However, meaning
orientation, as opposed to reproducing orientation,
contained no element of pathology in its loadings.
The previous third factor of achieving orientation
was divided into two. Factor III had its highest

loading on disorganized study methods and negative attitudes to studying, a factor similar to that which had emerged from the earlier inventory of motivation and study methods (Entwistle, 1975). This factor,which can be seen as a non-academic orientation to studying, represents disorganised and dilatory approaches to studying.   Factor IV was closer to the previous achieving orientation with high loadings on strategic approach and both extrinsic and achievement motivations.   There was also an apparent readiness to adopt either deep or surface approaches, which is consistent with a previous finding (Entwistle, Hanley and Hounsell, 1979) that students with an achieving orientation will seek high grades, using meaningful or rote learning, whichever seems to produce the best results.

Table 4.4   FACTOR ANALYSIS OF APPROACHES TO STUDYING SCALES
(N=2208)

| | | Factors | | |
Variables	I	II	III	IV
Academic Performance				
School	(−02)	(−13)	(−15)	(−07)
Higher Education	31	−26	−39	(19)
Approaches to Studying				
(DA) Deep Approach	70			(22)
(RI) Inter-relating Ideas	65			
(UE) Use of Evidence	54			(23)
(IM) Intrinsic Motivation	72		−25	
(SA) Surface Approach		57	36	30
(SB) Syllabus-boundness	−41	58		(24)
(FF) Fear of Failure		50	34	
(EM) Extrinsic Motivation	−25	38		53
(ST) Strategic Approach	29			48
(DS) Disorganized Study Methods	−25		50	
(NA) Negative Attitudes to Studying	−39		52	
(AM) Achievement Motivation	(24)			45
(CL) Comprehension Learning	55	(−24)	30	
(GL) Globetrotting			52	
(OL) Operation Learning		62		44
(IP) Improvidence		68	(24)	26

Decimal points and most loadings less than .25 omitted.

Factor III (non-academic orientation) shows the highest (negative) loading on self-rating of academic progress. As expected, meaning orientation is positively related to achievement, while the reproducing orientation shows a negative relationship. Surprisingly, the achieving orientation itself shows only a slight association with the self-rating of academic progress. However, all these relationships will have to be re-examined subsequently, with a more satisfactory criterion of achievement (degree class).

FURTHER DEVELOPMENT WORK ON THE INVENTORY

The publication of an article describing results from the second pilot inventory (Entwistle, Hanley and Hounsell, 1979) created considerable interest among other researchers working in this field. As a result the final research version of the inventory has been used either in its original form or in a slightly amended form in studies at the Open University (Morgan, Gibbs and Taylor, 1980), at the Australian National University (Watkins, 1982) and is about to be used in Holland and Belgium (Van Rossum, personal communication).

In the Open University study, meaning orientation emerged as clearly as in our own analyses, but there was overlap between reproducing orientation, achieving orientation and styles and pathologies. The reproducing factor did not have significant loadings on extrinsic motivation, It did have loadings, not just on operation learning, but also on the two pathologies, and on disorganized studying and negative attitudes. The third factor linked together extrinsic and achievement motivation, while the fourth factor was not consistent in the two samples used.

As a result of our own factor analyses and those from the Open University, it was decided to carry out a reassessment of our sub-scales. The separation into sixteen sub-scales was designed to keep each dimension conceptually distinct; the separation could not be justified on the basis of empirical relationships. The later factor analyses made it imperative to see to what extent the current grouping of items, either within sub-scales or within four domains, could still be justified empirically. Thus alpha factor analysis was applied to data from the main study (N=2208) and 17 factors were extracted (to allow for 16 factors and the freedom to

rotate created by an additional factor).   Also a
five-factor solution was produced to examine membership of domains, and repeated for each of the six
disciplines separately.   The 17 factor solution
produced few identifiable groupings of items, so
Table 4.5 summarises the factors from the 5 factor
solutions.

Again the two main orientations were clear-cut
and identifiable in every discipline, being meaning
orientation and reproducing orientation.   The
clarity of the interpretation was blurred somewhat
where a separate style factor was created (history
and physics).   Then the meaning orientation could
be better described as 'deep approach out of
interest', while the reproducing orientation, with
operation learning removed, was more identifiable
with a surface, instrumental approach.   Conceptually
it was this distinction which had been expected.
Operation learning, with its emphasis on a cautious,
logical, controlled, approach closely reliant on
fact and detail, should not necessarily become a
surface instrumental strategy.   It was thus reassuring to find some empirical support for this
distinction.

The third main factor again differed from the
achieving orientation described previously.   Previously it was found that disorganized study methods
and negative attitudes were linked, while achievement
motivation was associated with both strategic
approach and extrinsic motivation.   In these analyses
the first two held together in most analyses, but
could be separated into distinct factors.   The
motivational sub-scales could also be found as
distinct factors, but more typically they were
grouped in the ways shown in Table 4.5.   An examination of these, together with earlier analyses,
suggests that the 'non-academic' groupings contain
two components - the rejection of academic values
and, in some students, an endorsement of alternative
goals - social, aesthetic or sporting.   It may
thus be necessary to describe motivation in terms
of four distinct sub-scales: achievement, extrinsic,
intrinsic and social.   Again in some analyses
'academic motivation', the combination of achievement motivation and intrinsic motivation, was also
related to strategic approach.   This combination
was commonly associated with elements of both deep
and surface approaches - thus describing the
separate 'achieving orientation' found previously.

It thus seems that there are perhaps four
distinctive orientations to studying which can be

Table 4.5   SUMMARY OF ITEM FACTOR ANALYSES

Groupings of Sub-Scales	English (N=282)	History (209)	Economics (450)	Psychology (402)	Physics (357)	Engineering (508)	Total Sample (2208)
Meaning Orientation (DA + CL + RI + UE) (also IM)	X	X	X	X	X	X	X
Reproducing Orientation (SA + IP + FF + SB) (also OL)	X X	X X	X X	X X	X X	X X	X X
Non-Academic Orientation (DS + NA + GL) (also −IM and −AM)			(two factors)			(two factors)	
Holist Style (CL + GL)		X			X		
Serialist Style (OL + IM)					X		
Academic Motivation (AM + IM)	X			X			X
Instrumental Motovation (AM + EM)		X					
Non-Academic Motivation (EM + C* − IM)	X		X	X		X	X

* C = maximum score on IM subscale (16)

identified empirically from the inventory and that these orientations are associated with character- istic forms of motivation, as Biggs has suggested:

Orientation	Motivation
Meaning Orientation (DA + CL + RI + UE)	Intrinsic (IM)
Reproducing Orientation (SA + IP + FF + SB)	Extrinsic and/or Fear of Failure (EM)
Achieving Orientation (AM + IM + ST)	Achievement
Non-Academic Orientation (DA + NA + GL)	Low levels of intrinsic combined with high ex- trinsic and/or social motivation

These orientations correlated with academic progress as shown in Table 4.6. Consistently the highest values are shown with the non-academic and achieving orientations. There is a subject area difference showing meaning orientation to be more effective and reproducing orientation (and serialist style) to be more heavily penalized in arts than science. The holist style is unrelated to achievement in any discipline, as is the serialist style in science and social science.

In parallel to these analyses of the final research version, work has also been progressing with a much shorter inventory of 30 items. This was devised initially for use in a book (Entwistle, 1981) to illustrate the type of scales available. For this purpose some of the items were slightly altered to make it appropriate for sixth-formers (16 - 18 year olds). The availability of this version of the inventory has allowed a pilot study* to be carried out in one school with a small sample of 51 pupils taking 'A' level (18 +) examinations. Table 4.7 shows the mean scores of pupils with the highest and lowest 'A' level performance on the shortened scales.

---

* We are grateful to Sean O'Conaill of Loretto School in Coleraine for collecting these data.

Table 4.6 CORRELATIONS BETWEEN STUDY ORIENTATION AND SELF-RATING OF ACADEMIC PROGRESS

Orientation/Style	English (N=282)	History (209)	Economics (450)	Psychology (402)	Physics (357)	Engineering (508)
Meaning	23	27	24	20	17	14
Reproducing	-39	-35	-24	-14	-26	-23
Achieving	27	24	38	38	40	28
Non-Academic	-36	-27	-39	-37	-44	-40
Holist	-02	01	-02	-00	-08	-06
Serialist	-23	-23	-06	-02	-06	-09

Decimal points omitted

Table 4.7   MEAN SCORES OF PUPILS WITH HIGH OR LOW 'A' LEVEL
GRADES ON SHORT 'APPROACHES TO STUDYING' INVENTORY

Orientation/Style	Science		Arts	
	High (N=5)	Low (7)	High (11)	Low (8)
Meaning Orientation	15.4	12.4	14.8	11.8
Reproducing Orientation	15.0	12.9	14.0	16.4
Achieving Orientation	15.2	12.4	14.4	6.6
Holist Style	13.0	11.9	14.1	13.0
Serialist Style	16.6	12.4	13.1	14.6

It was encouraging to find, even in this small
sample and using a much abbreviated inventory, a
pattern of results similar to those found with
students.   Of particular interest was a suggestion
that reproducing orientation and improvidence are
associated with success in science and with poor
performance in arts.

It is hoped that a schools version of the
published inventory will be produced and that in both
schools and higher education, the results can be
used for diagnostic purposes.   Linking this
inventory to schemes for teaching study skills in
schools and in higher education, (for example,
Tabberer and Allman, 1981; Gibbs, 1981) it is anticipated that students could be helped to develop
appropriate skills and to become more conscious in
using those skills strategically to improve their
levels of academic performance.   Such implications
of the findings of our research will be discussed
more fully in the final chapter.

Chapter Five

PERSONALITY AND COGNITIVE STYLE IN STUDYING

(Written in collaboration with Sarah Morison)

By now we have been able to establish clearly from the inventory data that students adopt distinctive approaches to studying - the most insistent contrast being between meaning and reproducing orientations. The question posed in this chapter is whether these approaches can be interpreted in terms of more fundamental psychological processes. The initial review sections introduce theories and psychological tests which were incorporated into the study reported in the second half of the chapter.

LEVELS OF PROCESSING IN THE MEMORY

Marton initially referred to deep level and surface level processing, and the idea of different levels of processing is already well established in the psychological literature on human memory and information processing. Models of human memory have described generally three distinct types of memory - a sensory register (which holds incoming perceptions only briefly), a short-term memory (STM - which holds a limited amount of information for up to about 20 seconds), and a long-term memory (LTM) which itself can be divided into episodic (storing episodes of experience) and semantic (storing and relating concepts).
Information can be held in store for longer periods by internal repetition (rehearsal) and if repeated sufficiently often (overlearning) it will become a permanent memory trace, presumably in

---

The early part of this chapter contains extracts from Entwistle (1981), Styles of Learning and Teaching. More detailed descriptions of the psychological literature will be found there in Chapters 7, 9 and

episodic LTM.   This process is what would normally
be called rote memorization or surface level processing.   But much incoming information is reassessed and categorized in STM before being passed to
semantic LTM.   This process is what is involved
in deep level processing.

It comes initially as a contradiction of everyday experience to hear that we have a memory which
is essentially unlimited in size and in which memories
remain almost indefinitely.   The apparent paradox
vanishes when we realize that the ideas which go in
may not necessarily come out.   Retrieval from memory
depends on the accuracy of a coding process which
determines where the incoming information will be
stored, and hence where it is expected subsequently
to be found.

The long-term memory has been compared to a
library, to sets of pigeon-holes and to a filing
system (Broadbent, 1966).   It contains what Lindsay
and Norman (1972) call a data base of concepts and
records of events tied together within inter-connect-
ing systems.   Each individual has a unique conceptual structure, although the linkages between concepts
(which constitute definitions) have enough in common
to allow effective communication of ideas.   Concepts
are built up by repeated comparisons of incoming
perceptions or information with pre-existing concepts
or linkages between images (for example, the sight of
a dog and the sound of the word 'dog').   If the
coding system is to be effective and recall easy, it
is essential that the data base should contain a
large number of clearly defined and well differentiated concepts which also carry a large number of
connecting links with other concepts, ideas or events.
The ability to think divergently or creatively will
presumably depend on the extent to which the memory
has developed a multiplicity of unusual, but valid,
interconnections.   It will also depend on the
availability of appropriate, perhaps leisurely,
search mechanisms to explore fruitful combinations
of ideas.

Another model of the memory has been developed
by Craik and Lockhart (1972).   They broke away from
the mechanistic, three-box model by proposing
instead different levels of processing.   Memory is
seen as involving a "hierarchy of processing stages
where greater 'depth' implies a greater degree of
semantic or cognitive 'analysis'".   Recall of complex material will also be enhanced by systematic
elaboration at the same level of processing   (Craik
and Tulving, 1975).

Elaboration can be seen as developing linkages between the new idea and previous knowledge and personal experience.

It is therefore possible to reconsider our two main study orientations within these models of the memory. An orientation towards understanding (deep approach and comprehension learning) depends on a deep level of processing and elaboration. Reproducing (surface approach and operation learning) is more likely to involve overlearning by repetition at a shallow level of processing with little use of elaboration.

Our research strategy has involved translating constructs derived from qualitative analyses of students' reported experiences of studying into specific items of typical study processes and attitudes. We have then looked for explanations of the emerging study orientations in terms of psychological theories. It is, of course, more common to extrapolate psychological theories into educational contexts, in the expectation that basic psychological processes will be utilized wherever learning and remembering are being demanded. It is interesting, and reassuring, to discover that this research strategy converges on a description of student learning recognizably similar to our own.

From the University of Southern Illinois, Schmeck and his colleagues have reported a series of studies using an Inventory of Learning Processes (see Schmeck, in press, for an extensive summary of this work). Their approach has been to identify the processes identified most clearly in major theories of human learning and then to produce items which describe those processes in relation to the "environment and activities of the typical college student". Factor analyses of these items have produced four main dimensions describing distinct learning processes - deep processing, elaborative processing, fact retention and methodical study. Examination of the individial items shows conceptual overlap between these dimensions and our study orientations described in the previous chapter. 'Orientation to understanding' covers both deep and elaborative processing, but also contains items relating to intention and intrinsic motivation. 'Reproducing' is made up partly of the 'fact retention' dimension, but is perhaps related more strongly to shallow processing (i.e. rote memorizing processes)*. The methodical study dimension cannot be equated with our 'achieving orientation'. Schmeck describes his scale as covering the activities recommended by a 'how to study manual'. In our

* (But see Appendix, table A4).

inventory this area would be covered in part by the sub-scale of 'organised study methods', but also by 'syllabus-boundness' which is within our 'reproducing' domain. One major difference between the Schmeck inventory and our own (and Biggs') is that it does not contain either attitudinal or motivational items, which in our analyses are found to be most closely related to academic achievement.

The similarity in findings does however indicate the utility of attempting to relate our orientations to more fundamental psychological processes. Our analyses have tried to distinguish approaches (perhaps more markedly affected by the learning context) from styles (implying links with persistent individual differences). The factor analyses did not allow this separation to be made clearly, but the conceptual distinction can be explored in relation to the existing psychological literature. A holistic style, the wide-ranging search for analogies and interconnections between ideas, could be seen as a new way of describing a more familiar term - 'divergent thinking'. Similarly serialism might be associated with convergent thinking.

STYLES OF THINKING

Hudson (1966) popularized the distinction between convergent thinking (as measured by conventional tests of reasoning) and divergent thinking, which is productive or imaginative rather than logical and analytical. Hudson used the simple 'Uses of Objects' test which asks for as many different uses as possible for such everyday objects as a barrel or a paperclip. Scores depend on both the number of responses produced and on their novelty or statistical rarity.

Hudson (1966) drew attention to the wide differences in performance on the Uses of Objects Test, even of sixth-formers who were all highly intelligent. The inability of some pupils to think of more than the most obvious uses led Hudson to designate them as 'convergers', while the superabundance of uses produced by other boys indicated that they could be called 'divergers'. The label given depends on which test score was higher - the verbal reasoning test or the open-ended test. Hudson illustrates how wide the differences can be by quoting two extreme responses. The boys had been asked to list as many uses as they could think of for a barrel. Both boys were highly intelligent, but one was a mathematician and the other was an arts specialist.

> "<u>Converger</u> - Keeping wine in, playing football.
>
> "<u>Diverger</u> - For storing old clothes, shoes,
> tools, paper, etc. For pickling onions in.
> For growing a yew-tree in. For inverting and
> sitting on. As a table. As firewood chopped
> up. As a drain or sump for rainwater. As a
> sand pit. At a party for games. For making
> cider or beer in. As a play-pen for a small
> child. As a rabbit hutch, inverted with a
> door out of the side. On top of a pole as a
> dove-cote. Let into a wall as a night exit
> for a dog or a cat. As the base for a large
> lamp. As a vase for golden rod and michaelmas
> daisies, as an ornament, especially if it is a
> small one. With holes cut in the top and sides,
> either for growing wall-flowers and strawberries
> in, or for stacking pots, and kitchen utensils.
> As a proper garbage can or wastepaper basket.
> As a ladder to reach the top shelves of a high
> bookcase. As a casing for a home-made bomb.
> Sawn in half, as a doll's crib. As a drum.
> As a large bird's nest" (Hudson, 1966, page 90-
> 91).

Hudson found that a majority of convergers
studied science, while divergers mainly specialized
in the arts. He also suggested that these interests,
and the cognitive abilities associated with them, have
their roots in child-rearing practices. The type of
responses made by convergers led Hudson to the conclusion that these pupils were emotionally inhibited
and he speculated that this inability to express
emotion overtly stems from cool, overdemanding
mothers. Divergent thinking is clearly a component
of problem solving, but logical thinking is also
needed. A combination of imaginative production and
analytic reasoning - the alternation of the curious
and the critical which marked Heath's 'Reasonable
Adventurer' - is often necessary.

One of the weaknesses of the Uses of Objects
test is that it accepts both plausible and implaus-
ible uses. Raaheim (1974) has developed a 'categorizing' test which avoids this weakness by demanding realistic alternatives. In this test the names
of successive groups of three objects are presented.
In each group one name is underlined and the task is
to indicate in how many different ways the underlined
object differs from both of the other ones. Raaheim
describes the test as measuring cognitive flexibility
It seems to be a concept similar to that used by

Bieri et al (1966) - cognitive complexity - which
also demands flexible alternations of categorizations
but which is described by Bieri as a cognitive style.
Raaheim sees it as an ability.
    The difference between divergent thinking and
convergent thinking is not just one of different
processes.   There seem to be, as Hudson hinted,
emotional and attitudinal components.   de Bono
(1971) has used the term 'lateral thinking' to describe the alternative to vertical, analytic thinking.
He likens problem-solving to digging holes.
Logical thinking often comes to the point of digging
deeper and deeper holes in quite the wrong place.
He suggests that 'lateral thinking' is more likely
to be effective - a series of shallow, exploratory
holes prior to 'deep drilling'.   Lateral thinking
seems to be closely allied to divergent thinking, and
de Bono sees it as being necessarily leisurely, often
having a dream-like quality where the emotions, as
well as the intellect, are given free rein.
Crutchfield (1962) suggests that

> "One source of original ideas lies in the ready
> accessibility to the thinker of many rich and
> subtle (emotional) attributes of the percepts
> and concepts in his mental world and to the
> metaphorical and analogical penumbras extending
> out from their more explicit, literal and purely
> logical features.   For it is partly through a
> sensitivity to such (emotional) and metaphori-
> cal qualities that new and 'fitting' combin-
> ational possibilities among the elements of a
> problem may unexpectedly emerge" (page 124).

    These strategies of thinking can be readily des-
cribed in the terminology of the information processing model.   Divergent thinking is a search
strategy which has a broad focus and allows
connections between ideas to be made, even when the
justifications for the associations are not obvious.
The wide sweep of relevant information encompasses
both semantic and episodic elements within the LTM.
The search is likely to be relaxed, slow, broad, and
not limited to a specific location in the information
store.   On the other hand convergent thinking will
tend to be narrowly focused, intense, fast and
limited to specific locations.   This distinction
between broad, leisurely, inclusive rambles through
LTM, compared with narrow, fast, and limited forays,
parallels Pask's distinction between holists and
serialists, and seems to be at the root of the more

general, but ill-defined, psychological term 'cognitive style'.

COGNITIVE STYLE

Cognitive styles, like personality traits, are considered by most psychologists to be fairly consistent, and lasting, modes of functioning:

> "The stability and pervasiveness of cognitive styles across diverse spheres of behaviour suggest deeper roots in personality structure than might at first glance be implied ... Cognitive styles may entail generalized habits of information processing, to be sure, but they develop in congenial ways around underlying personality trends. Cognitive styles are thus intimately inter-woven with affective, temperamental, and motivational structures as part of the total personality ...
>
> Cognitive styles differ from intellectual abilities in a number of ways ... Ability dimensions essentially refer to the content of cognition or the question of <u>what</u> - what kind of information is being processed by what operation in what form?
>
> ... Cognitive styles, in contrast, bear on the questions of <u>how</u> - on the manner in which behaviour occurs ... Abilities, furthermore, are generally thought of as unipolar ... (and) value directional: having more of an ability is better than having less. Cognitive styles are (bipolar and) value differentiated: each pole has adaptive value ... (depending) upon the nature of the situation and upon the cognitive requirements of the task in hand" (Messick, 1976, pages 6 - 9).

Two of the best known cognitive styles derive from perceptual tasks - Matching Familiar Figures (Kagan et al, 1964) and identifying Embedded Figures (Witkin, 1977). Figure 5.1 shows an item from one of Kogan's MFF tests which consists of a standard drawing and six or eight variants, one of which is identical to the standard, and all of which are similar. The respondent is required to answer as quickly as possible, but has to make another attempt after each incorrect response. There is thus a pressure to find the <u>correct</u> answer, but also to decide quickly. Kogan (1976) sees the situation as building up competing anxieties towards correct, or fast, responses. The average time to answer (response latency) is measured and also the number of errors. Two cognitive styles have been detected with this test. _Impulsive_ people succumb rapidly to the need to identify the matching figure: they choose hurriedly and make more mistakes. _Reflective_ individuals treat the task more analytically and cautiously: they are more accurate, but slower.

The second cognitive style has perhaps attracted the greatest attention. An item from an Embedded Figures Test (EFT) is shown in Figure 5.2. Witkin (1976; 1977) has reviewed the extensive literature on the use of this and other methods of measuring the dimension of field dependence/field independence. In the EFT the respondent is shown a simple geometrical figure and is required to identify it in a complex figure. The task is rather similar to the children's puzzle in which, say, a 'hidden rabbit' is discovered as part of the foliage of a tree. Some people can spot the embedded figure almost immediately: they are not distracted by the surroundings and are categorised as field-independent. Other people spend much longer even with the simple items. Witkin argues that the different scores on this test do not simply reflect perceptual skills. Like Pask he argues for the existence of underlying styles of thinking. Witkin labels these styles _articulated_ (field-independent) and _global_ (field-dependent), which seem, at first sight, to bear some resemblance to Pask's descriptions of operation learning and comprehension learning.

The articulated, field-independent style involves analysing and structuring incoming information; the global, field-dependent mode of operation accepts the totality of impressions. The problem of Witkin's description is that field-dependence is an _inability_ to impose structure. If it is to be a style, a rather more positive side can only be inferred from incidental characteristics such as tendencies to be sociable and to have an interest in other people. Field-dependent students express this interest in people by being drawn towards courses in the humanities and social sciences, and opting out of courses in science and mathematics. Field-independent students, while found predominantly in science faculties, are still capable of success in other areas of study. This facility raises the question of whether these students might be best compared with Pask's versatile learners, rather than with operation

63

Figure 5.1   Example of an Item from a Matching Familiar Figures Test

Figure 5.2   Example of an Item from an Embedded Figures Test.

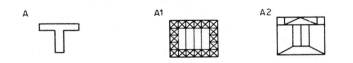

learners.   But here we run up against lack of
empirical evidence.
     From an educational standpoint perhaps the most
interesting studies reported by Witkin concern the
teaching methods adopted by teachers of contrasting
cognitive style.   It appears that field-independent
teachers or lecturers impose a tighter and more
logical structure on teaching material than do
'global' teachers.   They also prefer more formal
approaches to teaching.   Witkin argues that field-
dependent students need pre-structured information,
since they are less able to impose their own
analytic frameworks.   Hence field-dependent
students ought to be more successful with teachers
who have an articulated cognitive style.   To date
there is no evidence of differential success rates,
but there is a clear indication that students prefer
to be taught by teachers of the same cognitive style.
There is thus a possible conflict here between the
approach students prefer and what is considered to
be most effective in helping them to learn.

PERSONALITY

     Personality can be defined as "the dynamic
organization within the individual of those psycho-
physical systems that determine his characteristic
behaviour and thought" (Allport, 1963, page 28).
The term 'personality' is thus the broadest of all.
It can be taken to include cognitive abilities, but
these are generally excluded.   Styles of whatever
sort are certainly contained within this definition
and there are many indications in the literature
that distinctive behavioural or thinking styles are
a facet of personality.
     The description of personality, and its measure-
ment, has depended on the identification of what seem
to be relatively consistent 'common traits'.

     "Common traits are ... those aspects of person-
     ality in respect to which most people within a
     given culture can be profitably compared ...
     The scientific evidence for the existence of a
     trait always comes from demonstrating by some
     acceptable method the consistency in a person's
     behaviour" (Allport, 1963, page 343).

     A useful common trait must show the consistency
of representative groups of individuals both over
time and between situations.   A major problem is to
decide how much consistency is required to provide

evidence for the existence of a trait. People's behaviour, of course, is never _entirely_ predictable from one situation to another: it shows both con-sistency and inconsistency. Some psychologists have used this fact to argue against attempts to describe personality in terms of traits, or even against trying to measure it at all. Labelling can be seen as limiting human potentialities. Bronowski (1965) has rounded on these critics and asked them a series of awkward questions about human predictability.

> "(If) a man does not want to be law-abiding; very well then, it is time to ask him the rude but searching question "Do you want to be law-less?" You refuse to be predictable as an engine is, or an animal; do you aspire to be unpredictable? And if so, are you unpredict-able to yourself, the actor, as well as to me, the spectator? Do you base your claim to be a self on the proud assertion that your actions are arbitrary? (No) ... a self must have con-sistency; its actions tomorrow must be recog-nizably of a piece with the actions carried out yesterday" (pages 13-15).

The extent of such consistency is an empirical question. If important traits can be measured, and if these are also found, on the whole, to be consis-tently related to a variety of aspects of behaviour, then their use in psychology is surely justifiable. But which traits have proved most useful in des-cribing personality?

Jung (1938), from his clinical experience, identified what he considered to be two fundamentally different psychological types - people who viewed the world in opposite ways - the extravert and the intro-vert. The extravert, as the word implies, looks outward. His behaviour is predominantly orientated towards events in the outside world and his thinking is dominated by the search for objective facts. The introvert, on the contrary, looks inward. Out-side events are, of course, perceived but they tend to be judged by personal values and standards. The introvert's thinking is influenced by, even obsessed with, personal interpretations and theories. Jung sees dangers in both extreme ways of thinking.

> "For as in the former case the purely empirical heaping together of facts paralyses thought and smothers their meaning, so in the latter case introverted thinking shows a dangerous tendency

to coerce facts into the shape of its image, or by ignoring them altogether, to unfold its phantasy image in freedom" (pages 481-482).

In Jung's theory the extraverted and introverted tendencies are <u>both</u> present in every person. Whichever characteristic becomes dominant in a person's behaviour and conscious thought, its opposite continues to be represented in the unconscious as the <u>shadow</u>, and is thought to have a continuing effect on the development of personality.

In writing about personality theories, Jung pointed out that the choice of a particular type of theory, or an emphasis within that theory, was in part a reflection of the theorists's own personality. Thus Jung's theory, with its description of extraversion and introversion in terms of ways of <u>thinking</u>, perhaps reflects Jung's own admitted introversion. He was not much concerned with outside events. In contrast Eysenck (1965) has provided descriptions of extraverts and introverts which stress differences in <u>behaviour</u>.

"(The typical extravert is) sociable, likes parties, has many friends, needs to have people to talk to, and does not like studying by himself. He craves excitement, takes chances, often sticks his neck out, acts on the spur of the moment, and is generally an impulsive individual ... The typical introvert, on the other hand, is a quiet retiring sort of person, introspective, fond of books rather than people; he is reserved and distant except with intimate friends. He tends to plan ahead, "looks before he leaps", and distrusts the impulse of the moment" (pages 59-60).

Eysenck and Cattell have both used personality inventories and factor analysis in the attempt to determine which general traits are most useful in the description of personality. Both of them were students of Cyril Burt who had investigated aspects of children's personality in 1915. Burt (1965) claimed to have originally identified a general factor of emotionality, and later described two significant bi-polar factors, one of which appears to have been extraversion/introversion, while the other described the contrast between optimistic and pessimistic outlooks on life.

Cattell (1965) has identified sixteeen different traits, but these overlap to some extent. A

simplified description of these traits reduces the
number to five: anxiety, extraversion, tender-
mindedness, radicalism, and conscientiousness or
moral conventionality.   Eysenck's research has concentrated on the first two of these dimensions.   He
has also described the second two traits, although
he originally identified these as 'social attitudes'
(Eysenck, 1970).   Eysenck's most recent personality
inventories (Eysenck and Eysenck, 1969) now also contain a psychoticism scale (asocial or antisocial
morality) and a lie scale which measures the tendency
to give conventional responses.   At this descriptive
level there is a good agreement between the two
theories, but Eysenck sees extraversion and what he
calls neuroticism (similar to general emotionality)
as much more basic than the other descriptions of
personality.

Eysenck assesses levels of extraversion and
neuroticism through personality inventories which are
built up from a series of questions.   Each question
is an index of one particular personality trait, and
is chosen only after it has been proved to discrim-
inate between groups of people who are known to
exhibit extraverted or introverted patterns of
behaviour.   Respondents are asked to reply 'yes' or
'no' to questions such as

> Can you put your thoughts into words quickly?
> Are you mostly quiet when you are with other
> people?
> Are you an irritable person?
> Are you troubled by feelings of inferiority?
> Have you ever been late for an appointment or
> work?
> Do you sometimes boast a little?

Answering 'yes' to the first question and 'no' to
the second question are indications of extraversion.
The next two questions suggest aspects of neuroticism, while the final two items are part of a 'lie'
scale designed to detect people who are trying to
present themselves in a favourable light.   Considerable care and ingenuity goes into the design
of these personality inventories, and the strength
of the various traits is determined by the number
of responses given in the 'extraverted' or 'neurotic'
directions.   Although a person's response to any
individual item may be affected by the wording, or by
their mood at the time, their overall score on say
25 items remains fairly consistent over time, at
least among adults.

A considerable research literature has built up which reports personality in relation both to students' academic performance and to choice of subject area (see Entwistle and Wilson, 1977). It seems as if introverts tend to be more successful students, but as indicated in Chapter 4, this is probably attributable to better study habits. There are, however, clear differences in personality between students in different subject areas and these are presented diagrammatically in Figure 5.3.

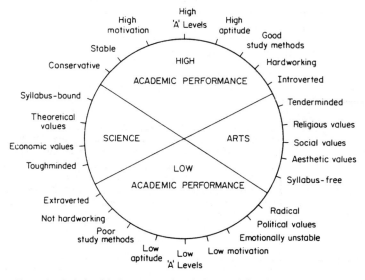

Figure 5.3 Relationship between students' characteristics, faculty membership, and level of academic performance (Adapted from Entwistle and Wilson, 1977, page 148)

The indication that cognitive styles and probably learning styles also differ by faculty reinforced the decision to include indices of personality in our investigation of the more fundamental psychological traits which may underlie approaches and styles of learning.

THE DESIGN OF THE STUDY*

The first step was to identify groups of students who had distinctively different orientations to studying. The second pilot version of the Approaches to Studying Inventory was used for this purpose. From the sample of 767 first year students, 130 were selected as having the highest or lowest scores on the sub-scales which most clearly measured meaning orientation and reproducing orientation. For this purpose the combined scores on deep approach plus comprehension learning were used. The dichotomy on each combined measure produced four groups.

The 130 selected students were sent the third version of the inventory to complete and were invited to take part in the test sessions. Seventy-two students agreed to participate and 60 finally came to the initial interviews. In spite of repeated reminders, no others came. The distribution of the 60 students between the four groups is shown below.

Surface/ Operation	Deep/Comprehension	
	High	Low
High	Strategic $N_1 = 13$	Reproducing $N_3 = 11$
Low	Meaning $N_2 = 15$	Unmotivated $N_4 = 21$

The terms used to describe the groups were chosen on the basis of the mean scores on the inventory. The smallest group (reproducing) were mainly scientists who showed a disappointing reluctance to be involved in the study. The largest group (unmotivated) were, paradoxically, very helpful and cooperative, yet their main characteristic was low scores on most of the sub-scales and subsequent tests. The tests were given in the order shown below over a period of some 15 months. Payments were made

---

* This study was carried out by Sarah Morison (née Burkinshaw)

to every student who completed some 7 hours of testing, spread over the 6 sessions.

Session	Test	Method of Administration
1	Approaches to Studying Inventory (Third Pilot Version)	Post
2	Interviews	Individually
3	(a) Omnibus Personality Inventory (b) Matching Familiar Figures (MFF)	Individually
4	Moray House Advanced Verbal Reasoning (MHA)	Small Groups
5	(a) Test of Categorizing (TC) (b) Uses of Objects (UO) (c) Test of Generalising and Abstracting (TGA) (d) Embedded Figures (EFT)	Small Groups
6	Spy Ring History Test	Microcomputer Individually

The initial interview was designed to create interest
and motivation. It was essential that every student
completed the whole test battery, yet the demands on
the students were very heavy. By establishing a
personal relationship with each student, by providing (optionally) information about test scores and an
interpretation of them, by explaining the relevance
and importance of the project, by encouragement
throughout, and eventually by offering a financial
reward for completion of the full set of tests, all
60 students were retained in the study throughout
a period of 12-15 months.

The tests used are described below in sufficient
detail to ensure that the meaning of each dimension
measured can be understood. The tests are introduced within five measurement areas or domains:

personality, reasoning ability, cognitive style, cognitive flexibility and learning style.

PERSONALITY

The test chosen was the Omnibus Personality Test (Heist and Yonge, 1968), as it had been specifically designed for use with students and contained sub-scores on 14 traits, several of which had, in the literature, been shown to be related to choice of subject area, and seemed also likely to be related to differences in learning style. The traits measured are as follows:

Thinking Introversion — high scorers show a preference for ideas rather than practical action; they have wide-ranging academic interests.

Theoretical Orientation — have a logical, analytical and critical approach to problems, an interest in science and theoretical concerns and problems.

Aestheticism — have wide interests and involvement in literature, music, painting, architecture, etc.

Complexity — show tolerance of ambiguity, enjoy novelty; adopt flexible approaches to problems.

Autonomy — distrust control and authority; are tolerant of other people's contrary views; prefer radical liberal thinking.

Religious Scepticism — reject conventional religious beliefs and practices.

Social Extraversion — enjoy being with people and attending parties or social functions; are happy to join in discussions or talk in public.

Impulse Expression — act on the spur of the moment; are ready to express their feelings; have an active imagination

Personality and Cognitive Style in Studying

Personal Integration — are not socially alienated or personally disturbed, having no strong feelings of paranoia, guilt, or inadequacy.

Anxiety Denial — do not see themselves as restless, tense, anxious, over-sensitive, or highly strung.

Altruism — show friendly concern for others; are trusting and ethical; have an interest in the community and social relationships.

Practical Outlook — have interests in practical things; value material possessions and facts; have a tendency also to be authoritarian and conservative in outlook.

Masculinity — have interests in science (not aesthetics); are calm, emotionally stable, and deny personal inadequacies.

Response Bias — are attempting to make a good impression (faking good); are socially conventional, content and relaxed.

It is important to note that some of these personality scales contain items quite similar to those contained in our Approaches to Studying Inventory. There is, in terms of content, an overlap between, for example, deep approach and both thinking introversion and theoretical orientation. But the overlap is small enough to be able to accept the personality traits as distinct. Thus the measure of theoretical introversion coincides with the personality construct, particularly as described by Jung, and the validity of the other personality dimensions has also been carefully established.

REASONING ABILITY

The main test used was the Moray House Advanced Test of Verbal Reasoning (Godfrey Thomson Unit, 1971), which is a conventional 'intelligence' test. It provides a score in terms of an intelligence quotient with a mean of 100 for the population.

In addition a test of Generalizing and Abstracting (Peel, 1978) was used. A set of three words is presented; four alternatives are offered as a description of what the target words have in common.

For example: <u>Charity</u>   <u>Sympathy</u>   <u>Tolerance</u>
Voluntary work; Humanity; Generosity; Lacking in some people

In each item the distracting alternative responses contain a word of similar meaning but at the same level of generality, a particular instance or example, and a non-essential attribute. The items are divided into concrete and abstract terms, providing separate estimates of the ability to abstract and generalize correctly.

COGNITIVE STYLES

Field-Independence

The Group Embedded Figures Test (described in Witkin <u>et al</u>, 1977) produces a single score of field-independence which represents the total number of simple figures correctly identified within the complex figures (see Figure 5.2). The simple figures are shown first, followed on the next page by the complex figures. The test is in two parts with nine items in each and an overall time-limit of ten minutes.

Reflectiveness/Impulsivity

The Matching Familiar Figures Test was used in a form suitable for young adults (described in Messer, 1976). Two scores were derived from this test - the average time taken to make the first response (which indicates reflectiveness) and the total number of incorrect choices made (inaccuracy).

Cognitive Flexibility

The Uses of Objects test was used to obtain a measure of verbal fluency (total number of uses) while the Categorizing Test provided an indication of flexibility. Both tests have been described in an earlier secton.

Learning Style

Pask (1976b) has used the Spy Ring History Test to provide indices of comprehension learning, operation learning and versatility. The test is lengthy and intellectually demanding. Students are presented with detailed information about the development of an imaginary spy network operating between several countries over a period of three years. Students have to rote-learn lists and interpret diagrams to work out the communication patterns and make predictions about future developments. Besides the three indices of learning style, the test also provides a score on 'knowledge of facts'.

Because of the demanding nature of this test and the lengthy administration time, the test was mounted on a PET microcomputer *. The computer controlled the appearance of lists and diagrams and also calculated the scores.

Students' reactions to this test were, on the whole, unfavourable. They found it difficult and boring. Many students resented the demands made for continuous rote learning, and the results indicated that few students had coped adequately with these demands. Those who found the test interesting were mainly studying science or engineering. Arts students seemed to find the type of learning required alien, and were often uncomfortable with using the PET. Even the scoring procedure seemed to penalize arts students. It thus came as no surprise that the results made little sense. The scores intended to measure learning styles had weak and contradictory relationships with supposedly equivalent dimensions from the Approaches to Studying Inventory. In an exploratory factor analysis Pask's test formed its own factor with high positive loadings on all three styles and on knowledge of facts. The only significant loadings elsewhere were on verbal reasoning, field independence, and accuracy. This disappointing set of relationships, which were contrary to the patterns demanded by Pask's own descriptions of the constructs, led the test to be dropped from the main analyses. It may be that our attempts to present the test in a more attractive

* We are grateful to Gordon Pask for making the computer program available and to Phil Odor for adapting it for use on the PET.

way on the microcomputer interfered with the validity of the test which has been used effectively by Pask in its original form in several studies. The microcomputer presentation may have misled students into believing they had learned the material more throughly than they had, thus preventing them responding to subsequent parts of the test.

CHARACTERISTICS OF STUDENTS WITH CONTRASTING APPROACHES

The main question being asked in this part of the research was whether students adopting contrasting approaches to studying showed equivalent differences in any of the more fundamental psychological characteristics included in the study. The simplest analysis thus examined the mean scores and standard deviations of the four contrasting groups, using analyses of variance to indicate whether differences between the groups were statistically significant. With such small groups there are a large number of insignificant differences. The results were thus treated only as indicative and other analyses carried out. In terms of personality, the first indications were that students high in meaning orientation have high scores, as expected, on thinking introversion and theoretical orientation, but also on complexity (very marked) and to a lesser extent on autonomy, aestheticism, and religious scepticism. The strategic group were characterized by high anxiety, less personal integration and a higher level of impulse expression. The reproducing group had high scores on practical outlook and masculinity, combined with low scores on thinking introversion, theoretical orientation, complexity and autonomy. The unmotivated group could only be described as unresponsive and conventional. The remaining tests showed no significant differences, although there was a suggestion that high scores on meaning orientation were associated with greater facility in verbal reasoning and verbal fluency. Students with high scores on deep/comprehension learning showed a tendency towards field dependence which nearly reached statistical significance.

RELATIONSHIPS BETWEEN APPROACHES AND PSYCHOLOGICAL ATTRIBUTES

The other main analysis involved looking at the correlates of deep/surface approaches and comprehension and operation learning. The statistically significant correlations found with each of these variables are shown in Table 5.1.

These simple correlations provide an initial indication of the extent to which there may be personality correlates of learning styles or approaches to studying. The impression created by Table 5.1 is that, as predicted, styles, rather than approaches, are more closely associated with psychological attributes. Students with high scores on comprehension learning tend to have high scores on a group of personality traits which relate to interest in ideas, but they also tend to be more ready to express impulses and admit feelings of anxiety and inadequacy. Operation learners have an opposite set of personality attributes associated with interest in practical, non-theoretical areas. They also showed caution (reflectiveness) and had lower scores on the abstract items of the generalizing test.

To make sense of the total set of interrelationships it is again necessary to carry out a factor analysis, but as there are 36 variables and only 60 students this multivariate analysis has to be treated as exploratory, rather than definitive. Given the small sample, care was taken to include only those variables which could create factors (at least two overlapping variables are necessary). After a series of exploratory analyses with different groups of variables, the clearest set of factors was produced by using principal component factor analyses with rotation to oblique simple structure to the set of variables shown in Appendix Table 3. Six factors had eigen values above unity.

The factors are mainly associated with the different measurement domains. Thus Factors I and II represent meaning orientation combined with positive attitudes to studying, while reproducing orientation is associated with strategic, achievement motivation. The personality inventory produces two factors, one of which brings together complexity, autonomy, and impulse expression (sceptical intellectual autonomy), while the other is dominated by anxiety and a lack of personal integration. Of the remaining smaller factors one seems to describe the ability to solve intellectual and perceptual

Table 5.1 SIGNIFICANT CORRELATIONS WITH APPROACHES AND STYLES (N = 60)

Deep Approach	Comprehension Learning	Surface Approach	Operation Learning
Thinking Introversion (48)	Thinking Introversion (52)	Practical Outlook (38)	Practical Outlook (39)
Theoretical Outlook (38)	Aestheticism (43)	Thinking Introversion (−31)	Complexity (−37)
Aestheticism (31)	Theoretical Outlook (39)	Theoretical Outlook (−26)	Aestheticism (−30)
Impulse Expression (28)	Complexity (33)		Abstract Generalising (−28)
Complexity (27)	Personal Integration (−31)		Reflectiveness (23)
Verbal Fluency (24)	Impulse Expression (30)		Thinking Introversion (−23)
	Practical Outlook (−23)		
	Verbal Reasoning (23)		
	Anxiety Denial (−22)		

Decimal points omitted

puzzles, while the final factor seems to describe the abilities of Hudson's 'diverger'.

It is, of course, particularly interesting to look for overlap between the final four factors and scores on the Approaches to Studying Inventory. Thus Factor III suggests that fear of failure and globetrotting, linked to disorganized surface approaches to studying, are associated with general feelings of anxiety, tenseness and inadequacy. Fransson (1977) has already shown that it is not so much a threatening learning situation which induces surface approaches to studying, as it is students' perceptions of that situation as anxiety provoking. These findings could be taken to indicate that it may be as much a student's underlying general anxiety which induces surface learning as the particular learning context experienced. But the direction of causality and the effects of previous experience cannot be determined from this type of analysis.

Factor IV is the main personality grouping of sceptical intellectual autonomy. Its fairly strong links also with degree class and deep comprehension learning are reassuring, although the element of disorganization and globetrotting is unexpected. Again it is clear that the general personality trait is reflected in approaches to studying (an indication of syllabus-freedom) and in tests of thinking (abstract generalizing and flexibility). The ability to solve puzzles links only with complexity and the use of evidence. The 'divergers' of Factor VI show readiness to express their impulses (as Hudson argued), but their deep approach, linked as it is with negative attitudes, is not associated with degree class.

Additional analyses were also carried out to identify correlates of high levels of academic performance. Overall it was clear that a deep orientation, combined with both intrinsic and achievement motivation, were the attributes most consistently related to degree class. However, anxiety was positively related to academic performance among women.

Drawing together the evidence derived from this part of the inquiry, it is possible to argue that there are underlying personality traits associated with the tendency to prefer comprehension or operation styles of learning. It also appears that a deep orientation involves, at least to some extent, the abilities to think both logically and flexibly, combined with the personality characteristics described as sceptical intellectual autonomy.

Personality and Cognitive Style in Studying

In spite of a certain circularity through similar items, the argument for personality correlates of styles of learning is still pressed, based on the validity of the traits identified in the Omnibus Personality Inventory.

STUDENTS' PREFERENCES FOR CONTRASTING STYLES OF WRITIN

The next section describes an experiment, carried out after the test sessions had been completed, in which students were asked to read, and answer questions on, three short articles. As part of this experiment students were also asked to read and comment on four essays. These essays were supposed to have been written by students, although in fact they had been specially written to exhibit extremes of serialism and holism. The topic chosen was 'Alternative Sources of Energy', a title which was expected to interest both arts and science students. The essays were written to fit as closely as possible the stylistic characteristics of holists and serialist as described by Pask and listed below.

Holist characteristics	Serialist characteristi
Comprehension Learning:	**Operation Learning:**
Creates an overall picture	Uses rules and procedur
Assimilates ideas from other subjects	Gives details in isolat
Invents description schemes	Keeps to one topic at a time
Uses analogies	
Has broad generalizations as hypotheses	Proceeds in stepwise manner
Relates ideas to everyday experience	Gives specific hypothes
Looks for alternative approaches to problems	
Globetrotting:	**Improvidence:**
Inappropriate links between ideas	Insufficient explanati of detail
Vacuous analogies	Failure to use common principles

The instructions given to students were as follows:

"You are to imagine that you are the tutor responsible for this course and are required to write evaluative comments on these essays indicating what you consider to be their stylistic strengths and

80

weaknesses and then to mark each of them on a scale
on which '9' indicates an outstanding essay and '1'
indicates one which is very poor indeed.   On this
scale '5' is the mid-point which should be used to
indicate 'reasonably good'.   Your comments should
make clear your reasons for allocating the mark you
decide.   Please also say which essay is most
like one you might have written yourself and
which one you found easiest to read."

The sample consisted of 47 of the 60 students
described in this chapter, divided as before into the
four categories - strategic (N = 10), meaning (9),
reproducing (9), and unmotivated (19).   In marking
the essays, the four groups of students showed clear,
and different, preferences for the four essays
(Serialist 1, 2 and·Holist 1,2), and also different
marking standards which made comparisons difficult.
The 'unmotivated' group,with low meaning and reproducing scores, were least critical, awarding much
higher marks without any clear preference for holist
or serialist essays;   they   marked Serialist 2 highest
and Serialist 1 lowest.   The reproducing group found
both holist essays relatively unsatisfactory, and
gave their highest average mark most clearly to
Serialist 2.   The meaning group also preferred
Serialist 2, but rated Holist 1 almost as highly.
Finally the strategic group, with high meaning and
reproducing scores, were the most critical group
(particularly of Serialist 1), but marked both holist
 essays more favourably than the serialist essays.
The marking pattern of the four groups is summarized
in Table 5.2 together with their indications of which
essay they found easiest to read and which was most
like their own style of writing.
In this small-scale exploratory study it was not
expected to find clear-cut differences between the
groups.   It appears that one of the essays (Serialist
1) was too extreme in its style for most of the
students, and another was generally thought to be the
best (Serialist 2).   However, if the high rating for
Serialist 2 is discounted, the two groups with high
comprehension scores (groups 1 and 2) show consistent
preferences for holist essays.   The unmotivated
group show in this analysis, as in earlier analyses,
no clear pattern.
Some indication of students' reasons for
choosing one or other style of writing was found
among their comments on the essays.   For example, the
reproducing group indicated their preferences for
the serialist essays by saying:

Table 5.2   PREFERENCES FOR SERIALIST AND HOLIST ESSAYS

Group	Marks Given		Easiest to Read		Most Like My Own	
	Highest	Lowest	Most	Least	Most	Least
1. Strategic	H1 H2 (S2)	S1	H1 H2	S1	H1 (S2)	S1
2. Meaning	H1	H2	H1	S1	H2 (S2)	S1
3. Reproducing	(S2) S1	H1 H2	(S2)	S1	S1 (S2)	H2
4. Unmotivated	(S2)	S1	H2	S1	H2	S1

H = Holist   S = Serialist

(The Serialist 2 essay was consistently judged to be the best and so the pattern shown is best interpreted by ignoring that essay – hence the brackets around it).

Personality and Cognitive Style in Studying

"Very readable. Some of the definitions, e.g. joule, are not strictly necessary but a clear and suitably brief account of the current dilemma. Quite probing and detailed but avoids dangers of being excessively political or technological".

"Covers most aspects briefly but adequately. Easy to read. Calculations relevant and understandable. Good beginning defining what energy is and present needs. Well organized and planned".

The comments they made against the holist essays included:

"Too vague, too many cliches. Uncritical. Attempt should be made to lose flowery style and concentrate on simple sentences which are lucid and precise".

"Clear concise style. Topical. Too much on background. Readable and a lot of relevant points made but could have gone into alternative technology in more detail".

The students who had high comprehension learning seemed to have enjoyed the relaxed, conversational style of both holist essays:

"Excellent. Included political analysis. Organized. Speaks with conviction and urgency. Easy to read".

"Very interesting and lively essay taken from an unusual and worthwhile perspective. Develops logically and clearly. Last paragraph seems a bit out of joint".

The 'strategic group generally disliked the serialist style, but also recognized that the holist style was light on detail:

"Written as if to include x no. of facts. One fact after another, not enough general writing to make it readable".

"Well structured, but certainly not to be read for pleasure. Not a style I like at all".

"Narrow. Doesn't look at social/environmental/ political problems. Too much mathematics leading to arbitrary factual statements. Dry to read, no personal comment".

"Good style. Pleasant emotive reading. Would be good for getting the point across to a difficult audience. Could perhaps do with more details".

This exploratory study has provided some indication of the ways in which students may differ in their preferred styles of writing essays. Although some of the differences here may reflect little more than arts/ science divisions, other analyses have shown that important differences in style and approach remain even within the distinct disciplines.

Chapter Six

APPROACHES TO READING ACADEMIC ARTICLES

(Written in collaboration with Sarah Morison)

A QUESTIONNAIRE ON OUTCOME AND PROCESS

Marton's original experiments on how students approached the task of reading academic articles relied on interviews to establish qualitative differences in what had been learned (outcome of learning) and what strategies students had used in tackling this task (process of learning). He and his colleagues had shown clearly a link between intention, process, and outcome. Students who intended to understand were likely to interact with evidence and argument, in relation to their previous knowledge and experience, and so come to a personal understanding of the author's conclusion. Students who were more concerned to answer correctly what they anticipated to be mainly factual questions on the article concentrated instead on question-spotting and rote memorization and often finished with very little grasp of the author's argument or conclusions.

Marton's research methodology is both time consuming and limiting in sample size. It could also be argued that students are being forced to respond to questions in an unfamiliar way. Certainly in Britain, first-year students would be more used to making written, rather than oral, responses to questions. It was therefore decided to develop a questionnaire variant of Marton's procedure, recognising that what was gained in sample size might be lost in the lack of opportunity to probe the levels of understanding and approaches to learning.

The early part of this Chapter is based on work carried out by Maureen Hanley and Garth Ratcliffe and reported in a previous article (Entwistle, Hanley, and Ratcliffe, 1979).

The categories identified in the questionnaire might thus be expected to be less clear-cut, and the relationships commensurately weaker.

The main problem in developing this variant was in finding a wording for the various questions on outcome and process which enabled students to understand what was required without also indicating what type of answer was expected. It also proved extremely difficult to find a way of coding students' responses which kept sufficiently close to Marton's categories to make a convincing test of his findings on the wider sample. A further difficulty was in finding articles which were general enough to be understood by students in a particular faculty, but demanding enough and detailed enough to present a sufficient intellectual challenge.

After two pilot studies a final form of the questionnaire was produced and three articles were selected as follows:

(1) Burt (1971) - The Mental Differences between
                    Children (4800 words).
(2) Pines (1976) - A Child's Mind is Shaped before
                    Age 2 (3200 words).
(3) Hoyle (1950) - The Expanding Universe (3800 words).

This version of the questionnaire contained the following questions designed to cover level of understanding, previous knowledge, knowledge of details contained in the article, and approach to learning.

(1) General Understanding 'Write down what you have learned from the article. Imagine you were going to describe what the article was about to a friend who hadn't read it. What would you say?'

(2) Attitude Statements (including an index of previous knowledge). 'Rate your attitudes to this article and the ideas it contains by underlining one of EACH of the three adjectives or phrases.'

Interesting   Average   Boring
Ideas familiar to me Average   Ideas unfamiliar to me
Enjoyable   Average   Not enjoyable

(3) Knowledge of Details 'Here are some specific questions on various aspects of the article. Try to answer each question as fully as you can

and where necessary explain your answer.'
Examples of typical questions in this section
are:
'How are the stars formed?
What evidence is there that the universe is ex-
panding?
Within the "new cosmology" what is the ex-
planation of the expanding universe?'

(4)   Approach to Learning   'Students tackle the task
of reading articles or books in many different
ways, and with different expectations of what
is required of them and of what they should be
getting out of their reading. How did you
tackle this article?   Was this approach typical
of, or different from, what you would do in your
normal studying?'

Procedure   Groups of students were invited to take
part in the experiment. The purpose of the study
was explained in general terms, students were then
asked to read the article as they would normally do
in preparation for, say, a tutorial.   There was a
generous time limit with no pressure to complete the
reading quickly.   Students could make notes, but
could not use them subsequently.   After reading the
article students were asked to complete a 'Uses of
Objects' test to avoid easy verbatim recall.   They
were then asked to complete the questionnaire.

Coding   Students wrote on average about 150 words
in response to the first question.   This was
effectively a short essay and thus created familiar
problems in coding the level of understanding reached.
The choice is essentially between impression marking
in relation to Marton's descriptions and a reliance
on specific marking criteria.   Since these studies
were carried out Biggs and Collis (1982) have published a classification system for coding the qualitative outcomes of learning (the SOLO taxonomy), and
this has been used in studies relating approach to
outcome (Biggs, 1979; Schmeck and Phillips, in press)
In the absence of a classification scheme, simpler
approaches were adopted.   In the first study the
number of main points mentioned was used to identify
'high' and 'low' categories, but in the third study
a more effective procedure involved impression marking against the specific criteria described by Marton.
The coder made dichotomous judgements of the response
against the following questions.

(a)   Has an attempt been made to integrate the presentation of the main points and/or facts? (i.e. has the student reinterpreted and re-organised what has been read, rather than re-calling points in the order read from memory?)

(b)   Have a 'sufficient' number of main points been mentioned?   ('sufficient' being defined so as to produce roughly a 50/50 distribution between categories).

(c)   Has the author's message been understood?

(d)   Are details (e.g. numerical facts, specific names) mentioned?

The sum of the first three codes was used as a summary variable indicating general understanding. The second question related to attitudes, and students responded on the three-point scales shown in the previous section.   Question (3) contained 12 specific questions.   These were divided into two groups for scoring: one group had questions about main points essential to an understanding of the author's argument;   the other questions concerned incidental facts.   Each question was scored on the basis of two marks for a full answer which was correct, one mark for an incomplete or partially correct answer.   The two groups of marks were summed separately to give totals for essential points and incidental facts.

The final question again creates great problems in coding.   The initial approach was impression coding into 'deep' or 'surface', but the last study used a similar procedure to the first question, where the coder was asked to make dichotomous judgements against a series of questions, three of which were indications of a deep approach and three which suggested a surface approach.

(a)   Was there a clear intention of trying to understand what the author was saying?

(b)   Was there an intention to integrate what was being read with other parts of the article, or with facts, or with previous experience?

(c)   Was there an intention to try to reach own con-clusion or make use of own personal experience?

(d)   Was there an intention to obtain facts or information?

(e)   Did the experimental conditions appear to have affected performance (for example, time limit, artificiality, consciousness of questions to be answered, anxiety etc.)?

(f) Was there an intention to memorise or try to
     learn by rote?

The sum of the first three ratings was used as
an overall indication of a <u>deep approach</u>; the sum
of the second three ratings provided a similar indication of a <u>surface approach</u>. A different coder
was used for each article, but a sample of each set
of questionnaires was checked to ensure that the
criteria were being interpreted consistently.

This version of the questionnaire was given to
248 first-year students from various subject areas
in two universities (N = 85), two colleges of
education (82) and first-year sixth-formers in a
further education college (81).

The articles proved to be different both in
difficulty level and ease of coding. There could
therefore be no comparison between the levels of
understanding reached in different articles: responses had to be analysed separately by article.
Table 6.1 shows the mean scores of students in' the
different types of institution.

There are some marked differences between the
university students and sixth-formers in the college
of further education. Note, for example, that while
on both the Burt and Hoyle articles the sixth-formers
rate themselves as almost as familiar with the ideas
as the students, they show on average only 0.77
indications of a deep approach (out of a possible
3), while the university students have 1.53 such
indications. The university students also have
higher scores on each of the three measures of the
outcome of learning.

The intercorrelations in Table 6.2 are shown
separately for the Hoyle and Burt articles. With
the Hoyle article, the pattern of relationships is as
expected, with general understanding showing a
substantial positive correlation with the deep
approach to learning (0.45) and a negative relationship with the surface approach (-0.29). The Burt
article showed much weaker relationships, as did the
Pines article (not reported).

To check on the justification for combining
codings within question (1) and within question (4),
and to look for further evidence of connections
between understanding and approach, principal components analyses without iteration were carried out
with oblique rotation using the SPSS program (Nie et
al, 1975). Application of the criterion of eigen-
values of unity was supported by scree plots to

Table 6.1   MEAN SCORES AND STANDARD DEVIATIONS BY TYPE OF INSTITUTION AND ARTICLES

Coding Category (N)	Burt			Hoyle		Pines	
	Univ. (16)	Coll. (25)	FE (46)	Univ. (36)	FE (35)	Univ. (33)	Coll. (57)
General understanding	1.31 (0.95)	1.36 (0.91)	1.04 (1.82)	1.75 (1.30)	1.34 (1.26)	1.94 (1.03)	1.72 (0.92)
Essential points	5.44 (2.48)	3.48 (2.16)	3.22 (2.22)	9.33 (3.96)	8.54 (3.70)	5.73 (1.84)	5.12 (1.59)
Incidental facts	5.63 (2.00)	2.52 (1.83)	2.91 (1.82)	3.03 (1.50)	2.57 (1.75)	8.33 (2.45)	7.88 (2.49)
Familiarity	2.19 (0.83)	2.32 (0.75)	1.98 (0.80)	1.94 (0.75)	1.91 (0.85)	2.06 (0.90)	2.19 (0.77)
Deep approach	1.38 (0.72)	0.72 (0.61)	0.70 (0.63)	1.67 (0.89)	0.83 (0.79)	1.45 (0.97)	1.42 (0.80)
Surface approach	1.19 (0.66)	0.92 (0.57)	1.04 (0.59)	0.83 (0.74)	1.20 (0.68)	1.21 (0.74)	1.18 (0.71)
Uses of objects	24.63 (7.54)	22.64 (9.86)	20.76 (5.59)	23.83 (7.22)	19.06 (5.52)	24.27 (7.27)	23.56 (6.90)

Table 6.2   INTERCORRELATIONS BETWEEN THE MAIN CODING CATEGORIES

	GU	EP	IF	FM	DA	SA	UO
General understanding	*	40	15	07	45	-29	15
Essential points	47	*	46	27	32	-25	29
Incidental facts	19	53	*	08	10	-06	08
Familiarity	20	07	05	*	17	-08	03
Deep approach	11	19	27	-01	*	-40	24
Surface approach	-05	07	12	04	07	*	07
Uses of objects	14	21	-08	11	13	-01	*

Notes: Correlations above the diagonal refer to the Hoyle article (N = 96);   those below the
diagonal refer to the Burt article (N =87).

Decimal points omitted.

Correlations significant at the 5% level where r = 0.20 (Hoyle) and r = 0.21 (Burt).

suggest that five factors should be extracted.
These factors accounted for 63% of the variance, on
average. These five factor solutions were not altogether satisfactory, as the components of general
understanding and approach to learning tended to be
associated together in rather different combinations
for the different articles. The connection between
approach and level of understanding can, however, be
seen clearly in the three-factor solution of the
responses to the Hoyle article (see Table 6.3).
Factor I combines the three indicators of general
understanding and both detailed knowledge variables
with the first two criteria for identifying the deep
approach. Factor III shows its high loading on
memorization, which is associated with a tendency not
to look for meaning, and a failure to mention the
main points when asked for a summary. Factor II
shows a greater weighting on those variables relating
to facts (with the rather important exception of
'incidental facts').

Table 6.3   FACTOR LOADINGS FOR THE HOYLE ARTICLE

Coding Categories		Factor Loadings		
		I	II	III
General understanding	Integration	61		-43
	Main points	52	21	-54
	Understanding	64		-43
	Factual details		27	
Detailed knowledge	Essential points	73	48	-24
	Incidental Facts	43		
Previous knowledge	Familiarity		32	
Deep approach	Looking for meaning	26		-56
	Use of experience	37	30	-51
	Relating facts and conclusion		40	
Surface approach	Looking for information			48
	Situational anxiety	-32		20
	Memorization			68

Decimal points and loadings below 0.20 omitted.

At least with the Hoyle article it was possible

to demonstrate the predicted links between the approach to learning and both the level of understanding reached and the extent of relevant knowledge retained. The value of keeping each index of either approach or outcome separate (as opposed to Marton's method of accepting any of three indicators as sufficient to categorize as overall deep or surface) was clear in the fuller interpretation of the relationships which became possible.

STUDENTS' COMMENTS ON APPROACH TO LEARNING

Besides the quantitative analysis, it was also possible to examine qualitatively the comments made by students about their approaches to learning. In many of the answers the distinction between 'deep' and 'surface' came through clearly, and in ways which paralleled Marton's own examples of students' comments (see Marton & Säljö, 1976a, p. 9).

Consider, for example, the following extracts in relation to the coding instructions. What approach has each of these students adopted?

Student A "Whilst reading the article, I took great care in trying to understand what the author was getting at, looking out for arguments and facts which backed up the arguments ... I found myself continually relating the article to personal experience, and this facilitated my understanding of it ... The fact of being asked questions on it afterwards made my attention more intense."

Student B "In reading the article I was looking out mainly for facts and examples. I read the article more carefully than I usually would, taking notes, knowing that I was to answer questions about it. I thought the questions would be about the facts in the article ... This did influence the way I read; I tried to memorize names and figures quoted etc."

Student C "I tried hard to concentrate - too hard, therefore my attention seemed to be on 'concentration rather than reading, thinking, interpreting, and remembering, something that I find happening all the time I'm reading text-books."

Student D "I read it in a casual interested manner, not being influenced by the fact that I was to be questioned, mainly because I did not expect the questionnaire to ask for any details from the

article.   Consequently I read it with impartial
interest - extracting the underlying meaning but
letting facts and examples go unheeded."

Although these are selected extracts chosen to
demonstrate particular types of answer, many of the
replies followed Marton's examples so closely that
it seemed almost as if the students must have read
about his ideas before - but they had not.

Using Marton's approach to coding (i.e. accepting one 'symptom' of the approach as a sufficient
indication), students A and D would be classified as
having adopted a 'deep' approach, while B and C would
be coded as 'surface'.   Yet students A and D have
clearly adopted very different approaches.   In each
of our studies there has been a distinct group of
students who look for meaning but do not interact
with the article, relating facts to conclusion.
This group has been labelled 'deep passive' to distinguish it from the 'deep active' approach shown by
student A.

One interesting point about the two students who
adopted the surface approach is that both of them
recognised that their approach had been rather ineffective.   A later question asked 'Were you satisfied with your performance (in answering the questions)?
to which student B replied: "I feel that some of my
answers are vague and need more detail ... I made the
mistake of trying to retain everything, rather than
just the important features."   There is at least a
hint here of the possible advantages of helping
students to become more consciously aware of their
approaches to studying.   The use of the questionnaire
proved fruitful, even though only one of the articles
seemed to be fully effective.   It has provided
evidence which, in conjunction with findings from the
approaches to studying inventory, has helped to
elaborate the concept of 'approach to learning' as
originally outlined by Marton.   More recent studies
at Gothenburg (Säljö, 1975; Fransson, 1977) have
independently confirmed the necessity to subdivide
approach to learning in terms of whether an active or
passive stance has been taken.   Säljö described a
'technified' deep approach in which the student
looked for meaning without interacting with the detail
or the argument.   This approach has since been
equated with Pask's learning pathology of 'globetrotting' or, in less extreme forms, an over-reliance
on comprehension learning to the exclusion of operation
learning.

The possible connections between the differing

categories of Pask and Marton were pointed up by the
factor analysis shown in Table 6.3. Taking the two
sets of categories together it seems likely that an
intention to approach learning initially in what
Svensson has called a holist (deep) or atomistic
(surface) way will reflect,in part, the characteristic learning style of the individual. Thus the
connection between a deep approach and comprehension
learning becomes inevitable. Similarly operation
learning, particularly where time or interest is
limited, is likely to become improvidence and so reflect at least one component of the surface approach.
A holist strategy (in terms of the questionnaire responses) should be shown by an emphasis on integration
and on the use of personal experience, while a
serialist strategy might be expected to show a greater
reliance on main points and factual details. Up to
a point, the distinction mentioned earlier, between
factors I and II in the three-factor solution shown
in Table 6.3, contains this characteristic difference in emphasis. This analysis continues the
pattern of results now familiar from previous
analyses. The empirical findings contain hints at
ways of conceptualizing learning styles, as distinct
from approaches to studying. But clear empirical
separation of these constructs is rarely possible.

In the study by Schmeck and Phillips (in press)
relationships between levels of outcome (as measured
by the SOLO taxonomy) were related to scales from the
Inventory of Learning Processes. They found that
deep outcome correlated 0.37 with 'deep processing',
but only 0.12 with 'elaborative processing'. Schmeck
comments that Marton's 'deep approach' includes "the
search for personal meaning" which is a part of elaborative processing. But the separation in Table
6.3 between two distinct types of deep approach re-
inforces our view that there are contrasting styles
in seeking understanding - one in which personal
meaning is emphasized, and one in which the evidence
is related carefully to the conclusions. In Schmeck
scheme, the first would be described as elaborative
processing and the latter might, at first, be thought
to be close to 'fact retention'. But there is a
major problem in accepting this equivalence. Examination of the items within the 'fact retention'
scale (Schmeck, in press, Table 1) shows that the
two items having loadings of above 0.5 are:
- "I do well on exams requiring much factual infor-
    mation"
- "I am very good at learning formulas, names and
    dates"

These items, and indeed all but two of the items in
the scale, are, explicitly or implicitly, self-ratings
of outcome: they do not strictly describe processes
at all. Indeed the nature of the items can be used
to explain the differential correlation with levels
of understanding. The 'elaborative processing'
scale is truly a measure of process - every item
describes a process, while 'deep processing' contains
an unfortunate mixture of process and outcome. Two
of the items in this scale (both with loadings of
over 0.40) are self-ratings of academic performance
- "I do well on essay tests"
- "I get good grades on term papers"

Thus the higher correlation between 'deep processing' and levels of outcome must, in part, be a
result of having self-ratings of prior learning outcomes within the scale.
This criticism becomes even more powerful where
Schmeck report that "the most successful college
students were deep, elaborative, fact retainers".
He comments that his inventory shows higher relationships with academic achievement than some other scales
of learning processes. In Chapter 4, we used
students' self-ratings of their academic progress
(which would be based on essay grades and test marks)
as our criterion. In relating process to outcome it
is essential to keep indices of process entirely
separate from criterion measures of attainment,
otherwise the circularity so produced interferes with
the interpretation of how the various processes and
styles relate to outcome. Only by a combination of
conceptual and factor analysis in scale development
can such circularity be avoided.

ALTERING STUDENTS' APPROACHES TO LEARNING*

Säljö (1975) reported an experiment in which
detailed factual questions about an article appeared
to shift students towards a surface approach to subsequent articles. He also showed that questions
about overall meaning moved some students towards a
deep passive (technified) approach, without making
an impact on the level of understanding reached. In
our questionnaire variant of Marton's original experiment we had shown how the content and level of difficulty of an article affected the clarity with which

---

*The research reported in this section was carried
out by Sarah Morison.

95

relationships between process and outcome could be demonstrated. Finally Fransson (1977) had shown how interest or perceived relevance affected the approach to reading an article.

These findings suggested that we should extend the use of the questionnaire variant of Marton's method of research by asking the student volunteers who had taken the psychological tests to carry out a learning experiment in which both content and question-type were varied. The materials and instructions were sent to the 48 students (out of 60) who agreed to continue their involvement with the programme beyond what had originally been negotiated.

Each student was sent three short articles, each of just under 2000 words. The first article was a shortened version of extracts from Hoyle's The Expanding Universe used successfully in the earlier study. The second was based on ideas presented by Geoffrey Ashe in his book Camelot and the Vision of Albion which described evidence linking the historical Arthur with an iron-age fort at South Cadbury. The final article was a summary of research on styles of learning and thinking, intended to have personal relevance to the students as it mentioned some of the tests they had taken during the previous year and provided the rationale for our research programme.

Students were assigned randomly to two conditions. One group was given entirely specific questions on ideas or facts presented in the article. The other group was given a general question asking them to explain 'to a friend' what the article was about. Both groups were asked after each article to suggest implications stemming from what they had read, and after the final article both types of question were given to all the students.

Both groups were also asked to comment on their approaches to reading and how the questions asked had influenced their strategies in tackling the second and third articles. They were also given a set of self-ratings about each article to indicate to what extent, on a five-point scale, they were familiar with the ideas, found the article interesting or difficult, were able to concentrate, felt tired, found illustrations useful, and could remember the main theme and the details. The instructions to the students asked them to read each article on a separate day. The instructions were as follows.

"Read this article carefully in your own time in the same way as you would if you were preparing for an examination. Take notes if you would do so normally, but you will not be allowed to use them afterwards. When you have finished reading the article put it back into the envelope together with your notes and reseal it. Take a break of 20 minutes, then open (the next) envelope and answer the questions in it, putting the questionnaire back in the envelope afterwards."

The general question was coded as before with dichotomous codes (1,0) on five indices of outcome describing whether or not the student had

(a) reinterpreted, reorganized or integrated material
(b) mentioned an above average number of main points
(c) understood the author's message
(d) used evidence appropriately
(e) used irrelevant facts

An overall indication of a deep outcome was obtained by calculating (a) + (b) + (c) + (d) - (e) on a scale of -1 to 4 (although no one obtained a score of -1).

The answers to the specific questions were scored right or wrong in two groups - essential points and incidental facts, while the 'implications' question was coded on a four-point scale.

Approaches to reading the first article were coded as before with three indices of deep, but in this case with four criteria of a surface approach. Criteria of a deep approach were

*   a clear intention to try to understand
*   an intention to integrate separate parts
*   an intention to reach own conclusion or to use personal experience

A surface approach was indicated by

*   being influenced by the anticipated form of the questions to concentrate on either (a) the general themes, or (b) the details
*   skimming through the article with likely questions in mind relying on memorization

The questions about changes in approach when reading the second and third articles were coded in ways which distinguished various reasons for an altered strategy - in particular the types of questions experienced, the different nature of the article, greater or less interest or familiarity.

In this exploratory study only simple analyses could really be justified. Four main questions were considered. Was there evidence that the four groups of students, as originally classified by the inventory of approaches to studying, were categorized in different ways in this experiment? Did students show consistency in the outcomes reached for all three articles? To what extent did the student appear to be influenced by the experimental treatment? How did students describe their reactions to the different articles?

APPROACHES AND OUTCOMES OF CONTRASTING GROUPS OF STUDENTS

Table 6.4 summarizes the outcomes and approaches of the four groups described in Chapter 5 - strategic, meaning, reproducing, and unmotivated - in terms of the percentage of occasions on which they had been coded into each of the categories. The differences are distinct and to a large extent make good sense.

In terms of <u>outcome</u>, the meaning-oriented group have the highest percentage of responses classified as showing reorganization or personal reinterpretation of the material and the lowest percentage of irrelevant detail. The reproducing group contains four times as many instances of irrelevant detail but is also coded as having an 'above average' number of main points almost twice as frequently. These two groups also differ markedly in the proportions of students who provide a 'good answer' to the implications question.

In terms of <u>approach</u>, the individual indices differ in their discrimination between these groups. The meaning orientated group have far and away the highest percentage of students classified has having a 'clear intention to understand' and 'an intention to reach their own conclusion or to use personal experience'. While the reproducing group do have the highest percentage of each of the three indices of a surface approach, the main difference is in the tendency to try to extract specific facts by skimming. Although the strategic group also uses this tactic, these students apparently do so without relying to the same extent on memorization. The strategic group showed a very high success rate in understanding the author's message, combined with very little use of irrelevant detail. Most correct answers to specific questions were given by the meaning and the strategic groups, while the fewest came from the reproducing group. The unmotivated group did reasonably well on the general question, but were remarkably unsuccessful in recalling incidental facts.

Table 6.4   PERCENTAGE OF STUDENTS IN EACH CATEGORY OF OUTCOME AND APPROACH

Groups (N)	Outcome — General			Implications	Specific	Approach — Deep		Surface	
	Interpret Points	Understood	Detail Evidence	Good Answer	Incidental/ Essential	Under-stand	Personal Integrate	Skimming	Memorize Questions
Strategic (12)	54	88	17	49	63	33	25	75	25
	39	46			89	25			75
Meaning (8)	57	60	13	53	63	88	88	13	38
	37	47			91	25			75
Reproducing (9)	48	58	55	39	60	44	17	78	44
	68	53			83	33			78
Unmotivated (19)	50	84	34	50	45	58	42	58	37
	42	50			91	16			68

(Note: the percentages are taken across all three articles read)

EVIDENCE OF CONSISTENCY OF OUTCOME AND APPROACH

Looking at the codings of the responses to the general question, it was possible to discover on how many occasions students were put into the same category for all three articles, thus providing evidence about consistency of outcome. This analysis could, of course, only be carried out for the 24 students who were given the general question each time. There were five codings made for each student and thus there were 120 occasions when three identical codings could be made. By chance a run of three identical dichotomous codings would be found on only 15 occasions. In reality three identical codings were observed on 49 occasions and 4 other times the difference was only a single 'undecided' code. There is here considerable evidence of consistency in the outcomes of reading articles, even under conditions deliberately arranged to encourage change. Nevertheless, it is possible to point to the fact that <u>different</u> outcomes are found more frequently (56%) than consistent ones, and evidence of deliberate changes in approaches can be found in the students' open-ended responses. Evidence of consistency was already implicit in Table 6.4 where there was a good deal of agreement between the assignment to groups on the basis of inventory scores and the codings made of the approach and outcome in the learning experiment. The agreement is all the more striking when it is recognized that the inventory was given a full twelve months before the experiment was carried out.

CORRELATIONAL ANALYSES TO IDENTIFY CONSISTENCY

Table 6.5 presents the correlation coefficients between the codings made of outcome. The stability of the values presented is low due to the small sample (N=23 for each group; one student had incomplete data). It is clear that there are some marked differences between articles. The historical article showed lower and less consistent relationships with the other two articles, while the correlations between 'The Expanding Universe' and 'Study Styles' were quite high and, with one exception (implications), consistent. It seems that the implications question proved unsatisfactory as students interpreted it in different ways in relation to the different types of article.
Table 6.6 shows the extent of consistency between the various measures of outcome derived from

Table 6.5   CORRELATIONS BETWEEN THE SAME CATEGORIES OF
OUTCOME FOR DIFFERENT ARTICLES

Categories	Expanding Universe		Arthur's Camelot
	Arthur's Camelot	Learning Styles	Learning Styles
General Question			
Personal Reinterpretation	11	20	-10
Main Points	04	65	39
Understood	-16	26	-08
Used Evidence	13	40	08
Irrelevant Detail	23	24	57
Specific Questions			
Essential Points	-09	31	-13
Incidental Facts	21	37	38
Implications	-20	-30	-26

(decimal points omitted)

the 'Learning Styles' article, for which a total set
of variables is available for all 46 students with
complete data.   Given the uncertain nature of
impression marking, correlations between different
indices of deep outcome would not be expected to
rise much above, say, 0.25 or 0.30.   In the complete
set of correlations some negative correlations might
be expected (for example between indices of a deep
outcome and both irrelevant detail and incidental
facts).   In practice rather more negative correlations emerged than anticipated.

The highest positive correlations came between
three of the deep outcome categories (main points,
understood and used evidence), as was hoped, but it
was not expected to find such high correlations between these categories and 'irrelevant detail' and
'incidental facts'.   These latter correlations imply
that a majority of the students were relying on
operation learning in seeking understanding, and this
is confirmed by the negative correlations between
'personal reinterpretation' and all of the other
categories with the exception of 'understood'.   This
pattern of correlations is in line with the two

factors within deep approach and outcome reported
in the earlier study (Table 6.3). It was thus
decided to run an exploratory factor analysis on the
'Study Styles' article with the complete set of
variables (including self-ratings and approaches),
although the sample size (N=48) hardly warrants the
use of this technique.

Table 6.6   INTERCORRELATIONS BETWEEN CATEGORIES OF OUTCOME
FOR 'LEARNING STYLES' ARTICLE

Categories	MP	U	UE	ID	EP	IF	IMP
Personal Reinter- pretation	-39	08	-14	-20	-23	-06	-21
Main Points	*	40	39	63	05	43	20
Understood		*	37	26	34	38	26
Used Evidence			*	31	05	49	19
Irrelevant Detail				*	-09	46	-06
Essential Points					*	-15	-07
Incidental Facts						*	-28
Implications							*

(decimal points omitted)

Table 6.7 shows the five-factor solution. The
first two factors show the distinction within deep
outcome already seen in the pattern of correlations.
Factor I is the clearest deep outcome factor and this
is also linked to self-ratings of 'finding the
article interesting' and 'easy to concentrate', together with an intention to reinterpret. According
to the codings of outcome, however, this intention
has not been fulfilled. Factor II shows a high
positive loading on the remaining main category of
outcome, 'personal reinterpretation', but it is
negatively related to 'main points' and to the
intention to 'concentrate on understanding'. The
'personal reinterpretation' coded here thus seems to
imply at most a 'deep passive' approach, perhaps
verging on casual globetrotting (note the use of
illustrations). Factors III and IV are the two
main 'approach' factors with what appears to be a
clear stylistic difference between them. Factor III
with its highest loadings indicating the use of personal experience, as opposed to skimming for likely

Table 6.7   FACTOR ANALYSIS OF OUTCOMES, SELF-RATINGS AND
             APPROACHES ON 'LEARNING STYLES' ARTICLE (N=48)

Categories	Factors				
	I	II	III	IV	V
General Question					
Personal Reinterpretation		59			
Main Points	58	-55			
Understood	45				
Used Evidence	59				
Irrelevant Detail	43				
Specific Questions					
Essential Points	34			41	
Incidental Facts	70				
Implications			42		
Self-Ratings					
Interesting	59		(29)		
Familiar				-30	44
Easy to Understand					43
Easy to Concentrate	43		35		37
Not Tired		36			44
Illustrations Useful		51			
Remembered Theme					91
Remembered Details	47				57
Approach					
Concentrating on Understanding		-54			
Intending to Reinterpret	39		(26)	-35	
Using Personal Experience			62		
Looking for Theme				-59	
Looking for Details				75	
Skimming		44	-73		
Memorizing			-45	32	

Decimal points and most loadings below .30 ommitted

questions or relying on memorization, can be described as deep holism.   Factor IV implies a surface
approach relying on looking for details rather than
for the theme, but the positive loading on 'essential
points' reminds us of the efficacy of operation
learning for some students.

EFFECTS OF THE EXPERIMENTAL CONDITIONS

The main differences between this experiment
and the previous one were the use of different types
of question and of contrasting articles.   Table 6.8
presents a summary of the categorizations of
students under the two experimental conditions
(general question about meaning and specific questions about detail) by article.
The initial impact of the first general question
on the meaning group seems, at first sight, to have
been as intended - with a rise in the percentage
reaching a deep outcome and a drop in 'irrelevant
detail' in relation to 'Arthur's Camelot'.   But
this pattern is reversed with the 'Learning Styles,'
article and the meaning group has an outcome almost
identical to the detail group.   If there has been
any general effect at all of the experimental conditions, it seems to have been to push students under
the detail condition towards remembering incidental
facts, yet being better able to discuss the implications.   However the large differences between
articles (with the historical article again being
most different) suggest that the effects of experiencing different types of question has been slight.
In order to explore this negative finding more
fully we need to look at the comments made by student
about their approaches.   After answering the 'Expanding Universe' article, there were marked differences in some of the problems reported by students
under the different experimental conditions.   By
chance, as an initial strategy, far more of the
detail group had concentrated on remembering the
theme than the meaning group (42% compared with 17%).
The general question created fewer problems than the
specific questions (46% had 'no problem' compared
with 21%).   Half the detail group reported difficulty in remembering details because they had concentrated on the theme.
The meaning group, with only one exception,
maintained their initial approach after experiencing
the first general question, while 46% of the detail
group changed or attempted to change.   This greater
emphasis on detail seems to have helped this group

Table 6.8 PERCENTAGE OF STUDENTS CATEGORIZED AS ANSWERING CORRECTLY OR IN DEPTH BY EXPERIMENTAL CONDITION AND ARTICLE

Category	Article/Condition				Learning Styles	
	Expanding Universe		Arthur's Camelot			
	Meaning (N=24)	Detail (N=24)	Meaning (N=24)	Detail (N=24)	Meaning (N=24)	Detail (N=24)
Deep Outcome to General Question (sum of four categories)	61		74		58	56
Irrelevant Detail	42		21		29	25
Essential Points		90		64	88	83
Incidental Facts		51		86	45	56
'Good Answer' on Implications	42	25	33	29	29	38

in answering questions on the final article.   71% (cf. 38%) experienced no problems, while the meaning group reported difficulties in remembering details because they had concentrated on the theme (46% cf. 8%).

The failure of the initial analysis to detect evidence of change can now be attributed to the fact that a majority of all these students seem more ready to concentrate on the theme rather than on the details.   But it also seems that the detail group managed to concentrate on remembering specific facts without sacrificing their overall grasp of the meaning.   This can be seen in several of the comments made by students which describe how they had read the article through as a whole first, and then gone through concentrating on remembering details which they thought might come up in the questions.   It should not be surprising, perhaps, to find students after two years in higher education adapting readily to specific demands without sacrificing understanding.   However, the general impression left from reading the answers was that few of the students had gone beyond a deep passive approach to these articles but again comments suggested that this in itself might have been a tactic based on an evaluation of the amount of effort that they were prepared to put into the experiment, or that these particular articles merited.

Although no systematic qualitative analysis was possible, given the rather brief comments made by most students, illustrative descriptions of approaches are worth recording.   In particular these show something of the 'thematized' interpretation of learning developed in higher education, and of the ways in which students recognize that their approaches are affected by assessmentdemands, subject content, and level of interest.

"I began to read the article and knowing I was to be questioned afterwards, I was immediately aware of examples and figures.   I noted these before reading on, but found that distracting. So stopped taking notes and read through the article twice.   Then I took notes again, but only when I understood the concept.   Then wondered if questions would want facts or explanation - too many numbers to keep in my head, (found the simpler illustrations eg. grapefruits, bees, much easier to remember than millions and billions) so I memorized a couple of important numbers and reread the theories.

"The latter were so clearly explained that I had
no difficulty understanding them and being able
to explain them to myself verbally.   I did not
attempt to memorize them or concentrate hard on
them.   They were straightforward, despite my
being completely ignorant of the subject.
Made sketchy notes on the theories but did not
re-read them having written them down.   Most
of the numbers had jumbled themselves up by
this time - glanced at the notes on the numbers
then put them in the envelope, thinking further
reading would confuse me."
*(Expanding Universe, student high on deep approach based
on inventory scores, detail condition)*

"I expected a few factual questions (eg. distance ones), therefore made notes of those.
Made a note of the content of the main theory -
expansion (bound to ask something on it).
However you wanted a recall of the article so
when I did this I also remembered things not
in the article but ones which jogged my memory
(eg. parsecs = light years) which made me
remember other related figures.   My general
plan was to note the important ideas, figures,
metaphors from each section.

I generally read articles in this way.   I try
to obtain a précis of the original.   If articles
are just a string of paragraphs without headings,
I find I try to include too much of the original.
If it is sub-headed, I just note the heading and
a few key words.   This works well if I'm
interested in the article and my concentration
is sharp.   Otherwise I stick to a lengthy
précis approach so that I have a good copy for
revision purposes.

The problem I would expect is that I'm bound by
facts.   Revision would be based on my strength
of memory.   Fortunately it works well, but I
have to work hard before exams, tests, etc.
It's a swot approach largely.   I would like to
be able to just write a page of notes (3-4 paras.)
and 'believe' I have everything there.   I
suppose this reflects a lack of understanding
in some way.   Nonetheless, my approach works
for me but from my reading and study habits it
is not particularly recommended.   I think I
need a better plan to get the most out of articles.
*(Expanding Universe, student high on surface approach,
meaning condition).*

107

"I concentrated more on the details since the article did not seem to be introducing new concepts in the way the first one was. They were more logical and easier to grasp (for instance I find it easier to understand how to date a piece of pottery than to understand how a star is formed). In this article the details did seem more important, dates and names were far more vital to the theme, since the essence of this article was the use of these details to solve a problem. In the first article details tended to be simply to help you understand something better, such as how great a distance actually was, the details could be disregarded and you'd still have your own representation of how great that distance was. But in this article if you disregard the detail (eg. the presence of Tintagel pottery) you lose a vital clue to the date and consequently you lose a part of the central theme."

(Arthur's Camelot, student low on both deep and surface, detail condition).

"Generally I go through slowly, often reading a paragraph over more than once if necessary, take notes on details, and prompts to (indicate) lines of thought. I basically try to understand the passage and get the idea 'mechanism' behind (it). If I can get that and learn the factual details, I can usually reconstruct the content.

As a scientist I generally expect questions requiring detail and so I tend to take note of such things and just try to get the 'feel' of the background. It is what I want out of an article (rather than its type) which dictates how I read it.

(This article was) psychology, which having done in Part I, I usually avoid like the plague! It was necessary to force myself to concentrate on it, and as you can see from the answers, I haven't done so well (and know it!) I find it difficult to find a way to tackle this kind of article. If I'm not interested in a subject it is rather doomed.

(I had a feeling that the style of questions might change! I don't think anything could

alter the way I read the article!)."
(Learning Styles, student high on both deep and sur-
face, meaning condition)

"I think I concentrated more on this one because the material wasn't as familiar as the
first one. If I get into it, it doesn't
really matter as far as questions are concerned
(whether they are detailed or not). The combined effort of memory, concentration, and
thinking enable me to answer your rather simple
task."
(Arthur's Camelot, student high on surface, meaning
condition).

"I thought I'd have to explain in more detail
about the theories ... and I'm sure this influenced the way I picked up information. I
skimmed over what I thought was irrelevant and
wouldn't be asked questions on ... if I (was
reading) for an essay I would read it with the
title of the essay in mind, only picking úp
related points. Therefore what influences my
approaches depends on my reason for reading the
article."
(Expanding Universe)

"I tried to pick up the names, because there were
so many I felt sure they'd be questioned, but I
couldn't remember them very well. Couldn't
keep my interest or concentration ... as I wasn't
all that stimulated by the article. (The main
problem was) that through trying to remember, it
seemed to help me forget. I was correct about
the type of questions being asked, but felt
unsure of my answers."
(Arthur's Camelot).

"(This time) I concentrated very hard and kept
going over paragraphs trying to work it out in
relation to what I knew and to the experiments
you had given µs - to try and find out which
cognitive style I had. Why? It was very
interesting and I feel I took it in better than
the others. I don't think I will forget the
main ideas, whereas I had already almost forgotten the other two. I could see its relevance to my own situation."
(Learning Styles, student low on both deep and surface,
detail condition: above three examples)

These quotations indicate some of the ways in which the context and content of learning influence students' approaches to studying. These comments came from a somewhat narrow experimental situation. The next three chapters report the attempts to look at studying in its broad natural context and to discover what aspects of departmental organization are most likely to affect students' approaches to studying.

Chapter 7

IDENTIFYING STUDENTS' PERCEPTIONS OF DEPARTMENTS

INTRODUCTION: THE STUDY OF DEPARTMENTS AS LEARNING
CONTEXTS

There are good reasons why a research programme
dealing with British students' approaches to learning should want to examine the academic departments*
in which they study. On theoretical grounds, it
has been argued that curriculum (what is to be
taught and learnt), pedagogy (how what is to be
learnt is transmitted) and assessment (what counts
as valid realization of knowledge on the part of the
learner) are those components of the academic environment which are most intimately related to learning
(Bernstein, 1971). British university and polytechnic departments possess a high degree of autonomy
in the organisation of courses, teaching and assessment. Moreover, European universities - unlike
American ones - are relatively homogeneous
institutions in which most students have little contact with more than one or two academic departments.
Although many American studies have compared
institutional environments in higher education (see,
e.g., Pace, 1967; Stern, 1970; Peterson, 1965;
Long, 1978), the relevant focus of analysis in
Britain is probably the main discipline students
study or the one department in which they spend most
of their time, rather than the university as a whole.
On a conceptual level, a number of distinctions
between departmental contexts might be drawn. A
department could be characterized in terms of its
relative commitment to teaching, to research and

* 'Department' is used here in the sense of 'smallest
basic academic unit'; it includes units called
faculties, schools, course teams, etc. in some institutions.

scholarship, or to technology (translation of
theoretical ideas into practice) (Becher and Kogan,
1980).   The structure of knowledge in the main
discipline the department is concerned with is
another possible analytic category - to what extent
is the knowledge studied relativistic and contextual,
or absolute, cumulative, and sequential?   (see e.g.,
Hajnal, 1972;   Schwab, 1964).   Other distinctions
which have been suggested include the cohesiveness of
curriculum content (Becher and Kogan, 1980), the
degree of control over what may and what may not be
learnt and taught, and the strength of boundary
maintenance between areas of knowledge in the
department (Bernstein, 1971).   The perceived
'quality' of a department (either in terms of its
reputation as a research unit or in terms of its
students' evaluations) is another possible basis for
categorization.   Each of these distinctions might
be thought to have correlates in the teaching, assessment, and course structure of a department - the
formality or informality of teaching methods, the
specialization or interdisciplinarity of the courses,
the openness of students' choices over content, the
use of final examinations or continuous assessment,
and so on.
     No empirical investigation, however, has examined
all or even a majority of these possible conceptual
distinctions.   Indeed, there are remarkably few
research studies of academic departments as such.
Two groups of related investigations throw some
light on departmental differences.   The first set of
studies has looked at the cultures of academic disciplines in terms of theoretical differences between
areas of knowledge and staff and student attitudes.
The most pervasive difference identified in the
modern literature is that between arts and social
science departments, on the one hand, and science
departments on the other: a version of the familiar
'two cultures' of C.P. Snow.   In fields of study
variously labelled paradigmatic, formal, or codified -
including the sciences - lecturers are more formal
in their teaching methods and less "permissive" in
their attitudes to students and student learning
than arts teachers: they are more likely, for
example, to see assessment as a way of motivating
and classifying students than as a way of providing
them with feedback.   (Roe, 1956;   Gamson, 1966;
Thompson et al, 1969; Wilson et al, 1975).   Corresponding differences have been observed in the
students attracted to arts and science departments,
differing student orientations and personality

variables being systematically related to field of
study. Arts and social science departments appear
to attract more nonconformist, radical, 'person-
orientated', neurotic, flexible, individualistic,
and divergent students; science departments are
populated more heavily with stable, 'thing-orientated'
convergent students; practical and applied fields
not surprisingly contain more students who are
vocationally-orientated.

The second group of studies has not been directly
concerned with learning contexts. These investigations have, however, identified what seems likely
to be another dimension of departmental contexts:
students' evaluations of teaching. The studies
reveal many similarities in the components students
use to assess the perceived quality of teaching.
Kulik and McKeachie (1975) reviewed eleven factor
analytic studies of ratings of lecturers and identified considerable overlap in the factors discovered.
The lecturer's skills as a teacher, his rapport with
students, the amount of structure in the courses,
and the amount of work students were expected to
tackle, were common components. Other investigations
(e.g. Payne and Hobbs, 1974: Entwistle and Percy,
1971: Brennan and Percy, 1977: Amir and Krausz,
1974) have noted the importance to students'
evaluations of lecturers' concern for student learning, the amount of choice available over method and
content of learning, social relationships between
students, interpersonal relationships between staff
and students, and clearness of grading procedures.
Taken together these investigations suggest that
teaching and courses are evaluated by students in
different countries and disciplines in broadly
similar ways, and indicate that it may be possible
to characterize departments in terms of students'
evaluations of the quality of the learning environment they provide.

Studies of academic departments themselves have
been few and far between. An early study which
suggested that the intellectual climate or ethos of
individual departments in the same field might vary
was carried out at Birmingham University (Beard, Levy
and Maddox, 1962). Two engineering departments were
found to differ in the demands they made on their
ablest students. Concommitant differences in student
attainment and attitudes to the subject were discovered.

Gaff et al (1976) conducted a promising study
of students in four departments at a Dutch university.
The authors used a questionnaire survey to examine

'atmosphere' in the departments, and concluded that:

> "Although there are some similarities among the
> four departments, it is apparent ... that they
> constitute markedly different learning environ-
> ments. The pressure-packed, heavily prescribed
> nature of chemistry; the relaxed somewhat un-
> certain climate in law; the memory-oriented,
> highly structured environment in medicine; and
> the free-wheeling, independent atmosphere of
> psychology - these distinctive 'atmospheres'
> of each educational environment are apparent
> from this initial analysis." (Gaff et al,1976).

A cluster analysis was then performed to identify groups of items which were answered in similar
ways. Ten scales were derived, ranging from the
amount of time students felt they must spend in
course-related activities, through the personal
attention given to students in the different departments, to the extent to which the course programmes
were prescribed by staff or defined by students.
The scales were used to identify educational 'problems
in the departments, and the authors concluded that
steps needed to be taken to offer more attractive
learning environments if the departments were not to
suffer high rates of student attrition. Hermans (1979
has since identified similar dimensions of departmental environments at another university in the
Netherlands.

RELATIONSHIPS BETWEEN DEPARTMENTAL OR COURSE CONTEXTS AND STUDENT LEARNING

Gaff et al remark that the effectiveness of
learning in the departments they studied might be
related to the type of learning context provided.
How does the context of a department relate to
learning? One obvious parallel is between the
different styles of learning described by Pask (see
chapter 2, pp 22-28) and the differing demands of
arts and science departments. Simply put, comprehension learners are likely to be attracted to
departments in which knowledge is most amenable to
personal interpretation (which are mostly arts and
social science departments), while operation learners will probably gravitate towards departments in
which the knowledge is hierarchically structured and
related to accepted paradigms (i.e., science departments). Similarly, it is likely that science
departments reward and encourage operation learning,

arts and social science contexts comprehension
learning. On the other hand, there may also be
differences within subject areas: different departments of engineering, for example, may favour
different styles of learning.

Another intriguing possible relationship is
that between the characteristics of a department -
its size, commitment to teaching, staff-student
ratio, its assessment and teaching methods, and so
on - and the quality and quantity of its students'
learning. Perhaps surprisingly, research has not
demonstrated any connection between objective
measures of learning contexts in higher education
and student learning. Dubin and Taveggia (1969)
found no consistent significant differences between
teaching methods in relation to student learning.
Hartnett and Centra (1977) used criterion measures
achievement tests to assess departmental 'effectiveness' in a study of American universities. They
then attempted to find correlates of effectiveness.
The analysis took into account various characteristics of the departments, including size, staff-
student ratio, staff interest in teaching (self-
rated) and salaries; students pre-entry levels of
achievement were controlled. Although large
differences in effectiveness were found between
departments teaching the same disciplines, no factors
consistently associated with effectiveness were discovered. The authors speculated that student perceptions may be more important in the explanation
of effectiveness. Student perceptions of departmental quality do not, however, appear to be
associated with other measures of departmental
differences. Gaff et al (1976), for example,
found that student-staff ratio and size were not
connected with students' descriptions and evaluations
of the departments in their study.

There is some evidence from the work on students'
approaches to learning carried out in Sweden and
elsewhere (see chapter 2) that levels of approach and
outcome are related to the organisation of teaching,
courses, and assessment. Fransson, for example,
(Fransson, 1977) has shown that deep approaches are
functionally related to interest in the learning
material, and surface approaches to threatening
assessment conditions, in one of the experiments at
Gothenburg. Laurillard (1978) shows how students'
approaches to learning tasks in their everyday
studies are associated with their perceptions of the
purposes of the task. It would seem worthwhile to
explore the deduction from these findings that

academic departments, particularly as perceived by their students, can encourage different levels of approach. There is certainly no shortage of historical and theoretical argument to support this possibility. Writers as diverse as Newman (1852), Pattison (1876), Veblen (1918), Whitehead (1932) and Rogers (1969) have variously argued that rigid assessment systems, impersonal staff-student relationships and lack of choice over method and content have damaging effects on the quality of students' learning experiences, while commitment to teaching amongst staff and freedom in learning facilitate student understanding.

There is also empirical evidence to suggest that assessment, teaching, and course structures in academic departments are critical variables in the determination of student learning, and that student perceptions are a useful way to measure these contextual characteristics. Becker et al (1968) studied Kansas University students' perceptions of their academic experiences. Using the sociological device of "perspective" (consisting principally, in this case, of the students' definition of the situation: "the ideas describing the character of situations in which action must be taken"), the authors argue that students react mainly to the environmental emphasis on grading.

Students learn the requirements of the social situation which rewards a high grade-point-average and turn themselves into the sort of persons the academic context demands. Grades are described by Becker as "the currency of the campus". High grades in assessment tasks are seen to be the most important goals by students, even though the members of staff deny they are so crucial. Students come to perceive a conflict between grades and learning and speak of using strategies to get good grades at the expense of understanding the material they are expected to learn. The process of assessment comes to have the unintended consequence of inhibiting rather than facilitating learning.

Snyder (1971) pursued the perceived conflict between manifest and latent functions of assessment a stage further. He argued (as a result of a study of students at M.I.T.) that the formal curriculum of universities emphasises academic values: a problem-orientated outlook, creativity, independence of thought, originality (c.f. Entwistle and Percy, 1971). The hidden curriculum, on the other hand, requires an answer-orientated outlook, rote learning, and memorization. Research in this country has

uncovered the operation of hidden curricula.
Miller and Parlett (1974) noted the 'bureaucratic'
assessment systems in some of the university departments they studied, and found that the academic
environment defined by examinations in one department
led to the distinctive strategies of adaptation
already described (chapter 2 , pp 12-13). Even the
cue-seeking students were often uncomfortably aware
that the strategies they used - although productive
of good degrees - were detrimental to learning.
Other studies have explored relationships between
students' attitudes to learning, student achievement,
relationships with staff, and perceived quality of
teaching. Ramsden (1976) found that a perceived
lack of any direction or helpful guidance by lecturers
in an independent study course led to the development
of negative attitudes to learning. One student
commented:

> "I don't think that they have really put enough
> thought into creating learning situations. I
> think they thought 'It's a good idea, 'student-
> centred education: we"ll apply it to higher
> education'. But it's not a very stimulating
> environment. Staff seem to expect students
> to generate everything ... they seem to have
> thought that students would do things like
> coming to them and asking for series of lectures.
> As I see it, an improved version of the course
> would be if students fitted into projects
> generated by staff. They ought to take more
> initiatives themselves... On an ordinary course
> 80 per cent of the lectures may be pretty use-
> less, but at least they can be a source of
> stimulation".

When more guidance was provided in subsequent
years of the course, although no compromises were
made about the amount of choice given to students,
their attitudes to learning and to the department
improved. Students in Miller and Parlett's study
(1974) spoke of the way in which a quite different
kind of context - impersonal, highly formalized, with
'bureaucratic' staff-student relationships - could
have similar effects in discouraging learning.
Pascarella and Terenzini (1977; 1978) studied the
association between student-teacher informal
relationships and educational outcomes. Informal
relationships were defined as out-of-class, not
formally arranged contacts, for any purpose. A
positive correlation between these relationships

and three dependent variables - academic performance, personal development, and intellectual development - was found. The first of these variables was a conventional assessment (students' performance in examinations and assignments as measured by the department); the others were students' self-ratings. Students who interacted more with teachers were also found to be less likely to withdraw before the end of their courses. The authors include in their discussion of these results, however, a caveat on the direction of causality in these relationships.

Recently, Fearn-Wannan (1979) has attempted to develop a path analysis model to explain Australian students' performance in chemistry. Students' perceptions of their lecturers' behaviour and satisfaction with the teaching were found to be small, but significant, mediating variables in the determination of performance. Research also exists which seems tentatively to support some of the assertions of writers like Newman and Rogers, to the effect that learning in higher education is facilitated when students are permitted greater freedom over methods and content of study, and that negative attitudes are developed when choice is perceived to be absent. Brennan and Percy (1977), reporting the analysis of data from a large-scale investigation of students in English universities and colleges, remark on the disjunction (noted also by Becker et al, 1968, and Snyder, 1971) between the avowed aims of lecturers to promote 'critical thinking' and the relatively few opportunities students said they were given to work in ways which would enable the aim to be realized. Moreover:

> "It seems clear from our research that students in all fields of study believe that they would learn more, and enjoy learning more, if they had greater control over the pace of their learning, more chance to determine the subject matter of their courses and were less rigidly inhibited by traditional conceptions of disciplinary boundaries and what constitutes the proper study of a particular subject. Students very often made comments describing the 'most satisfying aspect" of their course as 'the work which I have been allowed to do myself' and were highly critical of a curriculum structure which imposed a logic and sequence of learning on them which they felt was less educational and less motivating than one suggested to them by their own developing intellectual interests". (Brennan and Percy, 1977).

Subsequently Percy and Ramsden (1980) investigated two independent study schemes in a polytechnic and a university. It was found that most of the students who were interviewed in the study valued very highly the opportunity to work independently, that some students would have left university if they had not been able to use the independent study programmes to pursue their own interests, and that the standard of students' work produced in both schemes was generally acceptable and in some cases outstanding.

IMPLICATIONS OF PREVIOUS WORK FOR THE PRESENT STUDY

Studies of academic departments as learning contexts are unusual and few of the possible discussions suggested theoretically have been explored. What does seem to be clear from the work which has been done on academic contexts in higher education is that students' perceptions and evaluations are associated with their approaches to studying, while systematic differences exist in the environment provided by arts and science departments. Little has been done to disentangle the effects of different subject areas and perceived 'quality" of departments or courses on students' approaches. Limitations of time and resources in the programme meant that all the possible distinctions between departments which have been suggested could not be examined. It was decided, in view of the clear importance of these variables in earlier investigations, to concentrate in particular on students' perceptions of disciplinary and other differences in the departments in which they studied. However, exploratory work on defining departmental environments was carried out in the preliminary stages of the programme, and this is described below.

PRELIMINARY WORK

During the first year of the programme, a number of interviews were held with staff and students in two university departments. One of the purposes of these semi-structured interviews was to see whether differences in departmental learning contexts could be identified. Ten social science staff, thirteen social science students, three applied science staff, and nine applied science students were interviewed. The staff were asked about their aims as teachers, the structure of their courses, how they thought students tackled the learning tasks they were set, their perceptions of differences between students and the reasons for their success or failure, and the kinds of contact they had with students. The students were asked, _inter alia_, about the characteristics of the courses, teaching and assessment in their department. Specific questions were put about the content of lectures, seminars, and tutorials, and about the student's relationship with members of staff.

The staff interviews were complemented by a study of course documents in the two departments. These included recent examination and test papers, syllabuses, and course handbooks outlining the second year courses for students. It was hoped that these documents might provide a source from which an understanding of the context of the department might be gained.

The interviews revealed that students in both departments used similar constructs to describe the environments in which they were learning. These constructs were consistent with previous research on students' perceptions of departmental environments (c. f. Gaff _et al_, 1976). Particularly important to students were the effects of their lecturers: the extent to which they seemed to encourage learning, lectured effectively, and offered help with study problems. Assessment methods and workload were also important to students in both departments, although they were seen rather differently; the applied scientists felt that a great deal of pressure was needed in order to 'get through' the syllabus, while the social scientists would have preferred a much lighter workload. Formality or informality of teaching and learning (e.g. lectures versus discussion methods) were also often mentioned by the students. Although students could identify differences within departments on all these criteria (e.g. between the teaching abilities of different lecturers) they were also able to speak meaningfully about the department as a whole. Moreover, students related their approaches to studying to a number of characteristics of the learning context. On occasions the use of a deep or a surface approach was attributed by the students to the influence of the environment. The periodical tests used in the social science department, for example, seemed to encourage surface approaches. These relationships between perceptions of the context and approaches are described in detail in chapter 8.

It was more difficult to discern any clear patterns in the staff interviews. There were wider

differences in the comments made by staff in the
same department than by students in the same department.   It was, however, apparent that many staff
had little knowledge of how students actually tackled
learning tasks.   The study of course documents
yielded information about the structure of the
courses which was useful briefing material to help
focus the student and staff interview questions.
But again it was not clear how the information could
be used to define differences in departmental contexts.   In view of the demonstrated effectiveness
of the student interviews, and the parallels between
the results they provided and previous work on
academic learning contexts, it was decided to concentrate attention on identifying the characteristics
of departmental environments by means of students'
perceptions.

DEVELOPMENT OF THE COURSE PERCEPTIONS QUESTIONNAIRE
(CPQ) - 1.

     Similarities in the constructs used by students
in both departments in the preliminary interviews
suggested that a questionnaire might be an appropriate instrument for identifying and comparing the
course perceptions of larger groups of students in
a number of departments.   The first task was to
collect together a number of items descriptive of
the context of learning through students' eyes.   The
items came from two principal sources: the preliminary student interviews and an earlier study of
students' perceptions of courses (Ramsden, 1976).
The 47 items thus derived were sorted into scales
reflecting hypothesized dimensions by which students
were expected to characterize their learning environments.   An attempt was made to choose scales which
would be capable of distinguishing between subject
areas or distinguishing between departments in other
ways (e.g. quality of the teaching).   The components
were as far as possible related to previous work in
associated fields.   The concept of frame strength
(Bernstein, 1971), which refers to the amount of
control over what may and may not be transmitted in
the pedagogical relationship, was incorporated into
one scale.   The recurrent notion of "rapport" in
teachers' understanding of students as a component
of effective teaching (see, e.g., Rogers, 1969,
Kulik and McKeachie, 1975; Gaff et al, 1976) was
included.   Most of the scales used in the most
closely corresponding study (Gaff et al, 1976) could
be incorporated, while two of the distinctions

between subject areas discovered in one of the
American studies of lecturers' perceptions - existence
of a paradigm and concern with application (Biglan,
1973) - also found a place.
   The items were provisionally grouped into the
following eight scales:

Staff understanding: the degree to which students
feel their teachers to provide an acceptant, understanding, and sincere environment for learning.
Sample item: "Lecturers here frequently give the
impression that they haven't anything to learn from
students". (negatively scored)

Formal relationships: the extent of formality or
informality in staff-student relationships.   Sample
item: "Lecturers in this department seem to go out
of their way to be friendly towards students".

Relevance to work: how closely students feel the
curriculum relates to vocational requirements.
Sample item: "Much of the work I do here will be
relevant to my future job".

Frame strength: items thought to relate most closely
to the amount of discretion possessed by students in
organizing their learning, selecting its content, and
evaluating their progress.   Sample item: "The
courses in this department are highly organized".

Formal instruction: the extent to which the
department emphasizes individual learning or atten-
dance at lectures and classes. Sample item: "A great
deal of my time is taken up by formal classes
(lectures, practicals, tutorials, etc.)".

Workload and External pressure to work: the extent
of pressure placed on students to conform to deadlines
for submitted work, and the amount of material which
students feel they are expected to cover in the
syllabus.   Sample item: "There seems to be too
much work to get through in the courses here".

Homogeneity of the department: the degree to which
students perceive themselves to be in a department
in which the goals of their study are clear to them
and shared by most other students.   Sample item:
"It can be hard to know how well you're doing compared to other students in this department".
(negatively scored)

The first version of the CPQ was administered to second year students in four university departments - psychology, engineering, history, and physics - during 1977-78. A slightly amended form was used in two further departments (English and independent studies) in 1978.

The results were examined by means of item analysis: item-scale correlations and percentage agreements to each item were calculated, and alpha factor analysis (chosen because it is specifically designed for use in scale development) was carried out, using the SPSS programs.

All the significant item loadings in the first factor were from the original 'staff understanding" scale or the 'formal staff-student relationships' scale. This factor clearly represents students' perceptions of the quality of teaching and staff-student relationships in their department. The second factor appeared to identify a dimension relating to the amount of work students are faced with in their department: with one exception, all the loadings werefrom the 'workload' or 'external pressure to work' scales. The third factor combined items from the 'formal instruction', 'relevance to work', and 'strong framing' scales, suggesting that this dimension was one of clearly relevant curriculum contents transmitted in a formal way.

The next factor was concerned with the social climate or amount of interpersonal contact in a department. All the significant items were in the 'homogeneity' scale, but referred to aspects of students' relationships connected with their work. Factor V was similar to Factor IV, while the sixth dimension identified clear goals and standards in a department's teaching and courses (item 40, for example, is "You usually have a clear idea of where you're going and of what's expected of you in this department"). Only two items reached significance in the last two factors extracted. The first, item 38, was "Students have a great deal of choice over how they are going to learn in this department"; the second (in Factor VIII) was a relevance to work item.

A second analysis was run after removing a number of the weaker items and produced similar results. The CPQ scales were now revised to produce eight dimensions (Figure 7.1). The 'staff understanding' and 'formal staff-student relationships' scales were re-ordered to the two new scales of commitment to teaching (dealing mainly with the teaching climate of the department) and relationships

with students (referring chiefly to the quality of
relationships between students and staff). It
seemed useful to maintain a conceptual distinction
between formal teaching methods and relevance to
work; although these two aspects seemed to be
empirically inseparable in the factor analyses, it
might be that other samples would reveal a different
picture. The former 'workload' and 'external
pressure to work' scales were combined into one
scale of workload. The earlier 'homogeneity' component was subdivided into two scales: social climate
and clear goals and standards. The former strong
framing items were mainly redistributed through the
other scales, and another dimension of freedom in
learning was added, corresponding to Gaff's 'room
for student interests' and 'prescription in the
program" scales (Gaff et al, 1976).

Figure 7.1   DIMENSIONS OF LEARNING ENVIRONMENTS DERIVED FROM
FACTOR ANALYSIS OF THE FIRST VERSION OF THE CPQ

DIMENSIONS	MEANING
Relationships with students	Closeness of lecturer/student relation- ships; help and understanding shown to students.
Commitment to teaching	Commitment of staff to improving teaching and to teaching students at a level appropriate to their current understanding
Workload	Pressure placed on students in terms of demands of the syllabus and assessment tasks.
Formal teaching methods	Formality or informality of teaching and learning (e.g. lectures v individual study).
Vocational relevance	Perceived relevance of courses to students' careers.
Social climate	Frequency and quality of academic and social relationships between students.
Clear goals and standards	Extent to which standards expected of students are clear and unambiguous.
Freedom in learning	Amount of discretion possessed by students in choosing and organising academic work.

Inspection of the CPQ results in terms of the eight dimensions in Figure 7.1 revealed that students saw the process of learning and teaching in quite different ways in the six departments (see Ramsden, 1979). The engineering department was thought to have very formal teaching methods, clear goals of study, high vocational relevance, and an extremely high workload, combined with close and cooperative relationships between students. Physics students also experienced a fairly formal curriculum, with little personal choice over method and content; the psychologists worked in an environment which was thought to be friendly and informal, but felt they had a heavy workload and only a very small amount of freedom over what and how they learnt. English and history students said that much individual study was required in their departments and that the courses had little relevance to their future employment; relationships with staff were rather formal in history, but informal and helpful in English. Independent studies was thought to have the best teaching, and not unexpectedly, the highest freedom in learning. Staff were said to be friendly and to make real efforts to understand difficulties students were having with their work, although the goals and standards expected of students were perceived to be unclear and students worked in a poor social climate.

DEVELOPMENT OF THE COURSE PERCEPTIONS QUESTIONNAIRE - 2

Further interviews of a sample of students who completed the CPQ in its original form showed that the eight main components of perceived learning environments appeared to be stable and replicable (Ramsden, 1981), although the relationships with students and commitment to teaching scales could not be clearly separated. A revised version of the questionnaire was next constructed, consisting of eight six-item scales. Items in the previous version which had not had significant loadings in the factor analysis, or which had low item-scale correlations, were deleted; other items were added to some scales (especially to the freedom in learning scale) in order to produce six-item scales in all cases.

This revised CPQ was administered to a sample of 767 students in nine departments at three universities during 1978. Item analyses largely confirmed the integrity of the revised scales, although the distinction between the relationships with students and commitment to teaching scales again failed to emerge

empirically. Alpha-factoring of the items, extracting eight factors, followed by oblique rotation, produced a clearly comprehensible structure: Factor I
represented relationships with students plus commitment to teaching; Factor II, vocational relevance;
Factor III, formal teaching; Factor IV, clear goals
and standards; Factor V, workload; Factor VI,
social climate; Factor VII, commitment to teaching
and relationships with students; Factor VIII, freedom in learning (together with smaller loadings on
several relationships with students items). In
spite of large differences between individual items
in terms of percentage agreements for the nine
departments, item-scale correlations did not differ
greatly between the departments, suggesting that the
dimensions tapped by the scales were generally
applicable.

Mean scale values for the departments, disciplines and subject areas were calculated. These confirmed the ability of the questionnaire to identify
different departmental learning contexts. The
scales of formal teaching methods, vocational relevance, and (to a lesser extent) clear goals and
standards, social climate, and freedom in learning,
distinguished between science and arts and social
science departments. The other scales mainly
seemed to differentiate between departments rather
than disciplines. The scales were understandably
related to each other. Freedom in learning, for
example, was negatively related to formal teaching
methods (freedom in learning and informal teaching
are both more common in social science and arts), but
was also positively associated with relationships
with students (i.e. it is also an evaluative
dimension).

The final research version of the CPQ was
developed by re-ordering the items in the relationships with students and commitment to teaching scales
into two new scales of good teaching and openness to
students. The questionnaire as a whole was shortened
to 40 items in eight scales by deleting the weakest
item in each scale, and some of the items were rewritten.

This questionnaire was administered to 2208
students in 66 departments at the same time as the
approaches to studying inventory (see chapter 4; the
relationships between these two sets of scales will
be examined in chapter 9). It was expected - from
the earlier work described above - that some of the
dimensions of the CPQ would describe differences between subject areas and disciplines, while others

would represent students' perceptions of differences between departments.   The second group would be evaluations of the learning context in the departments.

On the whole the results confirmed these expectations.   As will be seen from Table 7.1, formal teaching methods, vocational relevance, and clear goals and standards were found to be very much related to subject area;   much more so, incidentally, than any of the approaches to studying subscales. The highest scores on all three of these CPQ scales were found in the engineering departments, and the lowest in the English or history departments.   It was equally clear that the two evaluative scales, good teaching and openness to students, were not related to subject area.   The wide ranges of departmental means within each discipline on these scales illustrate how different the departments were perceived to be by their students (see Ramsden and Entwistle, 1981, for details).

The remaining CPQ scales appear to describe differences between departments and between subject areas.   For example, although the freedom in learning mean values were higher in arts and social sciences than in scientific subjects, the range of mean scores within each discipline was wide.

Factor analysis of the CPQ scale totals also revealed a familiar pattern (Table 7.2).   Factor I is the evaluative dimension suggested in the interview study and the preliminary work, with its highest loadings on good teaching and openness to students. The next highest coefficient in this factor, for freedom in learning, invites the explanation that this scale is also a component of students' evaluations of departments.   Social climate, clear goals and standards, and workload play lesser parts.   Factor II represents differences between subject areas.   The dimension is one which distinguishes between formal vocational teaching and loosely-structured informal teaching, the former being more common in science departments and the latter in arts departments. Departments with clear goals and standards, high vocational relevance, and formal teaching methods also tend to have good social climates.   These results are consistent with those presented in Table 7.1.

The scales and items of the final version of the CPQ are given in Appendix A5 together with Cronbach α values which indicate a satisfactory level of internal consistency for each of the scales.   An interpretation of the factor analysis of scale totals in conjunction with conceptual analysis based on the results of the

Table 7.1 STUDENTS' PERCEPTIONS OF LEARNING CONTEXTS IN DIFFERENT SUBJECT AREAS

Scale	Mean (1) Science (2) Social science (3) Arts	S.D.	Analysis of Variance F (df 2, 63)
Openness to students	(1) 9.04 (2) 9.31 (3) 8.36	1.47 1.82 2.14	1.42
Social climate	(1) 11.19 (2) 10.78 (3) 9.33	1.48 1.40 1.72	7.64*
Formal teaching methods	(1) 12.17 (2) 6.67 (3) 3.06	1.61 1.37 .77	232.86*
Clear goals and standards	(1) 11.83 (2) 9.62 (3) 7.35	.89 1.87 1.94	37.88**
Workload	(1) 11.19 (2) 8.86 (3) 10.58	2.26 2.71 2.33	5.95*
Vocational relevance	(1) 11.21 (2) 7.21 (3) 4.27	2.96 1.42	58.51**
Good teaching	(1) 11.63 (2) 11.74 (3) 11.63	1.02 1.48 1.65	.06
Freedom in learning	(1) 8.24 (2) 10.21 (3) 11.54	1.72 1.46 2.67	15.35**

* p < .01

** p < .001

Table 7.2   FACTOR ANALYSIS OF COURSE PERCEPTIONS SCALES
             (N = 2208)

	Factors (56% variance explained)	
Variables	I	II
Good teaching	76	
Freedom in learning	57	
Openness to students	76	
Social climate	42	32
Formal teaching methods		71
Clear goals and standards	30	57
Workload	(-24)	
Vocational relevance		72

Decimal points and most loadings less than .25 omitted

Factor I   Positive evaluation of teaching and courses

Factor II   Formal vocational teaching

---

interviews of 57 students in six departments (see Chapter 8), suggested that the second-order evaluation dimension - Factor I in Table 7.2 - might usefully be subdivided into two components each containing two scales. Good teaching and freedom in learning were combined into the scale of perceived student-centredness (α = 0.75), while freedom in learning and workload (the latter scale negatively keyed) were joined to form a scale of perceived control - centredness (α = 0.75) in a department. These measures of a department's learning context were found to be significantly associated with characteristic approaches to learning; the relationships will be discussed in Chapter 9.

CONCLUSIONS

The course perceptions questionnaire appears to provide a useful means of describing certain important and consistent differences in the way students perceive departments. The relationships between the present results and previous research into academic environments in higher education seem to make sense. Dimensions of teaching quality, workload, and clarity of goals have been found to occur

129

consistently in factor analytic studies of student ratings of teachers. The only other research directl comparable to the investigations reported in this chapter (Gaff et al, 1976) discovered similar dimensions (and relationships between the dimensions) to those of the CPQ, with a sample of Dutch students. Studies of differences between the disciplinary 'ethos or 'culture' of different fields of study have also produced findings compatible with those of the CPQ (see, e.g., Smithers, 1969; Gaff and Wilson, 1971). It is hoped that the questionnaire may prove to be a valuable instruments for use by academic departments as a means of obtaining information about students' reactions to assessment and teaching methods.

The limitations of the CPQ are also apparent, however. Firstly, the picture provided of the perceived learning context is incomplete, because the questionnaire is unable to examine the detail of the relationships between an individual student's approach to a learning task and his perception of its context. Nor can it allow for differences between lecturers and courses in a department. Exploration of these matters requires a different methodology, and attention is turned towards them in the next chapter.

Secondly, the examination of students' perceptions offers only one way (although a demonstrably valid one) of describing departmental environments. Within the compass of the present research programme it was not possible to examine other potentially important distinctions between departments except in a very limited way. Lecturers' attitudes and experience, curriculum structure, research and teaching orientation, and the type of institution in which the department is situated, are among the differences which might fruitfully be explored in future research.

Chapter Eight

STUDENTS' EXPERIENCES OF LEARNING

In the previous chapters we have dealt mainly
with research findings arising from methods
traditionally used to investigate student learning.
The approaches to studying inventory made use of
typical psychometric techniques; tests of ability
and personality were the focus of chapter 5;
chapter 6 reported experimental data on reading
academic articles.

These approaches to understanding student learning have a common factor. They are all to some
extent removed from the immediate reality of being a
student in the natural setting of an academic
department. Even the development of the course
perceptions questionnaire inevitably tended to con-
strain students' experiences into a mould shaped by
the researcher. Although indications of the effects
of the context and content of learning were given in
the students' comments in chapter 6, these comments
themselves came from a rather narrow experimental
situation.

It is important that our choice of research
methods does not undervalue the dynamic, tentative
character of student learning in favour of a static,
consistent view. Nor must we exclude potentially
critical variables in the real world of a student's
encounter with a learning task in order to achieve
experimental precision. The research methods used
by Marton and his colleagues (see chapter 2) offer
an experiential, phenomenal perspective on student
learning which can be seen as an alternative to the
experimental and correlational approaches. Typically, each student's unique experiences are examined
by qualitative analysis of interview data. A
potentially richer and more accurate picture of the
links between student learning and its context and
content is the chief return to an investment in this

approach. Of course, the qualitative approach is not without weaknesses of its own, perhaps the most important of which is the danger of bias from the subjective and impressionistic way this sort of data is sometimes handled. But careful controls can be used to minimiz e these difficulties.

This chapter describes the findings of a series of interviews designed to draw upon the strengths of this qualitative, experiential perspective. The interviews were used to examine students' approaches to academic tasks and their assessment strategies, and to provide a detailed picture of students' perceptions of the contexts of learning in which they worked. The results extend previous work at Lancaster, and the research of Marton (see, e.g., Marton and Säljö, 1976a, b) and Laurillard (1978; 1979) in several directions. The analyses which follow will show how categories of levels of approach, types of context, and individual differences in approach and strategic study methods were developed and subsequently used to identify differences between students and contexts. Relationships between the content and perceived context of the students' work and their approaches to academic tasks, and between approaches and degree results, will also be examined in detail.

METHODS

This is not the place to begin a discussion of the complicated issues surrounding the use of qualitative methods (see Marton and Svensson, 1979; Entwistle, 1981; Ramsden, 1981, for more extensive examinations of the relevant issues). It is, however, important to bear in mind that a qualitative perspective assumes that it is valid to consider categories of description - e.g. of different approaches to a learning task to which meaning is attributed through the learner's own perspective - as results in themselves, and not only as sources of categories to be later used in a quantitative way.

In the present study a total of 57 Lancaster University students was interviewed. Table 8.1 shows the composition of the sample, which was selected by examining students' scores on one or more subscales of the approaches to studying inventory; students with extreme scores were those chosen. The final degree results of the students, and in the case of the engineering students, the distribution of the chosen group's second year marks as well, suggested that the sample was at least broadly representative of different levels of ability.

Table 8.1   COMPOSITION OF THE INTERVIEW SAMPLE

Discipline	Year of Study	Dates Interviewed	N
Psychology	2	February–March 1977	13
Engineering	2	June 1977	9
Physics	2		10
History	2		11
English	2	January–June 1978	5
Independent Studies	2 & 3		9
TOTAL			57

The preliminary interviews used a broad range of questions, and experience with these interviews led to the development of a shorter schedule for students in the main part of the study.   This contained three groups of questions.   The focus of the first group was on reading and essay-writing (for arts and social science students) and on problem-solving and report writing (for science students).   Appropriately specific questions about relevant learning tasks (How did you go about it?   Why are you reading it? Were you looking out for anything in particular? Did you do it differently from another task of the same sort?   Why? - and so on) were asked.   The second set of questions concerned assessment strategies and the perceived outcome of the student's course.   Finally, several questions about the learning context of the student's main subject department (teaching, assessment, purpose of lectures, relationships with staff and other students) were asked.
All the interviews used a semi-structured approach;   the order and phrasing of the questions varied somewhat depending on the way in which the student answered them, and exactly the same questions were not asked of every student.   The semi-structured approach did not, however, mean that the interviews were uncontrolled.   It was always ensured that the same main points - see above - were raised.   Great care was taken not to be over-directive.   At the

133

same time, the interviewer made a continual effort to be alert to comments made by the student which related to the hypotheses of the investigation, and which ought to be probed more fully.

The analysis of interviews of this kind presents perhaps a greater threat to the validity of the data than their conduct. At first, consideration was given to using methods such as network analysis and critical incident techniques, but the results obtained in a comparable study of students' approaches to learning (Bliss and Ogborn, 1977) seemed trite in comparison with the sophistication of the methods. More useful guidance was obtained from the methods of qualitative analysis used in the research carried out by Marton and his colleagues at Gothenburg. These techniques are designed to extract full value from the complexity of the interview data. Transcripts of the interviews are read and re-read until emergent qualities of students' experiences are consistently identified. The constructs are verified by several judges.

The present study adapted Marton's techniques to a different research situation. Practical constraints made it impossible to have all the interviews transcribed in full (a sine qua non of the Gothenburg approach). More importantly, it was felt important to avoid the dangers of a strictly inductivist approach by specifying certain guiding hypotheses derived from previous research, including the work of Marton. The categories of responses eventually used to classify the transcribed extracts were validated by means of inter-judge comparisons.

These constructs were used to direct the analysis:

1. Categories describing different levels of approach;
2. Evaluative and descriptive categories relating to the context of learning in different departments: in particular, categories relating to teaching, assessment, and course structures. The dimensions discovered in the factor analysis of the CPQ, those reported by Gaff et al (1976), and those reported in studies of lecturer evaluation (e.g. Kulik and McKeachie, 1975), were particularly considered;
3. Differences between individual students in "cue behaviour" (Miller and Parlett, 1974);
4. Differences between individual students in approaches to academic work (especially the holist-atomist dimension identified by Svensson (1977);

5.   Relationships between approaches and contexts
        (e.g. Becker's "selective negligence" in res-
        ponse to assessment pressures), including
        associations between the conditions of the task
        and the type of approach used (c.f. Fransson,
        1977).

        Fuller details of all the techniques used in
conducting and analysing the interviews can be found
in Ramsden (1981).

PRELIMINARY ANALYSIS

        A preliminary analysis was made by listening to
each tape-recording several times and making full (or
very lengthy) transcripts of a sample of interviews.
With the help of Marton's judgement instructions for
categorizing deep and surface level responses it
eventually became clear that deep and surface
categories of description could be applied to the
responses of students in every department.   Sub-
categories differing from those used by Marton were,
however, needed to classify the responses satisfactorily.   It was possible, in this analysis, to identify
different strategic approaches related to assessment
which distinguished among individual students.   For
example, a small number of students in all the departments took a highly strategic, assured approach to
assessment tasks, while others adapted to the constraints of examinations and assignments in less
positive ways.   Relationships between students' perceptions of particular tasks and the approaches they
used to them were also indicated in the analysis.
Students who described favourable conditions for
learning in relation to a subject or topic (e.g.
helpful teaching) were likely to describe a deep-
level approach to a task connected to it, while the
reverse was true if the conditions were unfavourable
(i.e. a surface level approach was described, often
by the same student).   An association between a
student's level of interest in a task, or his background knowledge of the subject to which it referred,
and level of approach, was also identified.   Poor
background knowledge (especially of concepts in
science) or a low level of interest (particularly in
arts and social science subjects) were associated with
surface level approaches.   These preliminary findings
have been described in greater detail elsewhere
(Ramsden, 1979).

CATEGORIES DESCRIBING DEEP AND SURFACE APPROACHES

The first task in the main analysis was to develop a model of deep and surface approaches which described the approaches used by students in a wide variety of tasks in different disciplines and departments. The framework was established by means of comparing students' responses to the interview questions dealing with approaches to academic tasks with two other sets of judgement instructions: those of Marton (1975) and Laurillard (1979).

Marton used one set of judgement instructions to classify social science students' responses to interview questions about their reading of academic articles under experimental conditions, and a somewhat different set to classify responses to questions about their normal studies. Laurillard interviewed science students about their approaches to several tasks forming part of their normal studies. She did not require students to work under experimental conditions, nor did she ask them questions about their general approaches to studying. The present study was similar to Laurillard's in that students were interviewed about their approaches to tasks carried out in their normal work. But the tasks described by students were much more diverse; they included problem-solving, project work, essays, reading of books and articles, and examinations, in a number of different subject areas. It seemed advisable, moreover, to leave open the possibility of identifying consistent approaches to studying by the same student.

It was found necessary to modify the categories used by Marton and Laurillard in order to provide a model which adequately described the variability in the present data. An effort was made to develop a set of sub-categories which was both theoretically parsimonious and generally applicable to all the departments. The definitions appear in Figure 8.1. Four categories used by the previous researchers to define a deep approach are generalized to become D_2 and D_3. D_1, which has no equivalent in Laurillard's descriptions, was found to be essential to classify students' indications of a close personal relationship with the academic material with which they were dealing. It resembles one of the sub-categories used by Marton and his colleagues to classify a student's approach to his normal work. This sub-category, which describes a tendency on the part of the student to see knowledge as part of oneself, is an important component of Marton's conception of a

Figure 8.1   CATEGORIES OF DESCRIPTION FOR DEEP AND SURFACE
              LEVELS OF APPROACH

D_1 Personal experience

Integrating the task with oneself.   Indicate desire
to relate the task or the subject to personal or real
life situations: to compare a task with personal
experience (outside the course);   to see a task as
part of oneself or one's personal development;   express a wish to use the knowledge forming part of the
task outside its immediate context in relation to
oneself.

D_2 Relationships

DEEP

Integrating the parts into a whole.   Indicate desire
to relate parts of the task to each other or the task
to other relevant knowledge;   indicate active attempts
to think about the relationships between different
parts of the material (e.g. relate evidence to conclusion);   try to relate material from different
sources;   try to see connections between previously
studied materials and currently studied materials.

D_3 Meaning

Integrating the whole with its purpose.   Indicate
intention to impose meaning: think about the underlying structure, or the intention of the whole task;
try to 'stand back' from the task and see it in a
wider perspective;   impose a pattern on the whole task.

S_1 Unrelatedness

Defining the task as separate or its parts as discrete.   Indicate intention or tendency to treat the
task as an isolated phenomenon: confront the
material as separate from other ideas and materials,
or from the general purpose of the task to which it
relates;   focus on the elements of the task rather
than the whole.

SURFACE S_2 Memorisation

Defining the task as a memory task.   Indicate
intention to memorize the material.

S_3 Unreflectiveness

Defining the task in an external way.   Indicate un-
reflective or passive approach to a task: indicate
intention not to extract meaning from the material;
see the subject-matter as external to oneself.

deep-level approach (see, e.g., Marton, 1976). The three surface sub-categories in Figure 5.1 closely resemble Laurillard's modifications of Marton's categories, although S_1 and S_3 are here more generally defined.

Figure 8.1 also shows the instructions used to classify students' responses. But the meaning of each of the categories is properly shown through the use of repeated instances from the student interviews. Given below are extracts from the interviews which exemplify the use of the sub-categories in relation to different tasks.

D_1 Personal experience

I think I tend quite a lot to relate (this reading) to my own experiences as well. Try and think of instances where these experiments would be proved right. So it takes a bit of time reading, yeah. I think if they're talking about things like field independence I try to think about whether people I know are field dependent or independent. (Reading academic articles; psychology, student 6).

I got into the poem and could feel what it means. I became part of it... I found it interesting because it had a deep theological meaning, and I'm interested in that subject. (Reading poetry; English, student 23).

I suppose I'm trying to imagine what the experiment is talking about, I think, in a physical sense. Sort of get a picture of what it's about... This one says an ultra-violet lamp emits one watt of power; it says calculate the energy falling on a square centimetre per second. I'm just thinking of the light and the way it spreads out, so therefore I know it's the inverse square law ... (Laboratory work; physics, student 8).

To start from scratch, to basically put together information and use it... and actually build it and test it and see that the thing, there is a fair degree of correlation between your test results and what you actually expected the thing to produce, I think is good... You select certain formulae to use, and by using them... and seeing that they produce the results you hoped they would, then, you know, you prove to yourself that those formulae could be used. (Project work; engineering, student 2).

D_2 Relationships

You read it, a section on precipitation hardening... and I think well, fair enough, the material is about as strong as mild steel or something, and I'll remember that if I can, but I'm not going to remember that it's 297 Newtons per square mm. if it's in such and such a state ... There are one or two

D_2 Relationships (continued)

things that do stick in your mind like the strength of mild
steel, and so on, because we've used it in the projects, so
you have a sort of relative scale whereby you can say it's
nearly as strong as mild steel ... (Reading textbooks;
engineering, student 6).

You know a method of approach, so you find usually the
thing simplifies itself greatly after you've removed a few of
the non-essentials and put it into a logical form which
relates to something you've done previously.   (Problem-
solving; physics, student 12).

I'm trying to relate it to the course as a whole.   It's
not just writing down a load of notes and thinking 'that's it
for my essay' ... You try to sort of keep a logical progression
in history, so you've some idea of the themes ... (Reading
texts; history, student 1).

You read it, you see what it's about, and usually it's
got, often it has some bearing on something else you've read
before.   It may confirm that or just add another side to it,
or be completely different.   (Reading academic articles;
psychology, student 2).

D_3 Meaning

The ideas are started by the actual question.   You realize
that it presupposes a few points that you must get into the
essay ... I list the ideas that have got to go into the essay,
because the essay, you know, entails these things.   (Essay-
writing; English, student 6).

If I feel that the article is going to be very relevant
to what I'm doing – and you can often glean that from the title
– then I'll tend to go through it fairly slowly.   Rather than
skim through it I'll read through it in a full way.   I suppose
I've got these various problem areas which I'll be looking into,
and I'll be looking, I'll be reading the article with these in
mind.   (Reading academic articles; independent studies,
student 6).

I was looking for a pattern which I could relate to the
script.   I was drawing graphs ... I knew from the script what
was supposed to be happening ... and I was looking out for it
to happen on the graph ... fortunately it did.   (Laboratory
work; physics, student 6).

You have to go through quite a few different designs to
get to the right one ... I'm sort of always thinking about
what I can put in the conclusion when I'm writing the project...

D$_3$ Meaning (continued)

I'll try and show what I have achieved, well, understand, from the project. (Project report writing; engineering, student 3)

It was a good chapter because it organised the readings that were to follow ... which led me off to further articles, and at the end of it, making notes on the things I was reading, I had a great wad of it, which by that time, I had an idea of how my initial conception of the problem could be used to sort out all the information I'd now got. And it all sort of fitted together quite nicely. Because I think as I was writing I was thinking about how I was going to, how the final product was going to come about, and that sort of directed my reading in fact. (Essay-preparation; psychology, student 5).

S$_1$ Unrelatedness

I don't exactly write down all the steps you should do. You should ... write down those sort of things — this is the result, did it work or not? If it didn't, did something else do it? That's the best way of going about it. Well, I just sort of write down what I've done. Just do the calculations and work back from there. (Projects; engineering, student 7)

This problem here, you're asked to say if it's an eigen-function, but you don't really know because he hasn't mentioned it in the lectures. He's mentioned what an eigenfunction is, but no way of telling how to work it out... You put in a formula to get the eigen energy, but to get the eigenfunction, whether it's applicable or not, there's no way of knowing (Problem-solving; physics, student 5).

I tend to give up on them. I tend to write very confused essays, because I have all these ideas going through my head, and I write them down, but I don't put them down in any particular logical sort of plan ... I tend to do better in exams, because the confusion doesn't matter so much, as long as the relevant points are there ... I don't seem to be able to link ideas together. (Essay writing; history, student 7).

I think it tends to be the case that I get bogged down in detail. I'm sure that's the case – I mean it explains why I'm so longwinded about any work that I do. I really don't find it easy to pick out the skeletal argument and just be satisfied with that. (Reading; psychology, student 10).

S$_2$ Memorization

Preparing for an exam, you learn your facts, then you have to memorize them, and sort of vague, sort of aspects of it... (Examination revision; history, student 2).

S$_2$ Memorization (continued)

I hate to say it, but what you've got to do is have a list of the "facts". You write down ten important points and memorize those - then you'll do all right in the class test. (Revision; psychology, student 5).

Formulae ... just go in (to the examination) with as many formulae as possible, so you learn those parrot-fashion. And approaches to the way you work out problems, techniques involved in maths ... I seem to remember, just sort of one day or two. (Revision; engineering, student 8).

I'm trying to remember it all - what's useful in exams. (Reading; physics, student 8).

S$_3$ Unreflectiveness

(This project) was just a matter of grinding the numbers out, getting some kind of solution. If it was adequate, fair enough. If it wasn't really, go back and pick different values. (Project work; engineering, student 11).

You just go straight for the section which is relevant to that particular question ... There'll be a topic in the book which the question comes under, and then you hunt through that section to see if they've got any ... Hopefully, they'll have the exact question and you can copy it straight down without doing any work at all ... Usually you have to hunt out the various related equations, then you just apply these to the problem. That's all, really. (Problem-solving; physics, student 12).

It's a bit confusing, (this subject)... I tend to rush through the books I'm reading for the essays, so I still don't really understand it when I've finished reading. And because there's such a lot of information I think you can oversimplify or go into too much detail. And I think I tend to over-simplify. (Reading; English, student 31).

You don't need to do as much background reading (for these essays). I just sort of set aside a day to do it and just write it. I don't think about it. (Essay-writing; English, student 38).

THE MEANING OF DEEP AND SURFACE IN DIFFERENT CONTEXTS

Analysis of the student interviews revealed important differences in the meanings attached to deep and surface approaches by students in different subject areas. In the previous section we looked at the concepts in a general form in order to identify differences which make sense in all the departments investigated; here we examine characteristic differences in the meanings of the categories in different learning environments. It is clear that what goes to make up a deep or surface approach in one disciplin is not the same as in another discipline. Moreover, while the meaning of the deep-surface dichotomy is fundamentally the same in different subject areas, there are important variations in emphasis. The analysis concentrates on the clearest distinction to emerge. This was (not unexpectedly) between arts and social science departments (psychology, history, English) and science and technology departments (physics and engineering).

Deep 1

In the physics and engineering departments, this sub-category is typically indicated by attempts to relate the experience of the <u>physical world</u> to theoretical concepts in the subject. Students frequently speak of "getting a picture of the problem" and linking theory to practice. Student 8 in the physics department provides the definitive example:

"I suppose I'm trying to imagine what the experiment is talking about, I think, in a physical sense. Sort of get a picture of what it's about ... I'm just thinking of the light and the way it spreads out, so therefore I know it's the inverse square law ..."(physics, student 8).

The category is also indicated by a student's expression of the experience of personal satisfaction while doing or in successfully completing a task:

"It's just seeing it work, you know. First of all it looks as though it's impossible to do and you just get, sorting through, the satisfaction of knowing you've understood what you're doing" (Project work; engineering, student 3).

Arts and social science students also speak of the experience of personal satisfaction; this may be combined with the linking of personal experience of <u>other people</u> to the subject matter of the task. For example:

"I'm very interested in social sciences generall I find it very enlightening, very entertaining, very satisfying, to learn theories and then to

observe them in reality.   Casually, to say,
"Christ, look, it's happening, you know, the
theory's there, that's what's going on," and I
think it adds so much, you know, to my life, to
be able to perceive what happens in everyday
society, through the eyes of a sociologist or
of a psychologist, and put a structure on what's
going on."   (psychology, student 7).

The important difference to be appreciated here
is the contrast between the emphasis in arts and
social science on personal contact with the learning
task derived from the student's experience of other
people and the emphasis in science on personal
experience of the physical world.   There is a
greater emphasis also on personal interpretation and
uniqueness of experience in the arts students' indications;   the interpretive element is most common in
English.

Deep 2

In the science departments, indications are most
frequently of attempts to relate together the various
aspects of a problem, particularly in a logical way
(to "see how it all fits together").   See, for
example, physics student 12 above, p.139:   you "put
it into a logical form which relates to something
you've done previously".
This extract also exemplifies another typical
indication: the connection of what is known about
another problem or topic to the new task - usually,
but not always, in a very specific way.   This also
happens in reading:

"You read it, a section on precipitation hardening ... and I think, well, fair enough, the
material is about as strong as mild steel or
something, and I'll remember that if I can, but
I'm not going to remember that it's 297 Newtons
per square mm. if it's in such and such a state
... There are one or two things that do stick in
your mind like the strength of mild steel, and
so on, because we've used it in the projects, so
you have a sort of relative scale whereby you
can say it's nearly as strong as mild steel ..."
(Reading textbooks;   engineering, student 6).

"I'm generally trying to relate what the book
says to what you know about it already".
(Reading textbooks;   physics, student 8).

143

"This book's about the relationship between the artist and society, which is quite relevant to the essay topic I'm doing, so I'm reading it very thoroughly ... I'm reading and underlining things that I think are important. And then I find it a bit difficult because sometimes it talks about some of the poems of the author that I haven't read, so then I go back and read the poems ... then afterwards I go back and make quite detailed notes on the book, looking back at the things I've underlined and trying to integrate it into the main topics that he's talking about." (Reading; English, student 5).

"One of the first necessities with essays is to have it well-planned ... I'm concentrating very much on the organizing aspects, trying to read through and see if it makes sense, you know, from point to point". (Essay-writing; history, student 8).

Indications of attempts to relate ideas from different topics or fields to the task in hand, or to relate ideas within the topic, are also commonly found (see, for example, history, student 1, quoted above, p. 139). The process of relating ideas appear to be done much more specifically in science tasks: concepts are related to particular problems in science, while in arts the focus is wider and ideas from different topics or fields are more freely related.

Deep 3

The expression of a sense of purpose in carrying out a task is common to both main subject groups. There is a somewhat greater emphasis in arts and social science on underlying meanings and uniqueness of experience, possibly because scientific fields are characterized by single paradigms and greater consensus about appropriate content and method (c.f. Biglan, 1973b). For example:

"It was a good chapter because it organized the readings that were to follow ... which led me off to further articles, and at the end of it, making notes on the things I was reading, I had a great wad of it, which by that time, I had an idea of how my initial conception of the problem could be used to sort out all the information I'd now got. And it all sort of fitted together quite nicely. Because I think as I was writing I was thinking about how I was going to, how the final product was going to come out, and that sort of directed my reading in fact." (Essay-preparation; psychology, student 5).

"What I'm trying to do is find out whether Tennyson compromised his art to the age or whether he just wrote what he really wanted to write. That's what I'm thinking about all the time as I'm reading it, and reading his poems as well." (Reading; English, student 5).

"There are always underlying themes in any period of history, and if you can sort of pick out these themes and really understand what was going on and what it was all about, then you've got a good chance of discovering it on an equal sort of basis with your tutor or in an exam." (Reading; history, student 1).

"You have to go through quite a few different designs to get the right one ... I'm sort of always thinking about what I can put in the conclusion when I'm writing the project ... I'll try and show what I have achieved, well, understood, from the project." (Project report writing; engineering, student 3).

"I was looking for a pattern which I could relate to the script. I was drawing graphs ... I knew from the script what was supposed to be happening ... and I was looking out for it to happen on the graph ... fortunately it did." (Laboratory work; physics, student 6).

"If you follow the instructions to the letter, it's not so interesting. The instructions are only one way of doing the experiment, but you can develop variations that get a better answer, if you just start from scratch, really ... You know what you're heading for - say this measurement of a nucleus - so that might imply measurements of field versus frequency, say. And that keeps you on the right lines." (Laboratory work; physics, student 10).

Surface 1

This sub-category is concerned with students' descriptions of not thinking about relationships in both science and arts. In science, however, students emphasize over-concentration on procedures in performing a task: using formulae, calculations, figures in tackling a problem without reference to their relationship to each other or to the purpose of the task. Two extracts already quoted above exemplify this sub-category (engineering, student 7, page 140 ; physics, student 5, page 140). It is sometimes difficult to separate this sub-category from descriptions of serialist strategies demanded by the type of task and the student's unfamiliarity with the topic. Particularly in science, it seems that it may be necessary to use procedures which are empirically inseparable from surface approaches as a stage prior to taking a deep level approach.

Engineering and physics students also describe a tendency to focus on factual details (in reading, lectures, and writing reports) which are deliberately unrelated to other parts of the course. This is unmistakably a surface approach:

"It's something completely separate from what we're doing in the lectures. It's just one very narrow subject ... it didn't relate to anything else at all really ... Facts, and just facts. Nothing else. You get the facts down so that anybody else can read them without any padding or anything else." (Project report writing; engineering, student 8).

In arts, the emphasis is more likely to be on detailed factual information which is unrelated either to the meaning of the task or to personal meaning. Arts and social science students are also more likely to speak in general terms about not relating ideas. For example:

"A point I didn't make about the essays was that, I think, you're meant to express an appreciation of diversity, whereas in the class test, if you can give a bit of factual information - so-and-so did that, and concluded that, for two sides of writing, then you'll get a good mark." (Tests; psychology, student 5).

"I tend to give up on them. I tend to write very confused essays, because I have all these ideas going through my head, and I write them down, but I don't put them down in any particular logical sort of plan ... I tend to do better in exams, because the confusion doesn't matter so much, as long as the relevant points are there ... I don't seem to be able to link ideas together." (Essay-writing; history, student 7).

Surface 2

Indications of this category among the science students' transcripts typically consist of descriptions of memorizing formulae, data, factual points in reading, or transferring lecture information or reading to the memory without thinking about it. The stimulus is often an impending examination, and the approach may be either calculated or simply anxious:

"Yes, a lot of preparation to get proofs off pat ... It's no good trying to work it out when you're in the exam." (Revision; physics, student 10).

"You've just got to go over, reading the notes ... There's not really any questions you can attempt ... It's just reading the notes and hoping it sinks in". (Revision; engineering, student 3).

Similar indications are given by the social scientists and artists, although these students also mention an emphasis on memorizing vague generalities as well as specific procedures and facts:

"Preparing for an exam, you learn your facts, then you have to memorize them, and sort of vague, sort of aspects of it ..." (Exam. revision; history, student 2).

"What gets tested in the exam is short-term recall, that's all. So in revising for an exam I just cram my mind with such facts as I consider to be pertinent, to be able to trot off these names of people or places, dates or whatever ... " (Revision, history, student 4).

Surface 3

This sub-category is very often combined empirically with S_1. The conceptual distinction, however, is between purposelessness and unrelatedness. S_3 is frequently seen by students to be dissatisfying, but necessary because of contextual constraints

(such as lack of interest in a required subject).
Indications of the sub-category in engineering and
physics are descriptions of the unthinking use of
procedures (e.g. equations) in solving problems, or
the glossing-over of the meaning of the problem:

> "The first one, well I know that formula off
> from last year. It's just a simple formula.
> You shove in a number and it comes out straight
> away." (Problem-solving; physics, student 5).

> "There'll be a topic in the book which the
> question comes under, and then you hunt through
> that section to see if they've got any ... Hope-
> fully, they'll have the exact question and you
> can copy it straight down without doing any work
> at all ... Usually you have to hunt out the
> various related equations, then you just apply
> these to the problem. That's all really."
> (Problem-solving; physics, student 12).

Alternatively, science students describe a process of sorting through data without trying to
understand it, just learning techniques, or "just
getting it done without enjoying it or thinking
about it". Psychology, history and English students'
indications of this category often consist of descriptions of a passive, unthinking, vague approach to
a task; for example:

> "The topic was causes and consequences (of the
> Reform Act) so I was sort of looking through for
> causes and consequences, as opposed to anything
> else that was relevant ... I wasn't really very
> interested, so I didn't spend a lot of time on
> it basically ... I just read what it said, I
> don't know really." (history; student 2).

A slightly different indication is of being
easily distracted by similar (but irrelevant) material
when reading, and of oversimplifying, or "going off
the point" when writing:

> "I have too many ideas running through my head
> and if I let myself run away with my ideas, I
> can completely come off the subject of the
> question, and I used to be really bad about
> that, but I'm not so bad about it now." (Essay-
> writing; English, student 6).

> "I tend to be a bit specific initially, but I

do find that I get misled very easily and as soon as another area comes up which is, perhaps, not quite to do with the topic that I'm wanting to look at specifically but has interesting connections, then I go off on tangents.   Very regularly end up sort of miles away from where I originally started."   (Reading books and articles;   psychology, student 10).

STYLES AND PATHOLOGIES OF LEARNING IN DIFFERENT SUBJECT AREAS

The differences we have described above are clearly related to the different nature of typical learning tasks in different subject areas.   It is difficult not to be aware of a parallel between the differences described by Pask (1976;   1977) in relation to learning strategies and styles and the present findings.   In arts and social science, it appears that a deep level approach relies relatively more - at least initially - on a holist strategy (an emphasis on personal experiences, uniqueness of experience, interpretation, illustration, the general relation of ideas).   In science, serialist strategies are more common (an emphasis is apparent, for example, on seeing relationships within the context of the task rather than in a more general way, or in making relationships between theoretical ideas).

It would appear that the holist-serialist and comprehension-operation distinctions describe differences not only between strategies and individuals within a subject area (Pask, 1976; Laurillard, 1978), but also differences between the demands made by learning tasks in different subject areas.   It is important to recognize the difference in the meaning of the deep-surface dichotomy which hinges on this distinction.   Deep approaches in science may contain elements which in arts terms would usually be classified as surface;   a serialist strategy may involve rote learning or a very narrow focus on procedures as a stage prior to a deep approach.   This strategy is not, of course, unique to science tasks;   but it is more common in science tasks than in arts ones.

It is also possible to see similarities between the surface sub-categories in the students' descriptions of their experiences and Pask's concepts of globetrotting and improvidence.   In so far as holist strategies are more commonly used in the first stages of arts and social science tasks or topics, and serialist strategies in science, it might be deduced that science students are more likely to display improvidence, and artists globetrotting. The evidence from the interviews is equivocal. Arts students are more "generalized" in their indications of surface approaches, but this is not the same thing as globetrotting. S_1 describes something close to improvidence (over-cautious reliance on detail and failure to use valid analogies or to see relationships), but it occurs at least as commonly in arts and social science as in science. On the other hand, S_3 contains some suggestion of globetrotting for the arts and social science students but not for the scientists. We shall look at further evidence concerning the presence of pathologies of learning in different subject areas in chapter 9.

CONTEXTS OF LEARNING

All the interviews included questions specifically concerned with the students' perceptions of the learning environment. The questions dealt with teaching, assessment, and course structures; a general question about the student's perception of the good and bad features of the courses and the department was included. Except in the psychology and engineering departments, the students were also asked about the context of specific learning tasks. For example, if a student indicated a surface approach to one task and a deep approach to another - or different approaches within the same task - he was invited to give a reason for the difference.

By far the most important category to emerge from the analysis of students' descriptions of their experiences was that represented in the earlier versions of the CPQ by the commitment to teaching and relationships with students scales. This category refers to the quality of teaching in the department and to the extent to which staff seem to understand the learning requirements of the students. It was apparent in the interviews of students in all the departments:

> "The thing with the independent studies staff is that they're all so amiable ... they're so helpful; if you go to them with a problem they can usually find some answer ... They all seem very committed to the idea of independent studies, th all feel that they're doing a worthwhile thing." (independent studies, student 2).

"Some (lectures) have been very good, partly because they've been, well, not flippantly delivered, but certainly humorously, and with an entertaining streak. Others have been putting across too many facts, and they seem to have been badly prepared and badly put across. There's one lecturer ... who is very clever, he knows it all, but I wish he'd try to share it a bit more with people, and just try and condense the things he's saying, because he often repeats himself and makes note-taking difficult." (history, student 5).

"There are some lecturers who will think about anything you say, and say, Oh, I hadn't thought of that, let's see what it leads to. And there are other lecturers who will just go on talking almost to themselves ..." (physics, student 10).

"As long as I'm doing a subject that I'm interested in, it doesn't really matter to me how they do it... I prefer departments to be organized and efficient, and also, more important, that's caring about their students. That to me is more important than the procedure of the coursework, you know, what they decide to do and what they decide to leave out from their courses doesn't bother me." (English, student 6).

"My criticisms will be very closely aligned to, I think, the lack of empathy that some of the staff have about the ability levels of the students relative to their subject. Not relative to being able to be good enough to be at university, if you like, but relative to the fact that the concrete knowledge that they have is virtually nil in some of the areas that we've talked about, at a very high level. So you can't attach anything that you've been told to something that you already know, which of course is a very important point in learning ... I think it's the overall problem of the experts coming in and having to give courses in a few weeks on their particular interest, and they have such a wealth of knowledge in that area that they start at too high a level. That's what I think happens. They've gone so far into their own area that they've forgotten that we know nothing, essentially, compared with them." (psychology, student 7).

The interview data reveal an aspect of students' evaluations which the CPQ does not: staff in the same department are compared with each other, and some are seen to be more effective than others. While students do not seem to experience difficulty in describing the characteristics of the department as a whole, the interviews show that these general descriptions hide important differences.

Several other categories of description emerging from the interview analysis appear to have an evaluative element. The first of these corresponds to the <u>freedom in learning</u> factor discovered in the questionnaire analysis:

> "I'm not sure where the system's failing but there isn't the exchange of ideas, the sharing of information ... It's this very formal or objectified way of looking at work, at what has been produced in work, instead of ... being more informal and relaxed about it, somehow stimulating much more beneficial discussion ... there isn't enough of that - you've got to stick to the structure and plough through it." (psychology, student 10).

The <u>assessment and workload</u> category corresponds to the workload factor:

> "If I have started in plenty of time, then I do start thinking about the subject itself, more than perhaps if I've got to hand it in, but basically it's all a bit of a struggle, just to hand things in, as opposed to being interesting; you're working against a time deadline instead of for your own benefit." (history, student 2).

> "The exams don't exactly fill me with enthusiasm particularly the electronics papers. We've got six papers for two units, which seems an awful lot. I know even the staff admit the workload in the second year is high, really tough on us." (engineering, student 5).

> "I look at (the topic) and I think to myself, 'Well, I can do that if I can be bothered to hunt through hundreds of textbooks and do the work' - and you sort of relate that to the value of the work in the course, which is virtually zero because it's so much exam assessment ... I just don't bother with it until the exams come round ... my revision is basically

for the exams, purely and simply aimed at passing the exams without bothering too much about
studying the subject." (physics, student 12).

Social climate and clear goals and standards
also seem to be evaluative, although perhaps not as
strongly so as the categories already described:

"The only thing I've got against it ... is the
isolation that's involved for independent
studies majors. I suppose to some extent that
is one's own bag, you know, and it's up to one
to make more contacts, but one finds oneself
rather isolated, because you're not going to
routinely convened classes, very often, and that
means you don't meet very many people. They
tried having seminars but they were very poorly
attended ..." (independent studies, student 29).

"We all do the same thing, we all talk about it
more than people in most departments. You can
learn a lot from this; everything's relevant to
everybody else. I know 95% of the other
students socially." (engineering, student 1).

"The first term, I seemed to have done a lot of
work, and I hadn't got anything back at all, and
I just had no idea how I was doing. I got
quite worried really." (English, student 5).

Two further categories derived from the interview analysis - formal teaching methods and vocational
relevance - correspond exactly to the CPQ scales of
the same names. They are descriptive rather than
evaluative categories.

In addition to the more general descriptions and
evaluations of teaching, assessment, and courses, two
categories referring to the context of specific
learning tasks were apparent in the analysis of the
interviews: the student's background knowledge of
the topic or subject of which the task forms a part,
and his level of interest in or personal commitment
to a task. These categories are intimately associated in the transcripts with the approaches students
describe to different tasks and will be discussed in
a later secton.

The interview analysis confirms the finding of
the CPQ analysis that the six departments provide very
different contexts of learning. The differences between the departments correspond closely to the

153

differences identified by the CPQ (see Chapter 7), and are not repeated here.

The categories of description themselves do not appear to differ in meaning from one subject area to another to the extent that the deep and surface approach categories do. The main evaluation variable, corresponding to the relationships with students and commitment to teaching scales (and their later refinements) of the CPQ, occurs in a similar form in all the interviews. One relatively minor difference is that social science students attach more importance to close personal relationships with staff than students in the other departments. There are more differences in emphasis in the other categories. Perceived excessive formality of the assessment system and a lack of flexibility in choosing assignments is of greater concern to arts and social scientists than to science students. In the vocationally-orientated engineering department, a heavy workload was not exactly welcomed, but was recognised as being necessary in order to fulfil the professionally-defined demands of the syllabus.

INDIVIDUAL DIFFERENCES IN STRATEGIC STUDY METHODS

We have so far focused mainly on differences between categories describing levels of approach and types of departmental context. We shall now look at some categories describing differences between individual students which emerged from the interviews.

The interviews included two questions taken from Miller and Parlett's study of students' examination strategies in a Scottish university (Miller and Parlett, 1974): "Do you think there is any technique involved in examinations, or not?" and "Do you think the staff get an impression of you during the year, or not?". To these questions were added others about techniques in essay-writing or project-report writing. The purpose of these questions was to see whether the kinds of strategies identified by Miller and Parlett would also be present in different environments - viz., in departments in which continuous assessment as well as assessment by final examinations was practised, and in science as well as in social science departments.

A preliminary analysis of the psychology students' interviews suggested that Miller and Parlett's findings were fairly closely replicated. Most students could be classified into one of the categories of cue-seeker, cue-conscious, and cue-deaf

using judgement instructions similar to Miller and
Parlett's modified to include continuous assessment
tasks.   Cue-seeking students, for example, not only
tried to make favourable impressions on staff, and
searched for cues to examination topics, but also
took special care to select essay topics, and write
essays, bearing in mind the likes and dislikes of the
particular tutor who had set them.

The engineering students presented quite a
different picture.   Cue-seeking, as defined by
Miller and Parlett, simply did not exist.   Some
students were more strategic than others, but instead
of using cue-seeking tactics, they used other methods
of maximizing assessment outcomes.   These included
paying special attention to the detailed requirements
of a tutor when presenting written work, and the
meticulous study of past examination papers.   These
students would probably be classified as cue-conscious
in Miller and Parlett's scheme, but this would fail
to distinguish a small group within this category
who displayed a particularly strong determination to
succeed by using these tactics.   Some of them were
aware that attempts to make good personal impressions
and to seek out favoured examination topics might
have the opposite effect in this environment to that
intended, because of the formality of the teaching
and staff-student relationships in the department.

These differences led to an attempt to develop
a more general model of strategic methods.   Miller
and Parlett's study represents a special case within
this model.

There are three main categories: most strategic,
intermediate, and least strategic.   Students who
consistently indicate active attempts to use selective effort in relation to assessment tasks (e.g.
essay preparation or examination revision) are classified as most strategic.   These students (n=6) often
also indicate the use of impression management.
They are frequently critical of the assessment system,
but see it as a game to be played and won.   An impression of a rather ruthless, calculating approach
is usually given (c.f. Wankowski, 1973; Entwistle
and Wilson, 1977).   Within this category, cue-seeking students can be identified in some departments.
The classic cue-seeking variant is best exemplified
in the psychology department:

"Sometimes I find myself writing for a tutor,
writing for a marker ... With that essay I was
just discussing, that reference group one, I
wrote with the image of the marker in mind, the

personality, the person, I find that's important, to know who's going to be marking your paper ... Question-guessing is the most important (examination technique).   Make a good stab at the questions that you think you are going to come up - just rationalize it and just work on the areas you think are going to be asked." (psychology, student 7).

"I like to give the impression that I'm out to get a First and hope that they'll treat me in that sort of way.   I think if I stress my intention often enough, they'll sympathize with me." (psychology, student 5).

It was also apparent in some of the history and independent studies students. For example:

"Staff certainly get an impression of me ... All essay marking is subjective.   I know of instances where I've handed in a good essay and got an indifferent mark for it.   I had a debriefing session with the tutor ... I thought, Well, my next essay I'll get a better mark for it.   And I wrote perhaps not such a good essay and got an excellent mark for it, which I didn't really deserve.   But in the context of the learning process the tutor has an impression of you ... it all adds up to your essay mark and your exam marks." (history, student 4).

In the engineering department the highly strate- gic approach was not at all like cue-seeking.   But the approach was related to an extrinsic, competitive motivation in this discipline more than in any other. Notice how the next student relates the absence of cue-seeking to the type of field in which he is studying, and at the same time illustrates his awareness of the assessment "game" in other subject areas:

"The lecturer told us his marking scheme, and 16 of the possible 20 marks went for the de- sign, building, and performance of the bridge. It was a model bridge, and only 4 marks, 20% of the marks, were available for the report. So obviously I didn't put much effort into that at all, obviously I didn't spend three weeks writing it up ... I'm well aware that I'm here to get a degree you know, you don't write what you think, you write what the tutor wants you to think. And in engineering in general there's not much room for that. I think there would be a lot more room for it in more subjective things, and I would do it even more then, presumably" (engineering, student 6).

The absence of cue-seeking in the engineering department appears to be related to the degree of formality in the learning context. While cue-seeking may be effective in a fairly personalized and informal environment, it is probably counterproductive in more formally-organized departments. Even a tactic such as selective revision of examination topics may be less effective in departments where knowledge is more hierarchically organised.

There were no students in the physics department who could be unambiguously classified into the most strategic category, but another student describes the association between strategies and subject area:

"You sort of hear people in arts subjects saying 'He's bound to ask a question on such a topic'. But in physics the thing's much more continuous in a way. You can answer a question on Gladstone's foreign policy, but there's lots of ways of setting up a question in physics. You can never be sure exactly what questions are going to come up." (physics, student 2).

The opposite extreme to the most strategic students is demonstrated by the transcripts of students in the least strategic category (n=20). These students do not use selective effort in relation to assessment tasks. They are often not interested in obtaining a good degree. The assessment system is typically externalized and reified: the students possess confidence in its reliability and validity as a means of classification. They think that the impression they make on staff will probably not affect their grades; they may or may not speak of using specific examination techniques.

A very small number of students from this category can be further classified as cue-deaf. Nearly all students in the present investigation, however, revealed at least a modest acquaintance with the idea that some students might be able to influence their grades by a judicious choice of assessment techniques. The following extracts examplify the least strategic category:

Just revise early, try and read through everything once ... I would have thought that (the staff's) impression of you couldn't affect your degree to any great extent. (physics, student 11).

You get this stuff about examination bias and all the rest of it, but I don't really think that teachers are that naive as to let their personal feelings about that person influence them in any way.   (psychology, student 4)

I'm not sure how they do go about marking essays and things like that.   I mean they might just go off what is there, but they could bear in mind, perhaps, if you didn't go to seminars ... I'm not sure.   (English, student 38).

(In writing up projects) as long as you get down all the facts you can, without padding it out too much, following some sort of given, you know, they give you what they think they want, and you try and follow the list, then I think that's what they want.   (engineering, student 8).

I: Do you think the impression staff get of you could affect your degree result?
S: No, it's not, sort of, the way I could work at all. If I do something I do it because I want to, not because I might get a 2i instead of a 2ii, or something.   That's not particularly important to me.   (history, student 2).

The largest group of students (n=28) was classified as intermediate.   Some of the students were very difficult to classify;   inevitably, doubtful cases have regressed to this category.   Some student were almost "beyond" cue-seeking, being fully aware of the possible biases of the assessment system, but determined to go their own way and study what they wanted to study, despite any harmful effect on their degree result;   others were hardly conscious of the assessment "game" at all, except for an occasional suggestion in their interviews that they might be aware that perfect objectivity in grading did not exist.   This category corresponds to cue-consciousness for students in some of the departments: there was an awareness of the effects of impression-management, and an understanding of the presence of cues to examination topics displayed by these students, without active and consistent attempts to seek out cues and make favourable impressions on staff being shown.

I think it's a favourable impression (that staff get of me)... If people know you, know your capabilities and how you normally work, if you're writing a question they read into it a lot of the time what they know you've meant ... I think it can have advantages. Although it shouldn't really. (independent studies, student 5).

If you really make yourself noticed it could have an effect (on degree results)... but I don't think it's significant in my case. (physics, student 13).

The main examination technique is to study past papers - as many as you can get hold of, and for as long as you've got the time ... the study of past papers is very essential. (engineering, student 2).

There's a lot of bluffing involved (in seminars). If you just know basically what you're supposed to be talking about, and throw a few intelligent comments in once in a while, you can create quite a good impression. But the impression couldn't affect my degree result much ... I'm a close friend of my tutor, but I don't play on it. (history, student 13).

You have to talk in seminars, and they hear what you say, and they can make a lot of inferences about you from what you say. And also, of course, from other things like your appearance and the way you speak, the way you put yourself over ... They know I know my stuff and that I speak when I've got something valuable to say. (English, student 6).

(Lectures are useful to get) a person's ideas, possibly, sometimes you get the lecturer's view on it, and you think - ah, that could come in handy for knowing what she thinks, playing the game or something. (psychology, student 2).

INDIVIDUAL DIFFERENCES IN DEEP AND SURFACE APPROACHES TO STUDYING

The major conclusion of Laurillard's resarch (Laurillard, 1978) was that students' strategies and approaches to learning were context-dependent: dichotomised descriptions of learning such as deep/ surface could not be applied to individual students but could be used to describe students in particular learning situations. It is nevertheless possible to maintain that while students are influenced by the demands of learning tasks and their contexts, they might also have relatively stable preferences for one approach or the other. There seems to be no logical flaw in this argument for consistency and variability in approach (Entwistle, 1979).

The interview transcripts were therefore examine
again in order to see whether consistent differences
between individuals could be identified, despite the
fact that every student had mentioned the use of both
deep and surface approaches. The following judgement instructions were developed in order to make
explicit the grounds for classification:

1.   What <u>general</u> approach to studying is mentioned?
     e.g.   "I <u>usually</u> find that I ..."
            "I <u>generally</u> try to ..."
            "<u>On the whole</u> I am able to ..."
            (see student 7, history, below, for a
             more extended example)

     If generally deep, classify as deep;   if
generally surface, classify as surface.

2.   What is the relationship between intention and
     process?
     i.e. Does the student speak of succeeding in
     carrying out deep intentions (classify as deep),
     or does he contrast intention and process?
     (classify as surface)

3.   Does the student concentrate in his responses
     on the technical aspects of studying when
     asked about how he goes about studying?
     e.g.   "I read this page, then I turned to the
             back of the book and spent ten minutes
             looking up the index ..." (= surface)

4.   Does the student make a distinction between the
     merely technical and the actual process of
     studying?   (classify as deep)

5.   Is academic knowledge seen as a part of the
     student?   Is an interest expressed in learning
     for learning's sake? (classify as deep).   Does
     the student talk of the excitement of learning
     and express a desire to learn?   Is he able to
     talk fluently about the process of learning
     (c.f. 4 above), as if it had been reflected on
     before the interview?   (= deep).

6.   Is academic knowledge seen as external, a threat
     a source of distress or anxiety, not part of
     oneself, something that happens to the learner?
     (classify as surface).

Categories 5 and 6 resemble the differences described by Saljo in his study of the development of subjective conceptions of learning (Saljo, 1979a, b,c). Learning in the "taken-for-granted" perspective is essentially a reproductive process (c.f. the earlier stages of development in Perry's model (1970)). Learning later becomes, for some experienced learners, "thematized": the learner becomes aware of the influence of the context of learning, is able to contrast learning "for life" with learning in school, and typically makes a distinction between rote learning and "real learning" (understanding).

The distinction between consistent deep and consistent surface approaches is perhaps most effectively illustrated by some rather more extensive extracts from the interview transcripts:

DEEP: I began to realize there, there was a structure in the things they were teaching us and it wasn't just a load of facts - that's only a recent, recent realization, perhaps only this term. I started to realize it when I realized that the English I'm doing for my free ninth, er, is very closely connected to psychology ... the novelist seems to be very close to the psychologist, only he writes it in a creative - no, not creative - a more artistic form. And when I realized that those were so close I suddenly realized how interrelated all the topics in psychology were. And that's when I also read some articles on creativity; that's when I suddenly realized that putting your own pattern on it would probably make a better essay, and a more enjoyable essay. And the little anecdote is that I got an A for the first essay done in the new way - so I've carried on. I can see Perry as being fairly relevant and I think, I couldn't have seen him as being relevant until I'd got into some of the stages myself. So being taught about it in the first year didn't really help because I didn't understand wha, what they were teaching, or I thought, I mean, I knew the facts sort of but I didn't know what was really meant 'cos you can't understand there are two sides to an argument - if that's what you're understanding - until you see there are two sides to an argument ... I've become more interested in the subject, I think. I've begun to understand more of the subject, and perhaps, learned, learned things that, can apply in my everyday life more successfully. I mean things like my learning. I've learned perhaps, perhaps a better way of learning ... (psychology, student 6).

SURFACE:
S: I don't really like seminars anyway.
I: Why not?
S: I don't know, er, they seem false to me, they, you've um, you all know that, that you're not enjoying them, you're just there because you have to, because they're supposed to be compulsory, your tutor's going to mark your essays anyway, so you might as well go and show willing but I don't like seminars ... I think there's a lot of bother involved in, er, I mean the two practicals count, and it's not just, I don't think it is, just the writing up the report at the end that you hand in − I mean that might be alright, but it's the way you go about organizing the practical. If you're in a state and, you go and see your tutor, and you say, er, "can't get enough subjects" or "something's gone wrong", then, it's not going to give you much. I mean you're going to feel like that aren't you − two inches tall, and you can't help but think, well when he's marking it he's going to remember that I came to him all in a state, I couldn't really organize it. I think, I think they give a lot of worry to people.
(psychology, student 8).

DEEP:
I: What sorts of things were going through your head as you were reading it?
S: Pleasure at somebody being able to handle such a complex subject as what's wrong with society with great lucidity and clarity; admiration at his achievement in identifying the failures of the industrial world-view and yet also positively being able to make positive suggestions about what might be done to correct deficiencies ... I was happy too that it linked in with what I'd been reading about the development of science and scientific traditions. It just really was a book which linked together lots of different things that I already knew in one pattern ... I was continually linking together different things.
(independent studies, student 29).

SURFACE:
I: Well, do you think you have to ... Do you think there' any special thing you have to do when you are preparing for them, revising for exams?
S: Um, definitely going through problem sheets and the worked solutions and that. I suppose to, find out, that way, you came across, all the likely combinations of things they're going to stick in, like rotten things ... Then you concentrate more on the, ins and outs of, the problems related to this part of the course. You know what might the prob, what might the er, what shall I say, mmm, awkward parts they are going to put in, you go through the past

problem sheets, then you can see what, um, intricate little pieces they are going to put in, you know to try and fool you and things like that. (engineering, student 7).

DEEP: I thought that was quite an interesting (essay) actually, because it was something like "What scope is there for individual initiative in a group?", and that makes me think, oh what, there's quite a few terms you've got to sort out here, er, this initiative thing, how can you take it, and I decided that, you can have initiative meaning freedom to act independently of the group and initiative being freedom to think independently of a group.   And I took that sort of line on it, which I thought would be a bit different – I know how boring it must be to mark thirty essays all the same ... At first I was a bit, I thought, Oh God, how am I going to start, I don't really know where my emphasis lies at the moment before I've done a bit of work on it.   I know roughly that I'm going to do this freedom to act/freedom to think bit, how does it interrelate?   So I just started reading, on the first chapter I think it was on that book called "Groups", and, er it was a good chapter 'cos it organised all the readings that were to follow – it was done by the editors themselves ... Which led me off to the readings in that, ah, which led me off to further articles, and at the end of it, making notes on my, on the things I was reading, I had a great wad of it which, by that time, I had an idea of how my initial conception of the problem could be used to sort out all the information I'd now got. And it all sort of fitted together quite nicely.   'Cos I think as I was writing I was thinking about how I was going to, how the final product was going to come about and, er, that sort of directed my reading in fact.   I'd read something and I'd think: well, how's this fitting in with what I've thought about so far, and once I'd got to that stage I'd think, well, where do I go from here.   And so I was using what I'd just read to determine what I'd read next, and I kept going until I had to go to bed. (psychology, student 5).

SURFACE: You look for different people's ideas, the different authors' ideas, and compare, then sort of work out what you think's relevant yourself ... I find it difficult trying to work out in my own mind what I think is relevant, because obviously so many people have written pages and pages on one subject.   I find it difficult to find what's relevant for myself.   Making my own mind up I find very complicated.   You spend such a short period of time – the other people have spent year and years ... (history, student 2).

> SURFACE: I sort of feel it's quite a challenge. I like getting a lot of ideas, I like to find a particular angle for it, make it a bit more interesting. But I tend to give up on them (essays), I tend to write very confused essays because I have all these ideas going through my head and I write them down, but I don't put them down in any particular logical sort of plan ... I tend to do better in exams, because there the confusion doesn't matter so much, as long as the relevant points are there ... I don't seem to be able to link ideas together ... (history, student 7).

It is possible to see a logical continuity between the consistent deep category, Pask's concept of versatility, and strategic study methods. Versatility in a "thematized" learner - shown by the ability to alternate between a grasp of the whole and its implications and the process of building up an understanding by working through details - is well demonstrated by this student:

> What I tend to do initially on an essay or a dissertation, I will make up perhaps a short or a long bibliography, depending on what it is, of books and articles that I think are relevant as source material, and then at first I'll tend to just go through those one by one, picking out out points which I think are relevant, giving me some sort of framework to work on. And then, after I've built up quite a large body of notes, possibly, from that, then I'll get to the stage where I've got a very good idea of how I'm going to organise the essay or the dissertation or whatever, and there'll be particular areas then which I'm looking for. There may be one or two particular points which I want to see what other people have written about. And so where previously I've been going through the source material perhaps one by one in a rather general way, then I'll get down to more specific details ... (independent studies, student 6).

Similarly, the concept of strategic study methods implies an ability to choose the most effective strategy for the task in hand (sometimes this might mean taking a surface approach) and an awareness of the purpose of the task and the way it relates to the course as a whole. Consistent deep approaches were found to be positively and significantly related to strategic study methods (Ramsden, 1981).

In the remainder of this chapter we shall examine some functional relationships between the categories that have been identified in the previous analyses. We shall deal first with students' perceptions of the relationships between different subject areas and strategies of learning.

STRATEGIES OF LEARNING IN DIFFERENT SUBJECT AREAS

We have seen that the subjective meanings attached to the sub-categories of deep and surface approaches differ from one subject area to another. The distinction between the arts and science subject areas is related to Pask's descriptions of differing styles and strategies of learning; it seems that different subject areas make different demands on the types of strategy used by students. Although the interviews did not measure styles and strategies of learning directly, history, English, and physics students were asked whether they felt that there were differences between the ways in which students in different subject areas studied. To what extent did the students themselves perceive differences in the type of strategy used in arts and sciences, and in the learning contexts provided by the different kinds of departments?

Learning tasks in science are typically described as hierarchical, logical, heterogeneous, and rule- and procedure-governed:

> (Science) seems to be a constant sort of building thing – they learn something one week and build on it ... knowing the formula, and using that, and applying it to solve another formula, etcetera. (history, student 9).

> A lot of our stuff is just sort of, you know, teaching us a logical flow of arguments, observing certain results, concepts and how they're related, whereas ... (physics, student 14).

> It's much more – exact isn't the right word – but in physics you're right or wrong ... here you can't think it, it happens. (physics, student 5).

> But for the sciences, they have to be more calculating, they have to know logical concepts, they have to know logical things and how an answer will come out of a calculation or a few statements which have been written down. (English, student 6).

Arts and social science tasks, on the other hand, are seen to be interpretive, comparative, generalized, more self-governed, and not as difficult or time-consuming:

(Arts students) seem to have a much easier time of it.
They read a lot more, of course, they've got to read all
these books, but ... it seems much easier ... it seems to
be just going on and on about what you yourself think ...
In these other subjects you can just sort of go on and on:
"I think this, I think that". (physics, student 5).

The work demands, in a way, a completely different
intelligence.   For us it's more interpretation, more
analysis, more penetration into the material ... They
have to look ahead to an answer: we have to look in ...
For English you have to see implicit meaning.   (English,
student 6).

The history or politics student is trying to interpret
facts;   the physics student is perhaps being more and
more precise whilst the history student is trying to
generali e more ... the history student is going round
and round, sort of thing.   (history, student 8).

It's hard to explain - you're not learning something one
week which will lead you on to something else, you tend
to skip about ... you can see things running through the
lectures, but they're very sort of tenuous ... It's
not something that you can build on.   (history, student
9).

A lot of (history) is just hypothesis, why did this guy
do this? and so on - it's a lot less certain. (physics,
student 14).

These subjectively-defined differences are surprisingly similar (the differences in workload and
difficulty excepted) to Pask's definitions of
operation learners and comprehension learners:

Operation learners pick up rules, methods, and details
... (the operation learner) assimilates procedures and
builds concepts for isolated topics.

Comprehension learners readily pick up an overall
picture of the subject matter ... (they) describe the
relationships between topics.   (Pask, 1976)

Moreover, although the two subject areas are
seen to require different ways of learning, students
in each field agree on what the differences are.
And both groups relate the differences they jointly
identify to characteristic differences in the environments of arts and science departments, as the following extracts show:

In physics, in the sciences, it's laid out in the lectures, everything that you do comes down, it's written on the blackboard, if you miss the lectures it's very important, really, because you miss out whole sections of the courses. Whereas with the arts you could to a certain degree, I think, be given a reading list and an essay list, and be left to tutorials and seminars ... just left to do it all yourself, with guidelines being set through the tutorials ... it's guidelines in the arts, in the sciences, it's just lines along which you have to work. There's no guiding - you have to do this, and you're not given any freedom of expression. (physics, student 12).

There is a big division between science and arts. My friend does biology, and she seems to have to learn so many more facts than us, and there's so much more pressure, especially this year. She's always being given exams, at the beginning of each term, so she has to work hard in the holidays, and you've got lots and lots of assignments to do each week, and the actual exam is a great vast area. She can't just revise particular topics, because there's a multiple choice (examination)... Sometimes she just has to memorize names, and things like that. I know sometimes she feels that she'd like to be able to think a bit more about things, critically ... It's a much more specific kind of subject, it's more systematic; we're left to ourselves a lot ... we have much more work to do outside the actual set hours. (English, student 5).

We do a lot more work than they do ... more often than not, you hear people say, "Oh, I'll get an extension for my essay for another two weeks" or something; if we asked for an extension for our tutorial sheets, we'd be three weeks behind ... (physics) is far more relevant to life than the study of history is. Admittedly, if you can see what's gone on in the past, you can, it might help you, but whereas if you get a science degree you can go directly into a scientific job, with history degrees, there isn't much you can do apart from teaching, if you specifically want to use history ... They perhaps don't take it as seriously, I don't think it perhaps means as much to them as ours does. (physics, student 11).

We can hand it in and compare it with some other guy, right or wrong, with fellow-students, but there it seems to be just going on and on about what you yourself think, so you can't really compare it with other students to see what they thought of it. (physics, student 5).

My lecture timetable is pretty sparse, whereas I've got a friend who does engineering, and he's got days just full

of stuff, but I've got to do a hell of a lot more reading.
I go to a lecture and it just introduces me to a subject,
whereas he, I suppose, gets an awful lot of it from
seminars, practicals, and so on. He gets a lot more
information, whereas I get an introduction to it, I
suppose. (history, student 11).

(In science) I think you have to learn things you don't
want to learn a lot more than in English; you can't
select as much, because it all fits together. (English
student 38).

These contrasting descriptions of tasks and contexts certainly support the view that Pask's concepts
effectively measure differences between subject areas
Subject area and learning strategy are functionally
related in the students' subjective conceptions.
The match is remarkably accurate and makes good
sense: science departments are seen to have clearer
goals, greater vocational relevance, less freedom in
learning, and more formal teaching; all these things
make for an environment in which serialist strategies
are encouraged (and probably rewarded), while the
reverse is true for arts students and in arts
departments. Although both science and arts tasks
may require both types of learning strategy (we have
seen that the ability to alternate between the two
is a characteristic of some competent learners), the
mixture is different. The students relate the
differences in learning strategies to the way in
which the departments are organized, as much as to
inherent differences in the subject matter. A
matching process, whereby students with a preference
for comprehension learning gravitate towards arts
departments, and operation learners towards science
departments, presumably takes place. It would
seem that the distinctions are continually reinforced
at university.

THE EFFECT OF THE LEARNING CONTEXT ON STUDENTS' LEVEL
OF APPROACH

Another important objective of the interview
analysis was the exploration of possible relationships between students' perceptions of the context
of learning and their levels of approach to learning
tasks. How do students explain the fact that they
take different approaches to different tasks?

Students' Experiences of Learning

Teaching, Assessment, Course Structure

For students in all the departments, the quality
of teaching and the extent to which staff gave help
and advice on approaches to studying were related to
generally favourable or unfavourable attitudes towards learning and students' interest in what they
were studying. The following extracts from the
interviews provide examples of these relationships:

(a) Interest in students, helpfulness of teaching

I certainly don't like it if you get tutorials where the
guy just comes along and sits down and makes you stand
up and do the work on the blackboard. Usually he picks
on people that can't do it, which I think is terrible
because you get stuck up at the blackboard and made to
look a fool, and it switches you right off... I think I'm
not going to do that if this guy's going to do that to
me, because I don't learn anything; nobody else learns
anything because it takes you so long to do one question;
and it makes you very unhappy with that particular
course, so I lose interest in the course. (physics,
student 12).

I find that the courses I do most work on are the courses
where I get on with the tutors best ... a tutor can put
you off the subject ... some of them don't like students,
so they're not interested in what students have to say
unless it's relevant to their approach. (English,
student 38).

Luckily I'm doing some courses with some good tutors on
them - you know, they make the books come alive because
they can talk about them and they can direct you to a
chapter or a passage, and that's important I think ...
you could spend an hour rooting through and then just
come to what you think is the essence of it all ... If
you get a guideline from the tutor, and I'm quite lucky
in having someone who can point the way, then it's a
godsend. (history, student 5).

(b) Commitment to the subject

If they (tutors) have enthusiasm, then they really fire
their own students with the subject, and the students
really pick it up ...I'm really good at and enjoy (one
subject) but that's only because a particular tutor I've
had has been so enthusiastic that he's given me an enthusiasm for it and now I really love the subject. But
at the beginning of (another course) the tutor was ...

169

a little bit passive for my liking ... something imaginative was lacking, there was something lacking in the seminar group ... (English, student 6).

(c)   Teaching at the students' own level

This problem here, you're asked to say if it's an eigenfunction, but you don't really know because he hasn't mentioned it in the lectures. He's mentioned what an eigenfunction is, but no way of telling how to work it out ... You put in a formula to get the eigen energy, but to get the eigenfunction, whether it's applicable or not, there's no way of knowing. (physics, student 5).

My criticisms will be very closely aligned to, I think, the lack of empathy that some of the staff have about the ability levels of the students relative to their subject. Not relative to being able to be good enough to be at university, if you like, but relative to the fact that the concrete knowledge that they have is virtually nil in some of the areas that we've talked at, at a very high level. So you can't attach anything that you've been told to something that you already know, which of course is a very important point in learning ... I think it's the overall problem of the experts coming in and having to give courses in a few weeks on their particular interest, and they have such a wealth of knowledge in that area that they start at too high a level. That's what I think happens. They've gone so far into their own area that they've forgotten that we know nothing, essentially, compared with them. (psychology, student 7).

(d)   Lecturing ability

The concepts are really difficult anyway. It usually takes, I think most people like, I certainly like to sit down on my own and go at my own speed. Now the lecturers certainly assume that we know it and they just keep going. People can say, "slow down" but people of course are reluctant to say they don't understand it. So he tends to keep going, and once you get behind it, you know, you can't really get back on terms. (engineering, student 1).

Recently we were doing Fourier analysis, and the lecturer mentioned in passing that it was something which they used when they transmit moon pictures back to earth ... that makes a lot of difference, you can see it being used. Another example he quoted was about why when you bang a drum you get lots of different sounds rather than when you, say, play a violin when you just get one note ... he said, if you look at this you can see why – and he was

right, you could see why, it did make sense.   (physics,
student 3).

(e)   Feedback on performance

You give an essay in – I gave in two at the beginning of
the second term and I didn't get those back till this
term ... you know, it's a bit difficult, when you're
writing the next essay, because you want to know where
you've gone wrong and the points that have been alright
... By the time you've got it back after waiting a whole
term you've forgotten what it's all about and it doesn't
really mean much then.   (English, student 31).

Unfavourable attitudes to studying, lack of
interest, and, significantly, surface approaches, were
related by the students to deficiencies of the assessment system (especially inappropriate assessment
methods), restricted opportunities for self-direction,
and excessive workload:

(a)   Inappropriate assessment methods

I look at (the topic) and I think to myself, "Well, I
can do that if I can be bothered to hunt through hundreds
of textbooks and do the work" – and you sort of relate
that to the value of the work in the course, which is
virtually zero because it's so much exam assessment ...
I just don't bother with it until the exams come around
... my revision is basically for the exams, purely and
simply aimed at passing the exams without bothering too
much about studying the subject.   (physics, student 12).

In independent studies you've got to do the coursework
and it's got to be good.   Whereas – I know some history
students who've just got phenomenally good memories and
have got a very good exam technique, and did very little
revision, and just got good marks on the basis of, you
know, parrot-fashion learning.   (independent studies,
student 7).

In this department, if (the design) fails that's like a
black mark.   It shouldn't be ... the French civil
engineer who was the world's leading authority on the
design of dams said there was more to be learned from
failure than success.   He's quite right of course.   So
if you have a failure, providing you can account for it,
then to me that's as valid as something that passed.
(engineering, student 2).

(b)   Excessive workload, lack of choice

> I'm disappointed in some respects that it isn't what I
> expected it to be ... All the time it's assessment,
> assessment, assessment.   When I got a place here I
> thought, great, this is marvellous ... I won't just be
> concentrating on ... doing it for assessment.   I'll be
> able to study ... just time to sit back and think and
> talk about a subject, and read about it.   No – it's all
> structured, you know.   When I leave here I'll go straight
> back to my room and I'll say, "Right, what've we got to
> do next?" ... It's good for individual teachers' images
> to get good marks out of their students on their courses.
> I don't think that is best achieved by following the
> academic philosophy of learning what you want to learn
> ... You've got to enforce a strong, very strong and
> carefully organized structure upon your learning, which
> is directed, aimed directly at, the assessment that exists
> ... I'm very disappointed ... that I can't just, you
> know, go through and really have a think and really work
> things out.   (psychology, student 7).

> In very few of the lectures was I picking (the principles
> up as we did them.   It took me all my time to get the
> notes down.   So, and this in a way, the pace is so fast
> that you get the notes down and that's it.   You don't
> really follow what's going on.   You can't do two
> things at once.   You can't sit back and listen to
> what's being said.   You spend an hour taking notes
> down ... I put this down to this very keen desire to
> cover that much work.   (engineering, student 2).

> If I have started in plenty of time, then I do start
> thinking about the subject itself, more than perhaps
> that I've got to hand it in, but basically it's all a
> bit of a struggle, just to hand things in, as opposed
> to being interesting; you're working against a time
> deadline instead of for your own benefit.   (history,
> student 2).

Departmental contexts which offer choice in
learning methods and topics to be studied seem to
be able to engender more favourable attitudes to
learning, although the freedom of choice also brings
with it greater responsibilities:

> If you're doing independent studies you're obviously
> interested in what you're doing.   Therefore you're in
> a much more relaxed mental state for approaching work: I
> am, anyway, and other people I know in the course are.
> (independent studies, student 2).

> You have to take responsibility for the work yourself.
> You're not, you don't have the advantage of a pre-
> existing framework of suggested reading and suggested
> approaches in independent studies, so you have to be
> damn sure that you are interested enough and confident
> enough to see it through those times when you come to
> sort of minor crises, when you realise suddenly that
> it's all on your shoulders and you've got no one else
> to go to ... It requires commitment and personal
> motivation.   (independent studies, student 29).

Two other context variables - clarity of goals
and standards, and social climate - were also related
by some students to favourable or unfavourable attitudes and to their sense of security as learners
within their department.

Level of interest and background knowledge

The student's interest in an academic task (or
his personal commitment to studying a particular
field) and his prior possession of some understanding
of the field or topic in which a task is situated
were found to be associated with the probability of
a deep approach to the task.   For example:

(a)   Level of interest

> It wasn't that interesting, there wasn't that much there.
> I wasn't reading it really intently, it was more skimm-
> ing through, looking for certain words, science, the
> industrial revolution, dates as well, just to sort of
> pick out the points that I wanted.   (history, student
> 14).

> I: Do you try to get a grasp of the, the whole thing
>   when you're reading an article, or ...?
> S: Yeah, I try, I try to, I don't often, sometimes,
>   depends what it's about, er, I try to.
> I: But you find it difficult?
> S: Mmm.   I wouldn't say I found everything, I would
>   say I found, found it difficult according to what
>   it was about.   I mean, the cognitive reading I was
>   telling you about, I just couldn't be bothered to
>   pay attention and see how one argument connected
>   with the other.   (psychology, student 8).

> It's a bit confusing, (this subject).   When it comes to
> writing essays, because I'm not very interested in it, I
> tend to rush through the books I'm reading for the essays,
> so I still don't really understand it when I've finished

reading. And because there's such a lot of information I think you can either oversimplify or go into too much detail. And I think I tend to oversimplify. (English, student 31).

(b) Background knowledge

(The best way to study) is to go through some work, and try and get some solutions. It's difficult. It depends on how well one knows the subject as well. It's easy to write questions for something you know well. You just sort of plod through and try and understand bits here and there in something you don't know. (engineering, student 3).

I think if I already know something about the subject about which I want to write, it helps. Because then I can write something out without having to refer to the books first, sketch something out in much more detail rather than just skeletal ... this question was about popular recreations, and were attitudes to them changing. Well, having been grounded in Folklore - a consuming passion for the last eight years - I know quite a lot about that already. So I just kind of wrote out 3 or 400 words which gave a basis for it ... mentally I was much more aware of accomplishing something useful. (history, student 3).

The actual question was a particle in a box, asking you what shape it would describe ... we have come across a similar problem in chemistry ... I know, I had a picture in my mind's eye of what I was doing, most definitely. I could see it. I think that is possibly because I've already done it in chemistry, and if I hadn't I'd just have thought it a lot of figures and a lot of complicated-looking formulae, and left it at that. (physics, student 3).

It was like one of the questions from a previous course, which I could relate. It was a Schroedinger equation for a particle in a box which we'd solved generally before in chemistry, so I could relate it, I could see a picture of what I wanted. I knew basically what sort of answer I should get, and from that I could work my way through it quite simply, no problem ...

The other bit was different: I couldn't do it. Basically I gave up with it, because it was a function, which I've never really understood ... I looked at it and I thought "That looks complicated" ... it was very short, it looked like it would need a lot of rearranging. (physics, student 6)

Of course, background knowledge and level of interest are not necessarily productive of a deep approach; they provide favourable conditions for it. As might be expected, background knowledge is most often related to level of approach in the science and technology departments: when knowledge is hierarchically structured and operation learning is favoured, an understanding of new concepts is often only possible if the previous stages have been fully grasped (c.f. Biggs, 1978). Level of interest is more commonly related to deep approaches in arts and social science tasks; this result is also understandable in the light of what has already been said about the greater informality of teaching and learning, and the more opportunities for choice, in arts subjects.

The two antecedents of levels of approach are related to each other, and both are partly explained by the perceived quality of the departmental environment. Good teaching and appropriate assessment methods are ways in which interest in a subject, and background topics relating to it, can be fostered. Moreover, the way in which a department is organized may permit student choice in methods and topics of study to a greater or lesser extent. All other things being equal, freedom in learning should make for a higher level of interest.

The relationships described above seem to make sense in terms of recent theoretical work and empirical research. The investigations at Gothenburg, which provided evidence of a connection between threatening assessment conditions and surface approaches (Fransson, 1977), were carried out under experimental controls; now, there is a clear indication that the same process occurs in the natural setting of students' everyday work. The arguments of authors like Becker (1968), Snyder (1971) and Rowntree (1977) -- to the effect that assessment procedures, heavy workload, and lack of choice in methods of learning and topics to be studied can have the unintended consequences of discouraging favourable attitudes to learning and encouraging rote learning instead of understanding - are strongly supported.

The connection between level of interest and level of approach has considerable intuitive validity. Both Fransson (1977) and Biggs (1979) note the coincidence of deep level processing and expressed interest. One of the second-order factors discovered by Biggs ("internalising": see chapter 4) contains both the student's interest in the subject matter and his attempts to interrelate ideas and impose meaning.

From an entirely different standpoint, a recent study of students' attributions of reasons for success and failure in essays and examinations has produced complementary results. Interest (or the lack of it) in an essay was found to be the most commonly attributed reason for a good (or poor) level of performance in it (Hughes-Jones, 1979).

A somewhat more unusual finding is the close association revealed in the interview transcripts between good teaching, favourable attitudes, and (by implication) the conditions for deep level approaches. The accepted view has been that quality and type of teaching is unrelated to student learning (see, e.g., Dubin and Taveggia, 1969). Recent evidence (Hartnett and Centra, 1977; Centra, 1976; Fearn-Wannan, 1979) does, however, seem to suggest that student satisfaction with teaching, and perceptions of lecturers' student-orientation, may be positively related to student achievement.

STUDENTS' ACADEMIC PERFORMANCE

Levels of approach and strategic study methods are known to be positively related to the outcomes of learning, measured either qualitatively or quantitatively (see Marton and Säljö, 1976a; Miller and Parlett, 1974; Svensson, 1977; Säljö, 1981). The final section of this chapter looks at relationships between outcomes and two of the categories derived from the interview analysis: consistent deep or surface approaches and strategic study methods. We should expect deep approaches and highly strategic methods to correlate positively with the measure of outcome used (degree result).

Final degree classifications were obtained for the student sample, after each student had been categorized on the approach and strategic dimensions. It was possible to obtain the results of all but three students. (At least one of the three - classified as consistent surface - withdrew before final assessment). The results were coded by the conventional dichotomized measure of good degree (First and Upper Second Class Honours) vs. other degree (Lower Second or below).

Level of approach and degree result

Tables 8.2 and 8.3 give the degree results and interview classifications of the 42 students who could be placed into the consistent deep or surface categories and for whom degree results could be obtained. The

pattern of the relationship is clearly in the hypothesized direction. Only 5 of the 16 surface
students achieved Firsts or Upper Seconds, while 16
of the 26 deep students gained good degrees.

Strategic study method and degree result

These results appear in Tables 8.4 and 8.5.
Table 8.4 shows that strategic methods are positively
but weakly associated with good degree results.
The size of the relationship is reduced by the large
"intermediate" category, which contains several
students who were difficult to classify. Comparison
of the two extreme groups reveals that five of the
six most strategic students gained good degrees.
Table 8.5 shows that the difference between the mean
degree results of the most and least strategic
students is statistically significant.

CONCLUSIONS

The results presented in this chapter have confirmed the remarkable explanatory power of the qualitative methods first extensively used in the
Gothenburg investigations of student learning. In
particular, they have demonstrated clear functional
relationships between the context of learning - the
type of task, the quality of teaching, and the
characteristics of academic departments - and the
approaches students use.
The next chapter returns to the quantitative
data collected in the survey of students' approaches
to studying in order to examine these educationally
important connections from another standpoint.

Table 8.2   LEVEL OF APPROACH AND DEGREE RESULT

| | APPROACH | | |
Result	Deep	Surface	Total
Good degree	16	5	21
Other degree	10	11	21
Total	26	16	42

Corrected χ^2 = 2.52 , p (one-tailed) < .06

Table 8.3   MEAN DEGREE RESULTS FOR DEEP AND SURFACE STUDENTS
            (n = 42)
            (where deep = 1, surface = 2, good degree = 1;
            other degree = 2)

Group	Mean	S.D.	T	p (one-tailed)
Deep	1.38	.50	-1.95	.03
Surface	1.69	.48		

Table 8.4   STRATEGIC STUDY METHOD AND DEGREE RESULT

	STRATEGIC METHOD			
Result	Most strategic	Intermediate	Least Strategic	Total
Good degree	5	14	8	27
Other degree	1	14	12	27
Total	6	28	20	54

X^2 = 3.47   n.s.

Table 8.5: MEAN DEGREE RESULTS FOR MOST STRATEGIC AND LEAST
            STRATEGIC STUDENTS (n = 26)

Group	Mean	S.D.	T	p (one-tailed)
Most strategic	1.17	.41	-1.92	.03
Least strategic	1.60	.50		

Chapter Nine

APPROACHES TO LEARNING IN CONTRASTING DEPARTMENTS

The development of instruments designed to measure students' perceptions of their courses and their approaches to studying was described in chapters 4 and 7. The next stage of the research examined possible links between the scales of the two questionnaires suggested by previous research and by the results of the student interviews (chapter 8). In what ways might contrasting academic contexts affect approaches to studying? The interviews had identified functional relationships between levels of approach and students' perceptions of the teaching and assessment they experienced; it was also clear that the way students tackled academic tasks was related to the subject area in which they studied.

The intention of the next part of the investigation was to test the validity of these connections, and to try to disentangle the effects of subject area and departmental organization, by using a contrasting methodology: the statistical treatment of quantitative data from a large sample of students.

METHOD AND PURPOSE

The results described in this chapter derive from the servey of 2208 students in 66 departments of engineering, physics, economics, psychology, history and English carried out in 1979-80. Students completed both the approaches to studying inventory and the course perceptions questionnaire; the methods used are presented in more detail in chapter 4. The scales of both instruments and their meaning are given in Figure 9.1.

This chapter is based on chapter 6 in Ramsden (1981).

Figure 9.1 SUBSCALES OF THE INVENTORY AND QUESTIONNAIRE

Subscale	Meaning
Deep approach	Active questioning in learning
Relating ideas	Relating to other parts of course
Use of evidence	Relating evidence to conclusions
Intrinsic motivation	Interest in learning for learning's sake
Surface approach	Preoccupation with memorization
Syllabus-boundness	Relying on staff to define learning tasks
Fear of failure	Pessimism and anxiety about academic outcomes
Extrinsic motivation	Interest in courses for the qualifications they offer
Strategic approach	Awareness of implications of academic demands made by staff
Disorganized study methods	Unable to work regularly and effectively
Negative attitudes to studying	Lack of interest and application
Achievement motivation	Competitive and confident
Comprehension learning	Readiness to map out subject area and think divergently
Globetrotting	Over-ready to jump to conclusions
Operation learning	Emphasis on facts and logical analysis
Improvidence	Over-cautious reliance on details
Formal teaching methods	Lectures and classes more important than individual study
Clear goals and standards	Assessment standards and ends of studying clearly defined
Workload	Heavy pressures to fulfil task requirements
Vocational relevance	Perceived relevance of courses to careers
Good teaching	Well-prepared, helpful, committed teachers
Freedom in learning	Discretion of students to choose and organize own work
Openness to students	Friendly staff attitudes and preparedness to adapt to students' needs
Social climate	Quality of academic and social relationships between students

The analyses were designed to investigate the following questions:

1. To what extent can differences in students' approaches to studying and perceptions of the context of learning by explained (a) by type of discipline studied (b) by type of department, after controlling for subject area?

2. What links between the two sets of scales can be identified by means of factor analysis?

3. Using departments as units of analysis rather than individual students, what associations between orientations to studying and course perceptions can be identified? In other words, do contexts of learning appear to influence approaches to studying?

4. Do some approaches to studying seem to be rewarded more highly (in terms of self-rated performance) in some contexts than in others?

DIFFERENCES IN STUDENTS' APPROACHES IN CONTRASTING SUBJECT AREAS

From previous work, including the interview study, it was expected that comprehension learning would be found to be more common in the arts and social science disciplines than the sciences, while the reverse would be true of operation learning. The two pathologies of learning would also be differentially related to subject area (although the interview results showed that both pathologies could be identified in science and arts students): improvidence should be more in evidence in science, and globetrotting in arts. The four sub-scales making up the meaning orientation scale (deep approach, relating ideas, use of evidence, and intrinsic motivation) would provide evidence of disciplinary differences if the interview results were to be replicated. Deep approach, intrinsic motivation, and relating ideas items are more characteristic of arts and social science approaches, while the use of evidence subscale is more descriptive of science approaches to learning tasks. Earlier work had also suggested that science students would be more likely to be extrinsically motivated and syllabus-bound (Entwistle and Wilson, 1977). The remaining subscales were not expected to show large differences between subject areas.

Table 9.1 MEANS OF SUBSCALES BY SUBJECT AREA

Scale	Mean (1) Science (2) Social science (3) Arts	S.D.	Analysis of Variance F (df 2, 63)
Deep approach	(1) 10.21 (2) 10.53 (3) 11.28	.90 .81 .67	8.41**
Relating ideas	(1) 9.55 (2) 10.54 (3) 10.35	.95 .77 .75	9.47**
Use of evidence	(1) 9.83 (2) 9.51 (3) 9.46	.54 .70 .46	2.51
Intrinsic moti- vation	(1) 8.05 (2) 8.29 (3) 9.06	1.26 1.50 .87	3.12
Surface approach	(1) 13.13 (2) 13.23 (3) 12.60	1.28 .94 1.19	1.64
Syllabus-boundness	(1) 8.96 (2) 8.18 (3) 7.22	.64 .84 .82	24.82**
Fear of Failure	(1) 5.87 (2) 5.91 (3) 5.73	.74 .74 .69	.29
Extrinsic moti- vation	(1) 6.93 (2) 6.01 (3) 3.08	1.69 2.01 1.09	25.45**
Strategic approach	(1) 10.37 (2) 10.27 (3) 9.80	.79 .55 .85	3.25
Disorganized study methods	(1) 9.74 (2) 9.70 (3) 8.77	.88 1.03 1.22	5.19*
Negative attitudes to studying	(1) 5.45 (2) 5.47 (3) 5.70	.75 .89 .63	.54

*p < .01
**p < .001

Table 9.1 (continued)   MEANS OF SUBSCALES BY SUBJECT AREA

Scale	Mean		S.D.	
	(1) Science			
	(2) Social science			
	(3) Arts			
Achievement Motivation	(1)	10.22	.88	
	(2)	9.45	.87	10.88**
	(3)	9.04	.64	
Comprehension Learning	(1)	8.09	1.11	
	(2)	8.49	1.09	14.16**
	(3)	10.03	1.35	
Globetrotting	(1)	7.45	.57	
	(2)	8.04	.57	6.87*
	(3)	7.48	.74	
Operation Learning	(1)	10.68	.92	
	(2)	9.91	.96	12.93**
	(3)	9.12	.99	
Improvidence	(1)	7.62	.90	
	(2)	7.82	.81	5.87*
	(3)	6.88	.93	

* p <.01
** p <.001

    The differences were examined in two ways.   The
mean values for each of the subscales by subject area
(science, social science, and arts) are shown in Table
9.1.   The means for each discipline and each department were also calculated.   It is clear from the
average scores for departments and subject areas that
operation learning and comprehension learning are
associated with types of discipline in the expected
way: operation learning receives higher scores in
science, comprehension learning in arts and social
science.   Globetrotting and improvidence are also
related to type of discipline, but less strongly.
    Globetrotting is highest in psychology depart-
ments, and improvidence in economics departments.
Globetrotting is no more common in arts departments
than in science ones.   On this evidence, it cannot
be unequivocally stated that learning pathologies
are a function of the type of discipline studied.
    Deep approach and relating ideas are most

common in arts and social science departments, confirming the predictions, but use of evidence and intrinsic motivation are only weakly associated with subject area, although in the expected directions. The other large differences between subject areas are in the subscales of syllabus-boundness, extrinsic motivation, disorganized study methods - rather surprisingly - and achievement motivation. Most of these differences conform with the theoretical predictions; for some reason, however, it would seem that arts students are less likely to have poor study methods.

Even when the effects of subject area and discipline are large and significant, it should be emphasised that there are still considerable differences between individual departments.

FACTOR ANALYSIS OF THE CPQ AND APPROACHES TO STUDYING INVENTORY

It will be remembered from chapter 7 that factor analysis of the CPQ produced two main factors: positive evaluation of teaching and courses and formal vocational teaching. Analysis of the approaches to studying inventory had revealed three principal orientations: meaning, reproducing, and achieving/ disorganized and dilatory. Factor analysis of the two sets of subscales together provides one way of examining the relationships between students' approaches and the context of learning in academic departments.

Table 9.2 gives the results of this analysis. Three factors (numbers I,III and V) are recognisable as the main studying orientations; factors II and IV are the formal-vocational and evaluative dimensions respectively; factor VI describes confident students with good entry qualifications. The interviews suggested that students respond to the departmental context in which they work by adopting different levels of approach. Although there is not a lot of overlap between the two sets of scales in this analysis, what there is makes good sense when compared with the interview findings. The reproducing orientation is associated with a heavy workload (factor III), disorganized and dilatory attitudes with perceived lack of clarity in goals (factor V), the evaluative factor with intrinsic motivation and use of evidence in learning (factor IV), and the formal-vocational factor with extrinsic motivation (factor II).

Table 9.2   FACTOR ANALYSIS OF APPROACHES TO STUDYING AND COURSE
PERCEPTIONS SCALES (N = 2208)

Variables	Factors (54% variance explained)					
	I	II	III	IV	V	VI
Academic performance						
School						29
Higher education	26		(-20)		-45	
Approaches to studying						
Deep approach	71			(22)	-29	
Relating ideas	67			(21)		
Use of evidence	52			28	-29	31
Intrinsic motivation	64			39	-27	-34
Surface approach			61			-30
Syllabus-boundness	-38	26	53			
Fear of failure			58		26	
Extrinsic motivation		47	37			-51
Strategic approach	27				-37	-26
Disorganized study methods					54	
Negative attitudes to studying	-28			-32	52	
Achievement motivation					-32	
Comprehension learning	60					
Globetrotting					44	
Operation learning			56		-29	-30
Improvidence			65			-33
Course perceptions						
Formal teaching methods		75				
Clear goals and standards		53		38	-25	
Workload			45	(-23)		
Vocational relevance		73				
Good teaching				77		
Freedom in learning		-28		50		
Openness to students				79		
Social climate		25		47		

Decimal points and most loadings less than .25 omitted

To what extent are the approaches to studying
factors, and the relationships between the CPQ and
approaches to studying scales shown in Table 9.2,
artefacts of area of study differences in the
relationship between learning and its context?   When
separate factor analyses by subject area are carried
out (Ramsden and Entwistle, 1981) meaning orientation
(factor 1) retains its emphasis on syllabus-freedom
and its stylistic component of comprehension learning

across all three subject areas.   This approach is
related to less formal teaching methods in science
and social science, to freedom in learning and good
teaching, and - in arts - to a good social climate
and clear goals.   Reproducing orientation (factor
III) is consistently defined in all the subject
areas.   It is related to a heavy workload.   Factor
V,   representing a disorganized and dilatory approach
to studying, is associated with the learning pathology
of globetrotting and, especially in arts, to comprehension learning.   This suggests that comprehension learning carried to extremes (and unleavened
by operation learning) in arts subjects may lead to
globetrotting.   A similar result was found for
certain arts and social science students in the
interviews.   On the other hand, operation learning
seems to be associated with improvidence in all three
subject areas equally (factor III).

Factor IV (departmental evaluation) was linked
to positive attitudes and meaning orientation in all
three faculties.   This result also conforms with
the interview data.

EFFECTS OF DEPARTMENTAL CONTEXTS ON STUDENT LEARNING

The next step was to examine in more detail the
relationships between context and approaches to
studying while controlling for the effects of subject
areas.   The interviews had shown that deep approaches
and favourable attitudes to studying were functionally related to students' perceptions of good teaching.   Unhelpful and uncommitted teaching was thought
by the students who were interviewed to encourage
poor attitudes to studying and surface approaches.
Surface approaches were strongly associated with perceived deficiences in the assessment system and with
a lack of freedom in learning.   In spite of the
controls used in the interview analyses, however,
these findings were still to some extent impressionistic and subjective, although the relationships
appeared to be important ones.   The connection
between surface approaches and assessment methods
was in accordance with deductions from earlier
findings, but the relationship betwen quality of
teaching and deep approaches had not previously been
demonstrated.   Indeed, Marton's work had shown how
difficult it was to induce a deep approach experi-
mentally (Marton, 1975;   Marton and Säljö, 1976b).

There are hints in the factor analyses that the
same processes identified in the interviews operate
in this larger sample of students.   But the

analysis so far described are based entirely on individual students as cases.   Clearly, it might be argued, poor students will attribute their inability to poor teaching and too much work.   A more convincing explanation would be provided if a unit of analysis representing departments, rather than individual students, were employed.

In order to do this, a set of analyses of covariance was performed on the departmental mean values of several subscales, students' pre-entry levels of achievement, and composite variables formed by combining subscales identified in the factor analyses.   It was predicted that departments which were positively evaluated by their students would:

(a)   have higher meaning orientation mean scores;
(b)   have lower reproducing orientation mean scores;
(c)   have lower disorganised and dilatory mean scores

than departments which were negatively evaluated.

Composite variables measuring different orientations and evaluation dimensions were formed as follows:

Meaning orientation	Deep approach + relating ideas + use of evidence + intrinsic motivation
Reproducing orientation	Surface approach + syllabus-boundness + fear of failure + improvidence
Disorganised and dilatory attitudes	Disorganised study methods + negative attitudes to studying + globe-trotting
Evaluation variable 1	Good teaching + freedom in learning
Evaluation variable 2	Freedom in learning - workload

These variables, all of which are measurements of departments' mean scores, were constructed after examining the results of the factor analyses and also took into account the interview findings.   A third evaluation variable was used in the preliminary analysis but later rejected.   It consisted of openness to students + freedom in learning + good teaching.   A preliminary analysis showed that openness to students was unrelated to any of the criterion variables;   it seems to be a measurement of students' satisfaction with the department but does not help to explain the quality of their learning.

We can summarize the main analysis of covariance results as follows.   The effects of the evaluation

variables on orientations and attitudes were similar
in all the disciplines (there were no significant
interaction effects).*   A heavy workload combined
with a lack of freedom in learning was strongly
related to an orientation towards reproducing in a
department's students (p < .001).   Meaning orientation
was related to the perceived presence of freedom in
learning combined with good teaching in the department (p < .01).   The way in which a department
organizes its courses, and its methods of teaching
them, seems to have a considerable effect on whether
its students develop an orientation towards meaning.
The effect is positive;   one of the central results
of the interview study is confirmed.

The interviews revealed that favourable
attitudes towards studying were associated with good
teaching and with choice over method and content of
study.   The inventory dimension apparently closest
to describing these attitudes is the disorganized
and dilatory component shown in the factor analyses,
with its high loadings on globetrotting, negative
attitudes, and disorganized study methods.   This
orientation was found to be unrelated either to
discipline or to the evaluation variables, but
positive attitudes to studying were found to be
associated with good teaching and freedom in learning
(p < .03).   This is consistent with the factor
analysis result linking departmental evaluation to
positive attitudes in all subject areas and, of
course, with the interview results reported in the
previous chapter.

Similar conclusions are reached following
multiple discriminant analyses of the departmental
mean scores.   Extreme groups of departments were
formed to see whether typical orientations could be
predicted by students' perceptions.   Groups were
formed by selecting the two highest and the two
lowest departmental mean scores in each of the six
disciplines, so that each group consisted of twelve
departments.   This procedure automatically controlled
for the effects of different disciplines.   One set
of departments was made up by choosing the highest
and lowest meaning orientation departments, another
by selecting the highest and lowest reproducing
orientation departments, and a third consisted of the
highest and lowest disorganized and dilatory attitude

---

* It was also impossible to detect any influence on
the relationship between orientations and contexts
of the type of department defined by mean 'A' level
grade score of its students.

departments.   Separate analyses were performed on
each.
     The functions discriminating between departments
which had high and low mean scores on the disorganised and dilatory dimension were not significant.
Extreme departments in terms of meaning orientation
were predicted best by good teaching and freedom in
learning.   Using these two variables alone, 71% of
the departments could be placed in their correct
groups, the prediction being better for the low
meaning orientation departments than the high ones.
This seems consistent with the Gothenburg findings
concerning the difficulty of inducing a deep approach
and the relative ease with which its opposite can be
encouraged.   It seems that departments without good
teaching and freedom in learning effectively act to
prevent the development of meaning orientation in
their students;   departments which are positively
evaluated encourage meaning orientation by providing
the right conditions for it to grow - but it is not
a necessary consequence.
     The discriminant function for the reproducing
orientation groups was defined mainly by workload
(.84), freedom in learning (-1.20), and vocational
relevance (.77), when all the CPQ variables were
included.   The prediction results for this group
were slightly more accurate, again in accordance
with the expectation suggested by the Swedish
research.

ACADEMIC PROGRESS IN DIFFERENT DEPARTMENTAL CONTEXTS

     Relationships between approaches to studying
and academic performance (both self-rated and as
defined by first-year grades) in the different
subject areas were examined in Chapter 4.   The use
of the course perceptions questionnaire provided an
opportunity to analyse possible interactions between
approaches to studying and types of context (defined
separately from subject area) in relation to self-
rated academic progress.   Do students with contrasting orientations to studying see themselves to
be performing equally well (or equally badly) in
departments of different kinds?
     In order to examine the effect of different
orientations to studying on performance while controlling for discipline, groups of departments were
formed in terms of different extreme contexts.   Thus
the two departments in each discipline with the
highest mean scores on good teaching were compared
with the two with the lowest mean scores on good

teaching, and so on. Correlations between self-ratings of performance and the composite variables representing meaning orientation, reproducing orientation, and disorganized and dilatory approaches, were then computed. For the purpose of these analyses, another composite variable, <u>accomplished learning</u>, was created. This was intended to represent more accurately the consistent deep + strategic approach identified in the interviews. It consisted of meaning orientation + strategic approach + comprehension learning + syllabus-freedom + positive attitudes to studying (compare the loadings on these variables in the factor analyses).

The correlations presented in Table 9.3 cannot be regarded as more than suggestive of the possible interactions between contexts and orientations, but they are of much interest. Meaning orientation is perceived to be related to academic progress most strongly in conditions of freedom in learning with light workload. Reproducing orientation is least penalized when the teaching is poor and there is little freedom in learning, while disorganized and dilatory approaches are least effective under the same conditions and are always fairly strongly related to poor performance. Accomplished learning is strongly favourable to progress in all conditions, but particularly so when the teaching is poor and there is freedom in learning.

All these associations are consistent with the results so far presented and with the interview data. It requires no great effort of imagination to picture the consistent deep-level, strategic students such as those identified in the interviews (for example, psychology, student 5) perceiving deficiencies in the teaching, and freedom of choice, as challenges to perform better; nor to see the disorganized student hoping that the helpfulness of his lecturers will enable him to progress more effectively. It remains disturbing that the reproducing students, responding to a context of restricted choice over method and content of study combined with ineffective teaching, feel that their strategy will not be too heavily penalized, while at the same time students orientated towards meaning feel themselves least likely to do well when the workload is heavy and there is little freedom in learning.

CONCLUSIONS

The results we have described in this chapter, taken in conjunction with the interview findings,

Table 9.3   CORRELATIONS BETWEEN ORIENTATIONS TO STUDYING AND PERFORMANCE UNDER DIFFERENT EXTREME CONDITIONS, CONTROLLING FOR DISCIPLINE

Conditions (types of department)	Orientations to studying			
	Meaning orientation	Reproducing orientation	Disorganized and dilatory approach	Accomplished learning
Highest freedom in learning	28	-25	-40	35
Lowest freedom in learning	25	-23	-35	29
Highest good teaching	23	-26	-28	27
Lowest good teaching	30	-18	-42	36
Highest freedom in learning and good teaching	30	-28	-37	36
Lowest freedom in learning and good teaching	26	-16	-47	34
Highest workload	23	-24	-43	31
Lowest workload	26	-21	-27	32
Highest workload with lowest freedom in learning	22	-20	-39	28
Lowest workload with highest freedom in learning	32	-26	-33	37

Decimal points omitted

show quite clearly that students' perceptions of
teaching and assessment methods in academic departments are significantly associated with, and probably
causally related to, students' approaches to studying.   Self-rated student performance is related
both to perceptions of courses and to orientations
to learning.   To have identified these effects and
interactions is not to imply that individual differences are unimportant variables in the explanation
of approaches and academic progress.   But these
findings do suggest that it might be possible to
make improvements in the quality of student learning
in higher education by alterations to the contexts
in which it occurs.   These implications are examined
together with conclusions drawn from the other parts
of the investigation in the next chapter.

LEARNING AND TEACHING IN HIGHER EDUCATION

INTRODUCTION

This final·chapter is an attempt to highlight
what we think are the distinctive contributions to
understanding learning and teaching made by our
research programme.   Our main aims were to explore
the contrasting ways in which students approach
studying and in what ways academic departments may
influence those approaches.   What can now be said
about these individual and contextual differences?
What practical implications can be drawn from this
research for improving teaching and learning in
higher education?   And finally, how successful was
the attempt to make use of different methodologies
in investigating how student learn?

HOW STUDENTS LEARN: APPROACHES AND OUTCOMES

The insistent contrast between students' ways of
studying revealed by this research is, of course,
between deep and surface (or meaning and reproducing)
approaches to learning.   Several different studies
within our research programme show how the distinctions suggested in the work of Marton and Biggs have
been developed.   Repeated factor analyses of successive versions of the approaches to studying inventory
confirmed the importance of the meaning and reproducing orientations in all the academic disciplines
we investigated.   Although it is also possible to
identify other orientations to studying, the evidence
here is less consistent.   The final analyses
suggested that the third main dimension - the
achieving or strategic orientation - would have to
be divided into positive and negative components
(strategic orientation and non-academic orientation).
The inventory has already been used with students
elsewhere - the Open University and Australian
National University - with similar but not identical

factor structures being reported.

The questionnaire variant of Marton's research method for investigating outcomes and processes of learning with academic articles also showed the deep-surface distinction between approaches to learning. In spite of difficulties in finding appropriate articles and in coding the responses, the analysis again showed the clear links between approaches and levels of understanding reported by Marton (Marton and Saljo, 1976a). Furthermore, it indicated that there were differences within the deep approach between students who were seeking personal meaning, and those who relied more on evidence and detail in building up understanding.

Qualitative analysis of the interview data (chapter 8) confirmed the importance of the funda-mental difference between deep and surface approaches. Although the distinction was seen to apply to many subject areas, it had to some extent to be re-interpreted within contrasting academic contexts. In other words, the meaning of the concepts subtly shifts in relation to different disciplines. In science departments a deep approach involves con-siderable emphasis on detail and procedures, and may even require a preliminary stage of rote learning difficult to distinguish from a surface approach. In humanities and social sciences, we saw how personal reinterpretation, related especially to experience of the world of people rather than things, was most important in carrying out a deep approach. A hint of a similar distinction was also found in the small-scale study of sixth-formers reported in chapter 4. Deep approaches were associated with high A-level grades in both arts and science, but successful scientists also used attention to detail and memorization.

Our research has confirmed the relationships between approaches and outcomes illustrated in the work of Marton and his colleagues. Approach and level of understanding are closely linked, not only in experimental situations but also in the realistic setting of conventional assessments. The learning experiments and the questionnaire on outcome and process (chapters 5 and 6) demonstrated the connection in a controlled context, while the inventory and interviews revealed similar relation-ships between approaches and either self-rated academic progress or degree classifications. Students in the interview study, for example, who used consistently deep approaches, and those who used high

strategic methods to handle assessment tasks, were
more likely to obtain First or Upper Second class
honours degrees. The reproducing orientation was
related to poor self-rated performance and the
meaning orientation to higher self-ratings in the
inventory survey; similar, although rather weaker
relationships between these orientations and first
year marks have been reported in the Australian study.
The strongest relationships with poor academic performance in the Lancaster research have been with
the non-academic orientation. It is also interesting
to see indications of subject area differences in the
correlations. Reproducing orientation is associated
with poor results especially in arts, while strategic
orientation has its strongest positive relationship
with progress in science subjects. These findings
undoubtedly confirm the usefulness of the inventory
scales and the deep and surface concepts for describing realistic differences in students' ways of
approaching their work.

INTERNAL AND EXTERNAL ORIENTATIONS TO STUDYING

It may be most helpful to see the difference
between deep and surface approaches to academic tasks
in terms of the student's intention. The deep
approach is internal - to the content of the article
or problem, and to the knowledge, experience and
interests of the learner. The surface approach is
external - towards the task and its requirements, and
implies a process of learning in which alien material
is to be impressed on the memory for a limited period
and with the specific intention of satisfying external demands. There is no expectation that the content will become a continuing part of the learner's
cognitive structure.
Using this distinction between external and
internal orientations to studying, we can see how
deep and surface approaches are a special case of a
more general tendency which can be found in several
very recent studies in addition to our own. For
example, Taylor, Gibbs and Morgan (1981) have discovered marked differences between students at the
Open University and a conventional university in what
benefits they expected to derive from higher education.
The Open University students showed predominantly
personal goals, but within these the orientation could
still be external (compensating for earlier academic
failure) or internal (broadening horizons, interests,
and capabilities). At the conventional university
the students showed mainly academic or vocational

goals, but again these could be subdivided into extrinsic (grades or qualifications)and intrinsic
(knowledge and skill) categories.
The distinction between external and internal
orientation is at the heart of our own meaning and
reproducing orientations as shown in the inventory
subscales making up the two main dimensions.
Students relying on reproducing information allow
staff to define learning tasks and are interested in
courses mainly for the qualifications they offer.
In contrast students looking for meaning are interested in the work itself and interact critically with
what they are learning.   The distinction can also be
seen clearly in a recent interview analysis (Thompson,
1981) which contrasted two groups of students high or
low in scores on syllabus-boundness (Parlett, 1970).
The attitudes of these "sylbs" and "sylfs" are
dramatically different.   The sylbs accept the
lectures and examinations without question; they
focus on the course as formally defined.   In contrast
all the sylfs reject, even abhor, examinations, and
actively dislike lectures (see Entwistle, 1981).
Other interview studies (Hodgson, 1981; Manook and
King, 1981)also bring out the way in which students
see teaching in terms of its external (assessment
orientation) or internal (personal interest and
knowledge) characteristics.
This distinction between whether a student
focuses in the intrinsic (internal) or extrinsic
(external) functions of educational experiences seems
to be the broadest way of conceptualising differences
in learning.   But by its very broadness it runs the
risk of oversimplifying the complicated differences
in how students learn.   We need to remember that
most students will be both intrinsically and extrinsically orientated at different times; that
students' approaches are strongly influenced by the
characteristics of the discipline studied and the
teaching received.   It is also important to recognize that students may have distinct preferences for
different (but equally effective) ways of tackling
academic tasks.   It is particularly important to
bear these complicating issues in mind if we seek to
apply the findings of this research to our own
learning and teaching, as will be clear in a moment.

HOW STUDENTS LEARN: STYLES, STRATEGIES AND INDIVIDUAL
DIFFERENCES

The research reported in this book has shown
that Pask's distinctions between styles and

strategies of learning (see chapter 2) are an additional dimension which needs to be taken into account when we try to describe how students learn. Some of the analyses of the approaches to studying inventory made it clear that separate holist and serialist factors could be identified. The questionnaire study of students' approaches to reading, described in chapter 6, revealed that the deep approach was better defined in terms of two dimensions One factor represented an emphasis on personal meaning, while the other showed higher loadings on previous knowledge and the use of detail. The result of the experiments in chapter 5 also seemed to indicate stylistic differences in studying. We saw how personal reinterpretation was again separate from concentrating on evidence, although it also seemed to be linked to a rather casual approach reminiscent of globetrotting - the overreadiness to jump to conclusions on scanty evidence. Where globetrotting is linked with a deep approach, it is clear that we are describing no more than a deep passive approach which will shade into a surface approach. In the main approaches to studying survey a surface approach was usually associated with both learning pathologies - improvidence and globetrotting. Thus stylistic differences are apparent not only in the way different students reach understanding, but also in the ways they fail to do so.

It also seems likely that students with different styles of learning are attracted to different subject areas. We saw in chapter 8 how contrasting styles of learning are part of the common-sense understanding of students. Students' own descriptions of differences in styles and strategies of learning in arts and science departments were strongly reminiscent of Pask's characterizations of comprehension and operation learning and of Hudson's (1968) descriptions of the stereotypes of arts and science teachers held by pupils.

How should we explain these contrasting ways of seeking understanding - one relying more on personal meaning and interpretation, and the other drawing more on previous knowledge, concentration on detail, and logical argument? Analyses of the relationships between learning styles and personality traits suggested that it does make sense to regard students' patterns of studying as being relatively stable and consistent. Although there were relationships between approaches to learning and both convergent and divergent thinking, the correlations were small. Much closer associations were found between the

indicators of styles of learning and personality
traits. The evidence must still be treated as
tentative, but it may be helpful to view styles as
being more a characteristic of the individual, and
approaches as being more obviously affected by the
context of studying. As approaches and styles are
themselves quite closely related, this separation
should be seen as no more than a convenient simpli-
fication. If we stick closely to the empirical
findings, we should be forced to accept that styles
and approaches are both relatively stable over time
and consistent over subject areas, but that both
are also importantly variable between tasks or
teachers. The apparent contradiction in this description may be difficult to conceptualize, but it
does reflect the complexity of the inter-relationships we find among the constructs used in research
on student learning.

Another attempt at simplifying the patterns of
results reported in the previous chapters will be
found in Figure 10.1. This framework indicates the
overlapping relationships between study orientations,
approaches to studying, styles of learning, personality, and probable outcomes of learning.

This framework may be helpful in summarizing
some of our main empirical findings, but it is also
incomplete and potentially misleading. It over-
emphasizes the relatively stable individual differences identified and presents a static model of
student behaviour. Yet our research contains
important additional elements. As we have already
argued, consistent differences in styles and
approaches to studying represent only part of the
whole picture of student learning. It is clear that
the content and context of learning need to be taken
into account: students often adopt flexible
strategies to cope with different academic demands.
Our theory would also need to incorporate the
developmental changes which students experience
through learning more effective approaches to studying.

HOW STUDENTS LEARN: THE EFFECTS OF LEARNING CONTEXT

A very important part of the studies of student
learning carried out in Gothenburg was the demon-
stration of connections between students' approaches
and the context of learning. Marton has stressed
that the approach to learning should not be seen as
a characteristic of the student, but as a response
to a situation. The 'natural' approach is a deep

one (Marton, 1976). Although we should also want to argue that it makes sense to speak of individual consistency in approaches, the results presented in the previous chapters show clearly the strong influence of the situation in which learning takes place. There are important interactions between the context and individual differences. For example, some students are better able than others to 'manage' adverse conditions.

The most crucial variable, as Fransson's original experiment showed (Fransson, 1977) is the student's <u>perception</u> of what he is required to do. The effects of contrasting perceptions can be seen at more than one level. For example, at the level of the learning task itself, perceived interest and relevance undoubtedly increase intrinsic motivation and make a deep approach more likely to occur. Tasks which are perceived as requiring only reproduction, or on which the student is mainly extrinsically motivated, increase the probability of a surface approach. These relationships, originally shown in Marton's work, were most apparent in the interview study described in chapter 8. It was also found that a student's interest in the subject matter of the task was a crucial component of a deep approach, especially in arts and social science subjects, while prerequisite knowledge was most often mentioned in relation to science tasks.

The second level at which the effects of learning context operate is that of the individual lecturer. The attitudes and enthusiasm of a lecturer, his concern for helping students to understand, and particularly his ability to understand the difficulties experienced by students in dealing with a new topic, are all likely to affect his students' approaches and attitudes to studying. It is perhaps important to note that our research deals only with students' perceptions of a lecturer's qualities, and the questionnaire covered only certain aspects of teaching. Further research is necessary to explore more fully the important influences of individual lecturers on their students' approaches to learning. It would also be necessary to explore whether effective learning depends on a correspondence between teaching style and preferred learning style.

The final level at which perceptions affect students' learning relates to departments. Of the differing ways in which departments are organized, the most crucial influences on approaches to learning concern the forms of assessment. It is

Figure 10.1   A FRAMEWORK SUMMARIZING DESCRIPTIONS OF STUDENT LEARNING

Study Orientation	Approach	Style	Stereotypic Personality	Processes	Probable Outcome
Meaning Orientation	Deep active	Versatile	Integrated and balanced personality	Uses evidence critically, argues logically and interprets imaginately	Describing, justifying and criticizing what was learned. (High grades with understanding).
	Deep passive	Comprehension learning	Impulsive introvert with a theoretical orientation	Intuitive, imaginative, thriving on personal interpretation and integrative overview but neglecting evidence	Mentioning overall argument, laced with illustration and anecdote. (Fairly high grades in arts).
Reproducing Orientation	Surface active	Operation learning (sometimes combined with improvidence	Converger with strong economic and vocational interests Neurotic introvert with obsessional characteristics	Attention to detail, cautious and limited interpretation, syllabus-bound and anxiously aware of assessment demands	Accurately describing fact and components of arguments, but not related to any clear overview. (Sometimes high grades in science)

(continued)

Figure 10.1   A FRAMEWORK SUMMARIZING DESCRIPTIONS OF STUDENT LEARNING (continued)

Study Orientation	Approach	Style	Stereotypic Personality	Processes	Probable Outcome
Non-Academic Orientation	Surface passive	Improvidence combined with globe-trotting	Social extrovert with few academic interests or vocational aspirations	Little attention to detail, over-readiness to generalize, superficial treatment and casual interpretation	Mentioning often irrelevant facts within a disordered, haphazard overview. (Low grades)
Strategic Orientation	Deep or surface as necessary	Strategic	Stability and confidence combined with competitive aggressiveness	Detail or meaning as perceived to be required by the teacher	High grades, with or without understanding

unfortunate that the most apparent effects are negative - students are pushed towards surface approaches by forms of assessment which seem to invite, and reward, reproductive answers.

These relationships were shown to be functional ones in the qualitative data from the student interviews. The correlational analyses of the course perceptions questionnaire and approaches to studying inventory, however, perhaps showed most convincingly the effects of departments and lecturers on student learning. It was clear that different departments teaching the same disciplines provided different learning contexts and that these contexts were closely associated with the typical approaches to learning adopted by the students. Perceived good teaching, and choice over methods and content of studying, were related to an orientation towards meaning and to positive attitudes to studying in a department's students. A lack of choice and a perceived heavy workload was associated with a reproducing orientation.

Besides noting the effects of departments on their students, it is also important to remember the characteristics which were not affected. The differences in departments were not related to either organized study methods or achievement motivation. These scales in the inventory are thus probably describing more stable individual differences or, at least, they represent aspects of studying not affected by differences in current departmental practice.

Taking these findings together, combining the impressions of causality from the interviews with the evidence of relationships from the questionnaires, we can begin to piece together a chain of causality which necessarily complicates the model of student learning presented in the previous section.

Positive attitudes to studying, a deep approach, intrinsic motivation, and academic progress are all related to good teaching, freedom in learning, and an avoidance of overloading. If students perceive the teaching they encounter to be effective, they are more likely to be interested in the subject matter to which it relates, and to be able to see its relevance to their everyday lives. They are, moreover, less likely to question the worth of the experience of higher education. Combined with assessment methods perceived to be appropriate, these contextual characteristics increase the probability that students will take deep approaches. The probability is further increased, especially in science subjects, if enough information and background knowledge associated with the academic task is available. But perceptions of inappropriate or excessive assessment, together with a too rigidly structured curriculum, encourage extrinsic motivation, engender poor attitudes, and thereby make surface approaches more likely. The quality of the outcome of learning is therefore likely to be lower as well. Of course, all these effects are mediated through the individual differences between students: each student will be affected in a different way. It should also be stressed that we are not simply arguing that freedom in learning is a guarantee of deep approaches. Elements of choice and a clear overall structure are both essential to this model of the effects of course contexts on student learning.

We must add yet another complication to the model. It is clear from the previous chapters that students' approaches and the effects of teaching have to be understood in relation to the subject area in which they take place. Disciplines differ in the "atmospheres" of learning they provide. Generally, science departments are seen to have more formal teaching, clearer goals, more vocational relevance, better social climates, and less freedom in learning than arts and social science departments. These differences are paralleled by typical styles of learning: operation learning is more common in science departments, comprehension learning in arts. We saw earlier how deep and surface approaches have to be redefined within contrasting subject areas. Added to that, it seems that styles of learning are differentially effective, depending on the subject area. Comprehension learning is most strongly related to self-rated academic progress in arts subjects, while operation learning is more effective in science. Versatility - the combination of operation learning with comprehension learning - is especially favourable to progress in science departments. Operation learning is apparently less necessary in achieving high marks in the arts and social sciences. These differences in contexts and styles of learning suggest rather different implications for encouraging deep approaches in different subject areas.

TOWARDS EFFECTIVE LEARNING

It should be clear by now that our current knowledge of student learning permits us to offer the component parts of a theory of the process of learning and teaching in higher education, although much work still needs to be done to reach a fully developed theory.   In chapter 2 we looked at research by William Perry showing that students report a process of intellectual and ethical development during their time in higher education.   The main direction of this change is away from dualistic, right/wrong views of knowledge towards contextual relativistic reasoning - the recognition of the tenative, permeable nature of academic knowledge and of the need to live with this uncertainty.   The research described in the earlier chapters of this book did not involve a longitudinal study of individual students over a period of several years, and so no direct evidence of development can be presented here.   However, there certainly are logical continuities between several of the concepts discussed in chapter 2, including Perry's, which our own investigations have demonstrated empirically.

The interviews of students in chapter 8 showed particularly well the links between versatility, strategic approaches, and successful learning outcomes.   Certain students seem able to choose to take either deep or surface approaches to academic tasks, selecting the approach most appropriate to the demands of assessment and teaching.   They adapt to, but are not dominated by, the departmental context. In chapter 9 we also saw how students who were orientated towards both meaning and achievement were apparently less affected by adverse teaching and assessment conditions.   Some students in the interview study were aware of a process of development in their approaches to learning in ways reminiscent of Perry's stages or Säljö's notion of thematization in learning.   Remember, for example, the psychology student who spoke of realizing that:

> "there was a structure in the things they were teaching us and it wasn't just a load of facts - that's only a recent, recent realization, perhaps only this term.   I started to realize it when I realized that the English I'm doing for my free ninth, er, is very closely connected to psychology ... the novelist seems to be very close to the psychologist, only he writes it in a creative - no, not creative - a more artistic form.   And when I realized that those were so close I suddenly realized how interrelated all the topics in psychology were.   And that's when I also read some articles on creativity; that's when I suddenly realized that putting

your own pattern on it would probably make a
better essay, and a more enjoyable essay. I've
become more interested in the subject, I think.
I've begun to understand more of the subject,
and perhaps, learned, learned things that, can
apply in my everyday life more successfully.
I mean things like my learning. I've learned,
perhaps, perhaps a better way of learning."

Perry's idea of the relativistic reasoner, Heath's
reasonable adventurer, Pask's versatile learner -
these are all ideal types of successful student. It
would be a mistake to extend these concepts too far
and to suppose that there is one ideal personality
profile or set of values and experiences which
characterizes the effective learner in higher
education. Just as labels denoting learning dis-
abilities in children or students (poorly motivated,
wrong family background, badly organized, and so on)
can all too easily become parts of self-fulfilling
prophecies, so models of ideal students may be unhelpful ways of encouraging effective learning. Our
research has shown, in contrast, that a bewildering
variety of approaches to learning exists in higher
education; different combinations suit different
students and can be equally successful or unsuccessful depending on the characteristics both of the
individual and of the learning context. It is
nevertheless true that the ability attributed by
Heath to the reasonable adventurer, to 'alternate
between the curious and the critical', or in our work
the alternation between a general view and the detailed examination of the evidence, is one which higher
education should aim to foster. The question which
then arises is how that ability is to be developed,
taking into account the individual, interdisciplinary,
and contextual differences, and the numerous roads
to understanding, which our research has revealed.

IMPLICATIONS FOR PRACTICE AND POLICY

The research described in this book does not
provide a blueprint for designing effective learning
in higher education. It does, however, offer a
much-needed theoretical and empirical rationale for
practical efforts to improve learning and teaching.
We have seen that the process of student learning in
relation to individual student differences and to its
context is much more complicated than lecturers and
students are often prepared to admit. The findings
of the research need to be reinterpreted by

lecturers in relation to the particular difficulties
of their students and their subject area.   Suitable
teaching strategies must take account of contextual
and individual differences.   We hope that one of
the most important messages to come from this
research is that commonsense theories of "good" and
"weak" students, conceptions of single "ideal"
methods of studying, and teaching technologies pur-
porting to be universally applicable in different
subject areas, are all of dubious practical value to
lecturers and students.   But what can now be said
about the steps which might be taken to improve
learning in higher education?

If universities and polytechnics seek to encourage greater versatility in their students, then
the evidence of this research is that a two-pronged
attack is needed.   On the one hand intervention
focused on <u>students</u> themselves is required;   on the
other, efforts to change <u>teaching and assessment</u> to
provide fertile conditions for the growth of
approaches aimed at understanding are necessary.

IMPROVING STUDYING

We have seen that students in higher education
use a variety of approaches to learning.   Not only
do the same students vary their approaches in response to different perceived requirements, but
different students differ in their individual preferences.   The finding that a deep approach can be
carried out with contrasting emphases on comprehension and operation learning suggests that we should
not try to change a student's learning style, except
as a last resort when it is creating serious difficulties for the student.   On the other hand it is
valuable to help students to become more aware of
their characteristic style and approach, to show
how they may most effectively capitalize on their
intellectual strengths and at the same time trans-
cend the limitations of a particular style.   The
improvident serialist needs help to practise the
skills of developing ideas and analogies;   the globetrotting holist ought to be given opportunities to
practise the handling of details to support his
ideas.   Students could also benefit from opportunities to become more confident in exploring
personal strategies which effectively cope with
different academic tasks and assessment requirements.
Some will probably need help with specific study
skills (reading for understanding, constructing
analytic essays, writing effective laboratory reports,

and so on).   But all students will gain from being
encouraged to raise their awareness and to think
about ways of developing flexible learning strategies
- the higher order skill of orchestrating the component techniques.

Many students will need a good deal of help in
recognizing the very different strategies required
to respond appropriately to the wide variety of tasks
set by lecturers.   Our first recommendation is that
direct teaching of study strategies, combined with
individual remedial help for students experiencing
special learning difficulties, ought to be provided
in our universities and polytechnics.   The incidence
of surface approaches in students shows clearly that
many have not mastered effective study processes.
Students take time to develop - if they develop at
all - a repertoire of strategies enabling them to
deal effectively with academic demands.   Although
many schemes have been devised to improve study skills,
few have taken seriously the wide range of strategies
which can be shown to be effective.   The increased
use of study skills programmes concentrating solely
on techniques, rather than on the development of
abilities to structure material with the aim of
understanding, would be worse than useless.

Inappropriate organizing techniques, for example,
are more of a hindrance than a help in studying.   An
"ideal" approach shown to be useful for one student
may suit others not at all.

Practical ways of running study skills programmes
which aim at increasing awareness have already been
developed, but they differ in their emphases.   Main
(1980) and Wankowski (Raaheim and Wankowski, 1981)
advocate individual counselling, Gibbs (1981) special-
izes in discussion methods, while Brew (1981) concentrates on helping students to organize and structure
both studying and learning.   We accept the value of
each of these approaches for particular purposes, but
would resist any suggestion that any of these
approaches was sufficient in itself.   Gibbs, for
example, avoids any direct teaching of study skills,
partly because the psychological justifications of the
'rules' for better studying are of dubious validity,
and partly because students are effective in such
different ways that no general rules could be described.   In our view it would be beneficial to provide students with the concepts and theories emerging
from the current research on student learning.   Such
a study skills course would draw attention to the
importance of organization and structure (in the ways
described by Angela Brew, 1981), to the existence of

207

contrasting styles and approaches, to the need to
adopt versatile and appropriate strategies, and to
the development of a personally satisfying style of
studying which is idiosyncratic but effective.   We
recognize the value of Gibbs' (1981) technique of
helping students to discover from each other the
variety of approaches being used in a situation
which is not threatening to self-confidence.   And
finally it is clear that some difficulties in studying experienced by students have deep emotional
roots, related often to home circumstances, which
can only be helped by a student counsellor with
specialized psychiatric skills, such as Wankowski
(Raaheim and Wankowski, 1981).   This individual
counselling may also be required by other students
who have 'blocks' created by particular academic
tasks, or who cannot make the connections from a
general course or workshop to their own problems.
Alex Main (1980) describes how such students may be
helped by a counselling service.

IMPROVING TEACHING AND ASSESSMENT

The usefulness of the sort of intervention described above is limited.   Study skills programmes
are usually the preserve of specialists outside the
everyday context of student learning - the teaching
and assessment processes of academic departments.
What the research reported in this book has repeatedly
demonstrated is the pervasive effect of this context
of learning on students' approaches to studying and
levels of understanding.   It would probably be more
effective to change the students' environment, which
is the source of many problems, than to concentrate
on helping students to find ways of coping with those
problems (see Wankowski, 1973).   It is sadly true
that disturbing conclusions reached by researchers
and other commentators on higher education during
the last hundred years or so (see, e.g. Whitehead,
1932) are confirmed in our findings.   The evidence
is overwhelming that the quality of student learning
is adversely affected by inappropriate assessment
methods, poor teaching, and the lack of freedom
provided by some courses.   Yet the detrimental
effects may not be visible in the outcomes of conventional assessments, as 'success' is defined by
the criteria adopted by the staff.   Nevertheless
the picture is not entirely sombre.   It is equally
clear that some departments, after allowing for
subject area differences, are more effective than
others at facilitating deep approaches.   We have

seen more than once how intrinsic motivation,
interest and relevance enhance the probability of a
deep approach, while threatening assessment conditions make surface approaches more likely.
Teachers can help to encourage intrinsic motivation
and point out relevant issues; they can equally well
encourage negative attitudes by a lack of concern for
the students' learning difficulties or by a lack of
commitment to their subject. Of course, deep
approaches cannot simply be created by effective
teaching and assessment; we can, however, ensure
that the conditions for understanding are as favourable as possible.

There can be no simple advice given to lecturers,
no magic training programme, which derives from our
research. The type of learning demanded by
different disciplines is clearly different, and so
no general recipe for better teaching and assessment
can be given. In arts, students should be encouraged
to search for personal meaning, which seems to depend
on empathy and openness from staff, informal teaching
(discussion) methods, freedom for students to explore
their interests, and yet, because of that freedom,
the setting of clear goals and standards. In science
and social science, good teaching seems to depend
more on pitching information at the right level and
being alert to student difficulties. A deep
approach in science depends more on operation learning, on relating evidence and conclusion, and on the
appropriate use of a certain amount of initial rote
learning to master the terminology. But this
versatility in learning will emerge readily only
where the workload is reasonable, and where freedom
in learning is allowed. The forms of assessment, the
types of questions, will also need to be consistent
with lecturers' attempts to develop critical thinking.
If factual reproduction of memorized answers is
implicitly encouraged and actively rewarded (through
the marks given), students will shift accordingly
towards surface approaches. Remember the psychology
student in the interview study in chapter 8 who said:

> "I hate to say it, but what you've got to do is
> have a list of the "facts"; you write down ten
> important points and memorize those, then you'll
> do all right in the test ... if you can give a
> bit of factual information - so and so did that,
> and concluded that - for two sides of writing,
> then you'll get a good mark".

Staff are often unaware of the effects that their

assessment demands have on learning.   Another
example comes from Gibbs (1981):

> "The scale of this problem quickly became
> apparent when, in an exercise on how students
> actually spent their time before and after the
> course started, it emerged that the students had
> actually been reading <u>more</u> psychology <u>before</u> the
> course started!   But the cause was not far
> away.   Three-quarters of all their time out-
> side class contact hours was spent writing up
> laboratory reports!   This turned out to be
> because laboratory reports were marked severely
> and the students were worried about passing the
> first year ... Their lack of reading was a direct
> consequence of a fear of failure and the per-
> ceived demands of the assessment system ...
> Apparent poor study skill was caused by teachers.

Onc of thc dilemmas in this area seems to be
that attempts to make assessments more reliable, by
using short-answer or multiple-choice questions, or
by introducing detailed marking schemes, are also
perceived as requiring mainly factual answers.   It
is certainly clear at school level that marking
schemes are more likely to reward the accretion of
correct pieces of information than evidence of integration and personal understanding.   Evidence of
personal understanding depends on the marker's judgement;   it is therefore impressionistic and liable to
be unreliable.   But it now seems that mechanical
marking schemes may affect not only the validity of
measurement, by concentrating too much on easily
measured aspects of the students' work, but also the
student's approach to learning.   It is, however,
possible to develop systematic marking schemes which
give appropriate credit to personal understanding,
based on repeated overall impression marks on
various criteria, or the use of appropriate classification systems for evaluating qualitatively
different outcomes of learning.   (Biggs, 1982).
There is, however, much work still to be done on this
problem.
The fact that lecturers in higher education
uᴿually have a great deal of choice over how they are
going to teach and assess means that, all too often,
approaches to teaching reflect a narrow view of the
'best' pedagogical method.   Frequently lecturers
will hold dogmatically to the view that one form of
teaching is necessarily superior - at one extreme,
it may be felt that computer managed instruction or

'Personalized Systems of Instruction' (Keller Plan)
are the answer to learning problems; at the other,
tutor-less discussion groups may be advocated as the
only "true" way of learning. The argument from our
research is that more, rather than less, variety of
teaching methods is likely to be beneficial.
Students are too rarely offered alternative ways of
learning: choice over the methods of learning available (independent work, essays, lectures, tutorials,
etc.) would seem to be not only highly valued by
students, but a logical implication of our model of
learning which stresses the wide variations among
styles and approaches they prefer.

How are we to encourage staff in higher education
institutions to respond to the challenge presented by
these findings? In part, as we shall see in a
moment, the answers must come from policy-makers, who
need to offer incentives and support for improving
teaching. Staff development programmes in Britain
have had only very limited success in the past. We
would argue that one of the reasons for their lack of
impact is an excessive emphasis on a model of
teaching and learning which focuses on lecturers'
problems - how to address an audience effectively,
how to prepare resource materials, how to run a
seminar skilfully. While these things are important,
they have tended to detract from the crucial links
between how tutors teach and assess, and how
effectively their students learn. Staff training
and development programmes need to discuss students'
problems, as well as those of the teachers - to
discuss how the students' difficulties may be created
by the staff in some instances. From the evidence
of our research, many lecturers show a lack of
sensitivity to students' study difficulties, while
they are not sufficiently aware of students'
approaches to learning or of the effects their
methods of assessment have on how their students
learn.

Future staff development programmes may thus
have to shift away from the concern with teaching
techniques towards helping lecturers to understand
the effects of their teaching on students' attitudes
and approaches. Good teaching, like effective
learning, can be realized in many different ways;
efficient techniques, either of studying or teaching,
are only useful if they can be incorporated within
an active and concerned approach, related to the
individual's preferences but not dominated by them.

In the last few pages we have looked in turn at some of the implications of our research for helping staff and helping students in higher education. But this separation between students, on the one hand, and teaching and assessment, on the other, is slightly artificial. In the real world improvements in teaching and learning are two sides of the same coin. Perhaps a practical attempt to improve student learning in higher education ought to consider both teachers and students at the same time. This suggests that it would be worthwhile to try to develop students' learning skills by encouraging staff to involve themselves in the process of improving their students' approaches to studying. While doing this, lecturers might also be expected to improve their teaching through a clearer insight into its effects on students.

The kind of staff development and study skills programme this approach would resemble in practice is demonstrated in a continuing project at the University of Melbourne (Frederick, Hancock, James, Bowden and Macmillan, 1981). The main aim of this project has been to develop the abilities and confidence of teaching staff in the faculties of the University so that they can take on what may be an unfamiliar role - helping individual students and groups of students to improve their learning skills. Staffed by a learning skills counsellor and two members of the University's Centre for the Study of Higher Education, the project began by making contact with faculty staff and explaining what it could offer. Its potential value was emphasized by the results of a previous survey of student learning skills in the university. In spite of a highly selective admissions policy and a low withdrawal rate, both students and staff had given evidence of widespread underachievement due to inadequate learning skills.

In several faculties joint activities involving teaching staff, the project team, and students have since become part of the teaching programme. The project's work has concentrated on staff development rather than on working directly with students - an approach which is more efficient and, from the evidence of our research, likely to be more effective. Activities have included shared tutorials, segments in lectures (outlining, for example, different note-taking strategies), staff workshops on studying and learning, learning skills topics in staff development courses and course team meetings, and providing resources to help staff understand better the learning skills difficulties of their students.

What distinguishes this attempt to intervene in learning and teaching is not so much the nature of its activities as its deliberate orientation towards integrating staff development and student learning. As this book went to press work was about to begin on a formal evaluation of the project, which will make use of several of the measures described in previous chapters to assess the effects of the interventions on the quality of students' learning. The results of this work will be awaited with interest by all who are concerned with teaching and learning development in higher education.

IMPROVING APPROACHES TO LEARNING AT SCHOOL

It is not only in universities and polytechnics that teachers need to take account of the research presented in this book. Teachers and examiners in secondary schools should be reminded of the importance of setting assessments which test understanding and demand independent thought, and do not seem to reward simple reproduction. Teachers should consider ways in which they can make explicit the type of learning that is expected and should adopt teaching methods which promote active thought within a clear structure. It is also of crucial importance that basic concepts and skills are thoroughly taught to ensure that deep approaches can be undertaken by pupils.

Orientations towards personal meaning or towards reproducing are brought to the experience of higher education by all students. Study methods and learning pathologies in university students are fully explained neither by stable individual preferences nor by the context of learning in higher education. It is clear that attitudes and orientations towards studying are powerfully shaped by experiences in school, in particular those associated with external examinations. The threat of formal examinations, and the revision associated with them, may push pupils towards memorizing: worse, it may leave them with the idea that learning is nothing more than reproducing other people's facts and ideas.

Students often refer explicitly to the problems created by inappropriate approaches to learning developed at school. For example, Mathias (1981) reports that many students felt that:

"their school experience had somehow distorted their view of learning ... Some (students) even gave fairly graphic accounts of how the 'O' and

'A' level system had inculcated an instrumental
view of learning. For instance ... "I used to
work for myself lots in the early days of
secondary school and it took a while to get back
into this habit because (during 'O'and'A' levels)
I was virtually being told what to do. And it
took me a while to get out of that and get back
into doing what I found interesting or if I
didn't find it interesting, to make it interesting"" (pages 6 - 7).

It is probable that a link between teaching
methods in school and approach to learning could be
demonstrated, and that again the twin attack of
modifying approaches to teaching and examining, and
developing in pupils a greater awareness of learning
strategies, could also beneficially affect the quality
of learning in schools. Indeed, it may be at school
level that the major initiative should be taken, to
prevent inappropriate learning strategies becoming
habitual before pupils move on to higher education
or employment.

POLICY ISSUES

How might the research findings presented here
be translated into policy terms, to be used in the
difficult planning issues facing post-compulsory
education in the remaining years of the century?
Educational planners and policy makers have shown a
wary attitude towards research into teaching and
learning in higher education in the past. It seems
likely that they may find themselves obliged to
change. The results of this research certainly do
not give specific procedural guidelines for policy,
but they do deserve to be taken seriously by
educational administrators and planners.
First, it is desirable that models of institutional and systems planning should build into their
analyses qualitative measures of student learning.
It is time to abandon simplistic notions of university
output couched solely in terms of quantitative criteri
- numbers of graduates produced - and to accept that
the effectiveness of a department or an educational
institution also has to take account of the quality
of understanding sought by its students. Second,
efforts need to be made to improve the learning contexts of departments and institutions. The evidence
that student learning can be improved by systematic re
appraisal of teaching and courses can no longer be
ignored. Inappropriate assessment methods,

unimaginative teaching, over-rigid courses, an excessive amount of curricular material - these weaknesses seem to act against a high quality of learning. Yet all are capable of being changed. An area deserving immediate attention is the assessment systems of our university departments. There is a need to develop assessment methods which genuinely test students' abilities to think critically and to understand the connections between activities in the real world and the material they learn in higher education. The capacity to reproduce information alone is of limited value in graduate jobs, either to employers or employees. Improved assessment methods might decrease the chances of the process and value of university education being ignored in the outside world (see Dore, 1977; Williams, 1978).

Another policy issue that should be faced is student choice of courses. There is a growing political pressure on institutions to encourage students to take courses of immediate benefit to the technical and commercial future of the country. This encouragement might well take the form of substantially reducing the number of places available in the arts, humanities, and social sciences. Such pressure is likely to be resisted, particularly by the universities, partly because they value a continued balance between disciplines, but more pragmatically because such changes imply redundancy for lecturers in the 'irrelevant' areas of study.

Our research, however, may suggest a reason for looking more closely at this issue in relation to students' academic interests. Many employers, it seems, are not looking to universities to supply specific technical skills: these are taught more effectively after graduation within the company. Employers are expecting degree courses to develop certain general qualities of mind, foremost of which seems to be the ability to think critically, objectively, flexibly, and quickly, and to apply that thinking to a wide range of problem situations. But for this 'deep' approach to occur, our research indicates that students must have an intrinsic interest in their content area. That terminology is perhaps too cautious. Students need to engage with the subject, to develop an intellectual passion to understand. If students are studying mainly to obtain a qualification - however relevant to society's anticipated needs - our evidence is that there is a greater likelihood that the knowledge will be obtained passively, in a way which would not engage those active critical 'faculties'. It is likely then that relevance, without commitment,

will provide employers with trained personnel without
the intellectual flair which higher education is
expected to awaken. Of course there is little known
about the extent to which intellectual skills
developed within an academic discipline are trans-
ferable to situations encountered in industry and
commerce. The experience of, say, the Civil
Service suggests that such skills are transferred,
but the evidence is largely anecdotal. The argument
that it would be better to develop those skills in
relevant disciplines (such as economics or law) fails
to distinguish two forms of relevance - to the anticipated needs of society and to the individual. For
intense involvement in studying, _personal_ relevance
is crucial, and policy makers who ignore this factor
could damage the central core of higher education.

This argument for student choice, should not,
however, be taken as a plea for the status quo. Our
evidence has pointed clearly to the fact that the
types of assessment and teaching predominating in some
departments are unlikely to encourage the intellectual
skills most prized by lecturers. But if systematic
reappraisal of teaching and assessment practices is
to occur, such activities must be rewarded. At
present, in universities time spent in improving
teaching may even be indirectly penalized. Research
output is the main criterion for promotion; the
investment of a similar proportion of one's time in
improving teaching receives no reward, and it is not
easy to do both things properly at once. The idea
that teaching might be evaluated is treated with out-
rage or dismay by many academics, although they accept
without question the judgement of others on the quali-
of their research. Yet if quality of research may be
judged, then the quality of a teacher's teaching (and
his students' learning) should also be open to similar
evaluation.

Our research can be taken to imply that resources
diverted into changing some established course
structures, and to staff development programmes, would
represent money well invested. The end to expansion
in higher education means that measures to maintain the
teaching vitality of staff are more than ever needed;
the spectre of an ageing academic population shot
through with cynicism about promotion prospects and
daily more uncertain of its future is depressing in
its implications for the standards of teaching in
higher education. But at the same time declining
employment prospects mean that attempts to institu-
tionalize staff development are likely to be treated
with growing suspicion and fear. Changes to well-

established course structures and approaches to
teaching will require increased expenditure on experiments in innovation and on programmes of staff
development concentrating on improving lecturers'
abilities to relate more effectively to their
students.   It cannot be expected that a diversion
of resources to these objectives will be accepted
readily.   It is important that changes rewarding
staff and departments which try to provide high
quality teaching, and which are strongly committed
to helping their students to learn, should be combined with an emphasis on the individual teacher's
responsibilities towards improving his own teaching.
A delicate task facing managers of higher education
institutions is to develop a climate of self-evalu-
ation and simultaneously to provide rewards for units
and individuals that try to enhance the quality of
their students' learning.

COMPLEMENTARY APPROACHES TO RESEARCH

    Our findings on the approaches to studying
adopted by students emphasize the importance of
flexibility and versatility; the need to adapt
approach to task demands and to alternate between
a holistic overall impression and the detailed
examination of evidence and logical argument.   These
findings on students' approaches apply equally well
to our own research strategies.   Not only have we
incorporated into the research design both qualitative methods (open interviewing of students) and
quantitative methods (multivariate analyses of
questionnaire responses), but there has been a
deliberate alternation between the two styles of
research.   Each has its strengths and its limiations.
The open interviews allow major explanatory constructs
to emerge out of the students' own descriptions of
their experiences of learning and teaching.   The
interviews cover, at least potentially, the whole
range of influences on student learning, and allow
both development and variability in strategy to
emerge and experience of causality in relationships
to be reported.   The questionnaires are designed to
measure dimensions defined in advance.   The questions
are closed and restrict freedom of expression.   But
the strength of relationships between the dimensions
of studying is determined by analyzing scale scores
and the multivariate analyses enable patterns of
relationships to be explored in more controlled and
sophisticated ways than are possible in the necessarily
impressionistic analyses of interview transcripts.

The alternation of qualitative and quantitative methods can be illustrated in two main ways - first, through the development of the inventory of approaches to studying. The inventory was developed from four main sources - a previous inventory of study methods and motivation, Biggs' study processes questionnaire, Marton's and Pask's descriptions of approaches and styles, and the pilot interviews with students. The previous inventory and Biggs' questionnaire contained,in part, items designed to indicate psychological traits - four forms of motivation. These items, it could be argued, lack ecological validity - they derive from theories of motivation rather than from the experiences of students. But this is only partly true. The early stages of development of such inventories involve asking students not only to respond to the items within the controlled format provided, but also to comment on the items and suggest areas not covered. The dimensions suggested by Marton have even clearer ecological validity; they represent descriptions made by the students themselves. The process of developing the inventory involved repeated reconsideration of the sub-scales, adding new items and omitting existing ones, on the basis both of factor analyses and of insights derived from the interviews with students. Thus the dimensions utlimately tapped by the inventory are firmly rooted in the experiences of the students.

The second illustration of alternation comes from the relationship between approaches to learning and methods of teaching and assessing. Repeatedly, in the interviews, students explained how their approaches were affected by lecturers and by the forms of assessment they experienced. The interview transcripts provide strong evidence of the perceived causality of these relationships, and individual quotations in the previous chapters have shown in detail what specific aspects of teaching are seen to influence students' learning under particular circumstances. The interviews enable the researcher not only to describe the relationships, but through empathy with the experiences reported, to reconstruct the students' perceptions of reality imaginatively and so to understand more fully the nature of student learning. The multivariate analyses have provided both a quantitative verification of the insights gained from the interviews, and have also provided additional insights into the complex patterns of relationships that exist, particularly between approaches and styles, and between the outcome of learning and combinations of personal characteristics (study organization and

motivation) and departmental contexts (workload and
freedom in learning).

We would argue that, in our experience, neither
qualitative nor quantitative methods of research
taken separately can provide a full and a convincing
explanation of student learning. It does not seem
possible to integrate the two styles of research:
they pull researchers in opposite directions. It
may not even be possible for a single researcher to
work effectively in both ways: some people have a
strong emotional attachment to a way of describing
the world which precludes one or other of these
styles of research. Research, like learning, is an
expression of pervasive underlying cognitive preferences and value systems. Nevertheless it seems
essential that an understanding of student learning
should be built up from an appropriate alternation of
evidence and insights derived from both qualitative
and quantitative approaches to research. In our
view the strength of our evidence on student learning
is the direct result of this inter-play of contrasting
methodologies, and has led to a realistic and useful
description of approaches and contexts of learning
in higher education.

REFERENCES

Allport, G.W. (1963) Pattern and Growth in Personality,
    New York: Holt, Rinehart and Winston
Amir, V. and Krausz, M. (1974) Factors of satis-
    faction and importance in an academic setting,
    Human Relations, 27, 211-223
Ashby, E. (1973) The structure of higher education:
    a world view, Higher Education, 2, 142-151.
Atkinson, J.W. and Feather, N.T. (1966) A Theory of
    Achievement Motivation, New York, Wiley
Bartlett, F.C. (1932) Remembering, Cambridge: Cam-
    bridge University Press
Beard, R.M., Levy, P.M. and Maddox, H. (1962) Aca-
    demic performance at university. Educ. Rev.,
    16, 163-174
Becher, A. and Kogan, M. (1980) Process and
    Structure in Higher Education, London: Heinemann
Becker, H.S., Geer, B. and Hughes, E.C. (1968)
    Making the Grade: the Academic Side of College
    Life. New York: Wiley
Bernstein, B.B. (1971) On the classification and
    framing of educational knowledge. In Young,
    M.F.D. (Ed.) Knowledge and Control, London:
    Collier-Macmillan

REFERENCES

Bieri, J., Atkins, A.L., Briar, J.S., Leaman, R.L., Miller, H. and Tripodi, T. (1966) <u>Clinical and Social Judgement: The Discrimination of Behavioural Information</u>, New York: Wiley

Biggs, J.B. (1976) Dimensions of study behaviour: another look at A.T.I.,<u>Br. J. educ. Psychol.</u>, <u>46</u>, 68-80

Biggs, J.B. (1978) Individual and group differences in study processes, <u>Br. J. educ. Psychol.</u>, <u>48</u>, 266-279

Biggs, J.B. (1979) Individual differences in study processes and the quality of learning outcomes, <u>Higher Education</u>, <u>8</u>, 381-394

Biggs, J.B. and Collis, K.E. (1982) <u>Evaluating the Quality of Learning: the SOLO Taxonomy</u>, New York Academic Press

Biglan, A. (1973a) The characteristics of subject matter in different academic areas, <u>Journal of Applied Psychology</u>, <u>57</u>, 195-203

Biglan, A. (1973b) Relationships between subject matter characteristics and the structure and output of university departments <u>Applied Psychology</u>, <u>57</u>, 204-213.

Birney, R.C., Burdick, H., and Teevan, R C. (1969) <u>Fear of Failure</u>, New York: Van Nostrand

Brennan, J.L. and Percy, K.A. (1977) What do students want? An analysis of staff and student perceptions in British higher education. In Bonboir, A. (ed.), <u>Instructional Design in Higher Education</u>, European Association for Research and Development in Higher Education, <u>1</u>, 125-152

Brew, A. (1981) Underlying themes in study methods teaching. Paper presented at the 5th International Conference on Higher Education, 1-4 September 1981, University of Lancaster

Broadbent, D.E. (1966) The well-ordered mind, <u>Am. educ. Res. J.</u>, <u>3</u>, 281-295

Bronowski, J. (1965) <u>The Identity of Man</u>, London: Heinemann

Burt, C. (1965) Factorial studies of personality and their bearing on the work of teachers, <u>Br. J. educ. Psychol.</u>, <u>35</u>, 368-378

Burt, C. (1971) The mental differences between childre In Cox C.B. and Dyson, A.E. (Eds.) <u>The Black Papers on Education</u>. London: Davis Poynter

Butcher, H.J. and Rudd, E. (1972) <u>Contemporary Problems in Higher Education</u>, London: McGraw-Hill

Cattell, R.B. (1965) <u>The Scientific Analysis of Personality</u>, Harmondsworth: Penguin

REFERENCES

Centra, J.A. (1976) Student ratings of instruction
        and their relationship to student learning,
        Princeton, N.J.: Educational Testing Service
Craik, F.I.M. and Lockhart, R.S. (1972) Levels of
        processing: a framework for memory research,
        J. verb. Learn. verb. Behav., 11, 671-684
Craik, F.I.M. and Tulving, E. (1975) Depth of pro-
        cessing and the retention of words in spisodic
        memory, J. exp. Psychol (Gen.), 104, 268-294
Crutchfield, R.S. (1962) Conformity and creative
        thinking In Gruber, H.E. Terrell, G., and
        Wertheimer, M. (Eds.), Contemporary Approaches
        to Creative Thinking, New York: Atherton
Dahlgren, L.O. (1978) Qualitative differences in con-
        ceptions of basic principles in Economics
        Paper read to the 4th International Conference
        on Higher Education at Lancaster, 29th August-
        1st September, 1978
Dahlgren, L.O. and Marton, F. (1978) Students' con-
        ceptions of subject matter: an aspect of
        learning and teaching in higher education,
        Studies in Higher Educ., 3, 25-35
de Bono, E. (1971) The Use of Lateral Thinking,
        Harmondsworth: Penguin
Dore, R. (1977) The Diploma Disease, London: Unwin
Dubin, R. and Taveggia, T. (1969) The Teaching-
        Learning Paradox, Eugene, Oregon: University of
        Oregon Press
Entwistle, N.J. (1975) How students learn: information
        processing, intellectual development and con-
        frontation, Higher Education Bulletin, 3, 129-148
Entwistle, N.J. (1979) Stages, levels, styles or
        strategies: dilemmas in the description of
        thinking, Educ. Rev., 31, 123-132
Entwistle, N.J. (1981) Styles of Learning and Teaching:
        An Integrative Outline of Educational Psychology,
        Chichester: Wiley
Entwistle, N.J. and Bennett, S.N. (1973) The inter-
        relationships between Personality, Divergent
        Thinking and School Attainment, Final Report to
        the SSRC on project MR 1346
Entwistle, N.J. and Entwistle, D.M. (1970) The
        relationships between personality, study methods
        and academic performance, Br. J. educ. Psychol.,
        40, 132-41
Entwistle, N.J., Hanley, M. and Ratcliffe, G. (1979a)
        Approaches to learning and levels of understanding,
        Br. J. educ. Res., 5, 99-114
Entwistle, N.J., Hanley, M. and Hounsell, D.J. (1979b)
        Identifying distinctive approaches to studying,
        Higher Educ., 8, 365-380

Entwistle, N.J. and Percy, K.A. (1971) Educational
    objectives and student performance within the
    binary system.   In Research into Higher Edu-
    cation 1970, London: S.R.H.E.
Entwistle, N.J. and Percy, K.A. (1974) Critical
    thinking or conformity? An investigation of
    the aims and outcomes of higher education. In
    Research into Higher Education 1973, London:
    S.R.H.E.
Entwistle, N.J.,Thompson, J.B.,and Wilson, J.D. (1974)
    Motivation and study habits. Higher Educ., 3,
    379-96
Entwistle, N.J. and Wilson, J.D. (1970) Personality,
    study methods and academic performance, Univ.
    Quart., 21, 147-66
Entwistle, N.J. and Wilson, J.D. (1977) Degrees of
    Excellence: The Academic Achievement Game,
    London: Hodder & Stoughton
Eysenck, H.J. (1965) Fact and Fiction in Psychology,
    Harmondsworth: Penguin
Eysenck, H.J. (1970) The Structure of Human Person-
    ality, London: Routledge and Kegan Paul
Eysenck, H.J. and Eysenck, S.B.G. (1969) 'Psychoticism
    in children: a new personality variable, Res. in
    Educ., 1, 21-37
Fearn-Wannan, H. (1979) Students' perceptions of
    lecturers as determinants of academic performance
    in first-year chemistry. Paper presented at the
    Annual Conference of the S.R.H.E., Brighton,
    December 1979
Fransson, A. (1977) On qualitative differences in
    learning. IV - Effects of motivation and test
    anxiety on process and outcome, Br. J. Educ.
*   Psychol., 47, 244-257
Gaff, J.G.,Crombag, H.F.M. and Chang, T.M. (1976)
    Environments for learning in a Dutch university,
    Higher Education, 5, 285-299
Gamson, Z.F. (1966) Utilitarian and normative orien-
    tations toward education, Sociology of Education,
    39, 46-73
Gibbs, G. (1981) Teaching Students to Learn, Milton
    Keynes: Open University Press
Glaser, B. and Strauss, A. (1967) The Discovery of
    Grounded Theory, New York: Aldine
Godfrey Thomson Unit (1971) Advanced Verbal Reason-
    ing Test, Edinburgh: University of Edinburgh,
    Department of Education
Hajnal, J. (1972) The Student Trap, Harmondsworth:
    Penguin
Hartnett, R.T. and Centra, J.A. (1977) The effects
    of academic departments on student learning,
    J. Higher Educ., 48, 491-507

* (Frederick et al - see end)

REFERENCES

Heath, R. (1964) The Reasonable Adventurer,
    Pittsburgh: University of Pittsburgh Press
Heist, P. and Yonge, G. (1960), Omnibus Personality
    Inventory, New York: Psychological Corporation
Hermans, B.M.J. (1979) Student and system: academic
    success and study problems in relation with
    characteristics of the academic environment and
    of the students.   In Van Trotsenburg, E.A. (Ed.),
    Higher Education: A Field of Study, 5 vols.
    Bern: Verlag Peter Lang
Hodgson, V.E. (1981) The use of stimulated recall in
    education research. Paper presented at the 5th
    International Conference on Higher Education,1
    - 4 September, University of Lancaster
Hoyle, F. (1950) The Nature of the Universe, Oxford:
    Blackwell
Hudson, L. (1966) Contrary Imaginations, London:
*   Methuen
Jung, C.G. (1938) Psychological Types, London: Kegan
    Paul, Trench and Truber
Kagan, J., Rossman, B.l., Albert, J., and Phillips,
    W. (1964) Information processing in the child:
    significance of analytic and reflective atti-
    tudes. Psychological Monographs, General and
    Applied, 78,(1, whole no. 578)
Kogan, N. (1976) Cognitive Styles in Infancy and
    Early Childhood, Hillsdale, N.J: Lawrence
    Erlbaum
Kogan, N. and Wallach, M.A. (1964) Risk Taking, New
    York: Holt, Rinehart and Winston
Kulik, J.A. and McKeachie, W.J. (1975) The evaluation
    of teachers in higher education. In Kerlinger,
    F.N. (Ed.), Review of Research in Education 3.
    Itasca, Ill.: Peacock Publishers
Laurillard, D.M. (1978) A study of the relationship
    between some of the cognitive and contextual
    factors involved in student learning.   Un-
    published Ph.D. thesis, University of Surrey
Laurillard, D.M. (1979) The processes of student
    learning, Higher Education, 8, 395-409
Lindsay, P.H. and Norman, D.A. (1972) Human Information
    Processing, New York: Academic Press
Long, S. (1978) Student types and the evaluation
    of the university, Higher Education, 6, 417-436
Main, A. (1980) Encouraging Effective Learning,
    Edinburgh: Scottish Academic Press
Manook, S. and King. A.R. (1981) Notetaking in
    lectures. Paper presented at the 5th International
    Conference on Higher Education, 1 - 4 September,
    University of Lancaster
Marton, F. (1975) On non-verbatim learning. II - the

223

* (Hughes-Jones - see end)

REFERENCES

        erosion effect of a task-induced learning algo-
        rithm, Reports from the Institute of Education,
        University of Gothenburg, No. 40
Marton, F. (1976) What does it take to learn? Some
        implications of an alternative view of learning.
        In Entwistle, N.J. (Ed.), Strategies for
        Research and Development in Higher Education,
        Amsterdam: Swets and Zeitlinger
Marton, F. and Säljö, R. (1976a) On qualitative
        differences in learning. I - Outcome and process
        Br. J. educ. Psychol., 46, 4 - 11
Marton, F. and Säljö, R. (1976b) On qualitative
        differences in learning. II - Outcome as a
        function of the learner's conception of the task
        Br. J. educ. Psychol., 46, 115-127
Marton, F. and Svensson, L. (1979) Conceptions of
        research in student learning, Higher Education,
        8, 471-486
Mathias, H. (1981) University learning and the
        school experience. Paper presented at the 5th
        International Conference on Higher Education,
*   1 - 4 September, University of Lancaster
Messick, S. and Associates (1976) Individuality in
        Learning, San Francisco: Jossey Bass
Miller, C.M.L. and Parlett, M. (1974) Up to the Mark
        A Study of the Examination Game, London: S.R.H.E
Morgan, A., Gibbs, G., and Taylor, E. (1980) Students
        Approaches to Studying the Social Science and
        Technology Foundation Courses: Preliminary
        Studies, Study Methods Group Report No. 4,
        Institute of Educational Technology, The Open
        University
Newman, J.H. (1852) On the Scope and Nature of
        University Education, London: Dent
Nie, N.J., Hull, C.H., Jenkins, J.G., Steinbrenner,
        K. and Bent, D.H. (1975) Statistical Package
        for the Social Sciences (2nd edition), New
        York: McGraw-Hill
Pace, C.R. (1967) College and University Environ-
        ment Scales, Princeton, N.J.: Educational
        Testing Service
Parlett, M. (1970) The syllabus-bound student. In
        Hudson, L. The Ecology of Human Intelligence,
        Harmondsworth: Penguin
Pascarella, E.T. and Terenzini, P.T. (1977) Patterns
        of student-faculty informal interaction beyond
        the classroom and voluntary freshman attrition,
        J. Higher Educ., 48, 540-552
Pascarella. E.T. and Terenzini, P.T. (1978) Student-
        faculty informal relationships and freshman year
        educational outcomes, J. Educ. Research, 71,
        183-189
224

* (Messer - see end)

REFERENCES

Pask, G. (1976a) Conversational techniques in the study and practice of education, Br. J. educ. Psychol., 46, 12-25

Pask, G. (1976b) Styles and strategies of learning, Br. J. educ. Psychol., 46, 128-148

Pask, G. and Scott, B.C.E. (1972) Learning strategies and individual competence, Int. J. Man-Machine Studies, 4, 217-253

Pask, G. et al (1977) Third Progress Report on SSRC Research Programme HR 2708 (see also Fourth Progress Report, 1978, and Final Report 1979), System Research Limited, 37 Sheen Road, Richmond, Surrey

Pattison, M. (1876) Philosophy at Oxford, Mind, 1, 84-97

Payne, D.A. and Hobbs, A.M. (1979) The effect of college course evaluation feedback on instructor and student perceptions of instructional climate and effectiveness, Higher Education, 8, 525-533

Peel, E.A. (1978) Generalising through the verbal medium, Br. J. educ. Psychol., 48, 36-46

Percy, K.A. and Ramsden, P. (1980) Independent Study: Two Examples from English Higher Education, Guildford: S.R.H.E.

Perry, W.G. (1970) Forms of Intellectual and Ethical Development in the College Years: a Scheme, New York: Holt, Rinehart and Winston

Perry, W.G. (1978) Sharing the costs in growth, In Parker, C.A. (Ed.) Encouraging Development in College Students, Minneapolis: University of Minnesota Press

Peterson, R.E. (1965) On a typology of college students Research Bulletin, RB65-9. Princeton, N.J.: Educational Testing Service

Pines, M. (1976) A child's mind is shaped before age 2. In Dentler, R.A. and Shapiro, B. (Eds.), Readings in Educational Psychology: Contemporary Perspectives, New York: Harper and Row

Raaheim, K. (1976) Do we need convergent thinking? Paper presented at the 21st International Conference of Psychology, Paris, July 1976

Raaheim, K. and Wankowski, J. (1981) Helping Students to Learn at University, Bergen: Sigma Forlag

Ramsden, P. (1976) Course evaluation in higher education, Unpublished M.Phil. thesis, C.N.A.A.

Ramsden, P. (1979) Student learning and perceptions of the academic environment, Higher Education, 8, 411-428

Ramsden, P. (1981) A Study of the Relationship between Student Learning and its Academic Context Unpublished PhD thesis, University of Lancaster

REFERENCES

Ramsden, P. and Entwistle, N.J. (1981) Effects of
    academic departments on students' approaches to
    studying, Br. J. educ. Psychol., 51, 368-383
Robertson, I.T. (1977) An investigation of some
    relationships between learning and personality,
    Unpublished PhD thesis, The Open University
Roe, A. (1956) The Psychology of Occupations, New
    York: Wiley
Rogers, C.R. (1969) Freedom to Learn, Columbus, Ohio:
    Merrill
Rowntree, D. (1977) Assessing Students: How Shall
    we Know Them?, London: Harper & Row
Säljö, R. (1975) Qualitative Differences in Learning
    as a Function of the Learner's Conception of
    the Task, Gothenburg: Acta Universitatis
    Gothoburgensis
Säljö, R. (1979a) Learning in the learner's pers-
    pective: I - Some commonsense conceptions,
    Reports from the Institute of Education,
    University of Gothenburg, No. 76
Säljö, R. (1979b) Learning in the learner's pers-
    pective: II - differences in awareness, Reports
    from the Institute of Education, University of
    Gothenburg, No. 77
Säljö, R. (1979c) Learning about learning, Higher
    Education, 8, 443-451
Säljö, R. (1981) Learning approach and outcome: some
    empirical observations, Instructional Science,
    10, 47-65
Schmeck, R.R. (in press) Learning styles of college
    students. In Dillon, R. and Schmeck, R.R.
    Individual Differences in Cognition, New York:
    Academic Press
Schmeck, R.R. and Phillips, J. (in press) Levels
    of processing as a dimension of difference
    between individuals, Human Learning
Schwab, J.J. (1964) Structure of the disciplines:
    meanings and significances. In Ford, A.W.
    and Pugno, L. (eds.) The Structure of Knowledge
    and the Curriculum, Chicago: Rand McNally
Smithers, A.G. (1969) A structural study of the
    occupational value orientations of engineering
    students, Voc. Aspect, 21, 129-134
Snyder, B.R. (1971) The Hidden Curriculum, New York:
    Knopf
Stern, C.G. (1970) People in Context, New York:
    Wiley
Svensson, L. (1976) Study Skill and Learning,
    Gothenburg: Acta Universitatis Gothoburgensis
Svensson, L. (1977) On qualitative differences in
    learning. III - Study skill and learning,

REFERENCES

Br. J. educ. Psychol., 47, 233-243
Tabberer, R., and Allman, J. (1981) Study Skills at 16 plus: an interim Report, Slough: National Foundation for Educational Research
Taylor, E., Morgan, A., and Gibbs, G. (1981) Students' orientations to study. Paper presented at the 5th International Conference on Higher Education, 1 - 4 September, University of Lancaster
Thompson, J.B. (1981) An Interview Study of the Attitudes, Expectations and Motivations of 124 students in Higher Education, unpublished PhD thesis, University of Lancaster
Thompson, J.D., Hawkes, R.W., and Avery, R.W. (1969) Truth strategies and university organization, Educ. Admin. Q., 5, 4-25
Veblen, T. (1957) (First published 1918) The Higher Learning in America, New York: Hill and Wang
Tankowski, J.A. (1973) Temperament: Motivation and Academic Achievement, Birmingham: University of Birmingham Educational Survey
Watkins, D. (1982) Identifying the study process dimensions of Australian university students. Australian Journal of Education, 26, 76-85
Whitehead, A.N. (1950) (First published 1932) The Aims of Education and other Essays, London: Ernest Benn
Williams, G.L. (1978) In defence of diplomas, Higher Education, 7, 363-371
Wilson, R.C., Gaff, J.G., Dienst, E.R., Wood, L., and Pavry, J.L. (1975) College Professors and Their Impact on Students, New York: Wiley
Witkin, H.A. (1976) Cognitive style in academic performance and in teacher-student relations. In Messick, S. (Ed.), Individuality in Learning, San Francisco: Jossey Bass
Witkin, H.A., Moore, C.A., Goodenough, D.R., and Cox, P.W. (1977) Field-dependent and field-independent cognitive styles and their educational implications, Rev. educ. Res., 47, 1 1-64

Frederick, J., Hancock, L., James, B., Bowden, J., and MacMillan, C., (1981) Learning Skills: a Review of needs and services to university students, Melbourne: Centre for the Study of Higher Educatio, University of Melbourne
Hughes-Jones, H., (1979) Attributional Analysis of Student Perceptions and the Reasons for academic success and failure. Paper presented at the Annual Conference of the S.R.H.E., Bright, December 1979
Messer, S., (1976) Reflection-Impulsivity: a review, Psychol. Bull., 83, 1026-1052.

Table A1   ITEMS CONTAINED IN THE FINAL RESEARCH VERSION OF THE
            APPROACHES TO STUDYING INVENTORY

MEANING ORIENTATION	Corrected* item-scale total correlation

Deep Approach (Cronbach Alpha = 0.56)

DA1	I generally put a lot of effort into trying to understand things which initially seem difficult	0.38
DA2	I often find myself questioning things that I hear in lectures or read in books	0.30
DA3	I usually set out to understand thoroughly the meaning of what I am asked to read.	0.37
DA4	When I'm tackling a new topic, I often ask myself questions about it which the new information should answer	0.33

Relating Ideas (0.47)

RI1	I try to relate ideas in one subject to those in others, whenever possible	0.31
RI2	In trying to understand new ideas, I often try to relate them to real life situations to which they might apply	0.24
RI3	I need to read around a subject pretty widely before I'm ready to put my ideas down on paper	0.20
RI4	I find it helpful to 'map out' a new topic for myself by seeing how the ideas fit together	0.30

Use of Evidence (0.38)

UE1	In reporting practical work, I like to try to work out several alternative ways of interpreting the findings	0.23
UE2	I am usually cautious in drawing conclusions unless they are well supported by evidence	0.13

---

* Corrected to remove contribution of that item to scale total

Use of Evidence (0.38) (continued)

UE3 Puzzles or problems fascinate me, particularly
where you have to work through the material to
reach a logical conclusion   0.19

UE4 When I'm reading an article or research report
I generally examine the evidence carefully to
decide whether the conclusion is justified   0.27

Intrinsic Motivation (0.72)

IM1 My main reason for being here is so that I
can learn more about the subjects which really
interest me   0.49

IM2 I find that studying academic topics can
often be really exciting and gripping   0.55

IM3 I spend a good deal of my spare time in
finding out more about interesting topics
which have been discussed in classes   0.44

IM4 I find academic topics so interesting, I
should like to continue with them after I
finish this course   0.56

REPRODUCING ORIENTATION

Surface Approach (0.49)

SA1 Lecturers seem to delight in making the
simple truth unnecessarily complicated   0.21

SA2 I find I have to concentrate on memorising
a good deal of what we have to learn   0.32

SA3 When I'm reading I try to memorise important
facts which may come in useful later   0.13

SA4 The best way for me to understand what
technical terms mean is to remember the
text-book definitions   0.24

SA5 I usually don't have time to think about
the implications of what I have read   0.28

SA6 Often I find I have read things without having
a chance to really understand them   0.32

Syllabus-Boundness (0.51)

SB1 I like to be told precisely what to do
in essays or other assignments   0.38

Syllabus-Boundness (0.51) (continued)

SB2 I prefer courses to be clearly structured
and highly organised   0.33

SB3 I tend to read very little beyond what's
required for completing assignments   0.27

Fear of Failure (0.45)

FF1 The continual pressure of work-assignments,
deadlines and competition often makes me
tense and depressed   0.30

FF2 A poor first answer in an exam makes me panic   0.30

FF3 Having to speak in tutorials is quite an
ordeal for me   0.22

Extrinsic Motivation (0.78)

EM1 I chose my present courses mainly to give me
a chance of a really good job afterwards   0.63

EM2 My main reason for being here is that it will
help me to get a better job   0.67

EM3 I generally choose courses more from the way
they fit in with career plans than from my own
interests   0.58

EM4 I suppose I am more interested in the qualifications I'll get than in the courses I'm taking   0.46

ACHIEVING ORIENTATION

Strategic Approach (0.32)

ST1 Lecturers sometimes give indications of what is
likely to come up in exams, so I look out for
what may be hints   0.16

ST2 When I'm doing a piece of work, I try to bear
in mind exactly what that particular lecturer
seems to want   0.16

ST3 If conditions aren't right for me to study, I
generally manage to do something to change them   0.18

ST4 One way or another I manage to get hold of the
books I need for studying   0.16

*Disorganised Study Methods (0.71) (reversed
scoring)*

DS1 I find it difficult to organise my study time
effectively   0.52

Disorganised Study Methods (0.71) (reversed scoring) (continued)

DS2 My habit of putting off work leaves me with far too much to do at the end of term   0.50

DS3 Distractions make it difficult for me to do much effective work in the evenings   0.46

DS4 I'm rather slow at starting work in the evenings   0.52

Negative Attitudes to Studying (0.60) (reversed scoring)

NA1 Often I find myself wondering whether the work I am doing here is really worthwhile   0.44

NA2 Continuing my education was something which happened to me, rather than something I really wanted for myself   0.37

NA3 When I look back, I sometimes wonder why I ever decided to come here   0.48

NA4 I certainly want to pass the next set of exams, but it doesn't really matter if I only just scrape through   0.25

Achievement Motivation (0.58)

AM1 I enjoy competition: I find it stimulating   0.43

AM2 It's important to me to do really well in the courses here   0.32

AM3 It is important to me to do things better than my friends   0.48

AM4 I hate admitting defeat, even in trivial matters   0.25

STYLES AND PATHOLOGIES OF LEARNING

Comprehension Learning (0.65)

CL1 Ideas in books often set me off on long chains of thought of my own, only tenuously related to what I was reading   0.45

CL2 In trying to understand a puzzling idea, I let my imagination wander freely to begin with, even if I don't seem to be much nearer a solution   0.39

Comprehension Learning (0.65) (continued)

CL3   I like to play around with ideas of my own even if they don't get me very far   0.47

CL4   Often when I'm reading books, the ideas produce vivid images which sometimes take on a life of their own   0.41

Globetrotting (0.36)

GT1   Although I have a fairly good general idea of many things, my knowledge of the details is rather weak   0.13

GT2   In trying to understand new topics, I often explain them to myself in ways that other people don't seem to follow   0.16

GT3   I often get criticised for introducing irrelevant material into my essays or tutorials   0.25

GT4   I seem to be a bit too ready to jump to conclusions without waiting for all the evidence   0.24

Operation Learning (0.49)

OL1   I generally prefer to tackle each part of a topic or problem in order, working out one at a time   0.32

OL2   I prefer to follow well tried out approaches to problems rather than anything too adventurous   0.29

OL3   I find it better to start straight away with the details of a new topic and build up an overall picture in that way   0.18

OL4   I think it is important to look at problems rationally and logically without making intuitive jumps   0.34

Improvidence (0.42)

IP1   Although I generally remember facts and details, I find it difficult to fit them together into an overall picture   0.25

IP2   I find it difficult to "switch tracks" when working on a problem: I prefer to follow each line of thought as far as it will go   0.19

Improvidence (0.42) (continued)

IP3   Tutors seem to want me to be more
adventurous in making use of my own ideas   0.22

IP4   I find I tend to remember things best if I
concentrate on the order in which the
lecturer presented them   0.26

Table A2   CORRELATIONS BETWEEN SUB-SCALES OF THE APPROACHES TO STUDYING INVENTORY

	Meaning				Reproducing				Achieving				Styles and Pathologies			
	DA	RI	UE	IM	SA	SB	FF	EM	ST	DS	NA	AM	CL	GL	OL	IP
Meaning Orientation																
Deep Approach		48	43	47	-09	-28	-05	-12	24	-22	-25	19	37	-03	06	-05
Relating Ideas			40	39	-03	-22	03	-11	22	-10	-17	13	39	08	03	02
Use of Evidence				36	-11	-15	-06	-03	21	-14	-22	20	24	-12	15	-01
Intrinsic Motivation					-20	-37	-08	-35	17	-22	-41	16	37	-07	-07	-12
Reproducing Orientation																
Surface Approach						37	32	28	18	18	23	11	-09	24	29	42
Syllabus-Boundness							27	32	06	24	22	06	-28	11	37	35
Fear of Failure								15	03	22	21	04	-01	19	22	39
Extrinsic Motivation									16	07	13	20	-19	04	30	27
Achieving Orientation																
Strategic Approach										-20	-17	25	03	-09	24	12
Disorganized Study Methods											30	-10	06	24	-05	13
Negative Attitudes to Studying												-24	-02	25	-02	13
Achievement Motivation													04	-02	19	08
Styles and Pathologies																
Comprehension Learning														18	-23	-12
Globetrotting															-07	19
Operation Learning																41

Decimal points omitted.
Total Sample N = 2208; correlations statistically significant with r > 0.06

Table A3 INTERCORRELATIONS BETWEEN INVENTORY SUB-SCALES AND PSYCHOLOGICAL TEST BATTERY

Test Sub-scales	Thinking Introversion	Theoretical Outlook	Aestheticism	Complexity	Autonomy	Religious Scepticism	Social Extraversion	Impulse Expression	Personal Integration	Lack of Anxiety	Altruism	Practical Outlook	Verbal Reasoning	Concrete Generalizing	Abstract Generalizing	Field Independence	Reflectiveness	Inaccuracy	Flexibility	Verbal Fluency
Deep Approach	48	38	31	27	14	21	18	28	-05	-07	12	-14	-03	-06	01	-21	20	-07	19	24
Relating ideas	36	28	33	27	26	15	10	21	-18	-19	-03	-09	03	09	13	-15	15	-03	14	17
Use of Evidence	04	15	07	-16	-09	-04	04	-04	-07	-16	-08	20	23	02	05	23	04	-13	-07	-07
Intrinsic Motivation	45	22	35	09	08	07	-11	08	-27	-22	10	-20	-16	06	01	-11	09	03	-14	-05
Surface Approach	-31	-26	-03	-18	-14	-12	01	10	10	-17	-18	38	07	-11	-11	04	12	-10	-10	-11
Syllabus Bound	-48	-30	-26	-37	-27	0	06	0	17	03	05	47	-13	-24	-23	05	-06	02	-05	-01
Fear of Failure	-04	-03	07	-10	09	-02	-25	11	-23	-38	-21	20	-24	02	-13	05	05	-13	03	-11
Extrinsic Motivation	-62	-19	-46	-47	-13	08	03	01	07	16	-08	57	-15	-10	-21	02	-17	07	-23	-14
Disorganized	-12	-13	-03	09	22	08	02	23	-08	-22	-20	-04	28	-03	16	-06	-07	-04	20	04
Strategic	02	20	13	-08	-07	20	28	15	01	10	06	37	-15	-12	-25	03	14	-15	11	11
Negative Attitude	-25	-22	-07	-07	04	-17	-15	08	-06	-26	-28	-03	28	-17	07	11	00	03	21	17
Achievement Motivation	20	18	13	-07	-17	-04	-14	03	-38	-35	-22	30	-01	-05	-02	02	10	-03	-03	-04
Comprehension	52	39	43	33	17	11	04	30	-31	-22	-06	-23	23	07	13	08	-02	-04	20	16
Globetrotting	15	-04	34	23	14	-06	-01	23	-27	-27	-31	02	10	-03	13	-06	09	04	18	-02
Operation	-23	-06	-30	-37	-16	01	-02	-13	-03	-02	01	39	-11	-07	-28	05	23	-11	-18	-09
Improvidence	08	06	14	-12	10	-11	-11	11	-07	-10	11	28	-26	-05	-08	-13	07	05	-09	-10

Approaches to Studying Inventory

(Continued)

Table A3 INTERCORRELATIONS BETWEEN INVENTORY SUB-SCALES AND PSYCHOLOGICAL TEST BATTERY (Continued)

Test Sub-scales	Theoretical Orientation	Aestheticism	Complexity	Autonomy	Religious Scepticism	Social Extraversion	Impulse Expression	Personal Integration	Lack of Anxiety	Altruism	Practical Outlook	Verbal Reasoning	Concrete Generalizing	Abstract Generalizing	Field Independence	Reflectiveness	Inaccuracy	Flexibility	Verbal Fluency
Omnibus Personality Inventory																			
Thinking Introversion	52	66	51	35	13	12	16	-05	-01	26	-36	02	08	19	-12	24	-15	17	05
Theoretical Orientation		24	40	34	45	30	30	11	29	17	02	05	19	05	05	15	-12	11	05
Aestheticism			52	34	24	22	30	-12	-02	04	-09	04	-06	02	-06	11	-14	24	01
Complexity				46	33	19	53	-01	01	04	-31	19	21	30	07	11	-11	14	03
Autonomy					42	13	26	07	12	18	-27	11	17	30	-08	-05	-11	18	-05
Religious Scepticism						33	44	05	26	05	10	09	-04	-09	08	01	-16	-05	-09
Social Extraversion							19	46	46	29	17	13	-05	-09	10	12	-19	14	14
Impulse Expression								-19	46	09	02	02	-07	09	03	-04	-10	14	05
Personal Integration									61	50	12	-06	05	-02	-14	00	06	25	21
Lack of Anxiety										49	20	-22	-16	-17	-04	-04	14	02	-06
Altruism											-04	-21	-04	02	-26	-05	12	-02	15
Practical Outlook												-21	-13	-18	00	04	-01	-10	-25
MHA Verbal Reasoning													39	48	50	19	-38	19	-02
TGA Concrete Generalizing														56	22	22	-31	-15	-32
Abstract Generalizing															07	18	-32	06	-37
EFT Field Independence																22	-42	-05	-04
MFF Reflectiveness																	-52	-01	-07
Inaccuracy																		08	20
TC Flexibility																			59
VO Verbal Fluency																			

Decimal points omitted
Correlations of above .22 are significant at 5% level

APPENDIX

Table A4   CORRELATIONS BETWEEN THE SCALES OF THE 'APPROACHES TO STUDYING' INVENTORY AND THE INVENTORY OF LEARNING PROCESSES (N = 269)

Learning Processes	Meaning Orientation			Reproducing Orientation					Achieving Orientation				Learning Style			
	DA	RI	UE	IM	SA	SB	FF	EM	ST	OM*	PA*	AM	CL	GL	OL	IP
Deep Processing	.14	.10	.23	.13	-.39	-.22	-.41	-26	.21	28	19	04	12	-34	-13	-40
Elaborative processing	36	39	34	33	-23	-22	-22	-19	18	18	15	06	26	00	02	-14
Fact retention	05	-03	06	05	-07	-07	-18	-08	26	16	16	12	00	-27	-06	-12
Methodical study	38	30	32	43	-07	-20	00	-05	34	49	26	24	00	-06	08	12

* The directions of scoring have been reversed to indicate organized study methods and positive attitudes.

This analysis was carried out at Southern Illinois by Dr. Schmeck, and became available too late to incorporate comments on these relationships in the text. These tentative findings confirm the suggestion that our reproducing orientation is similar to 'shallow processing'. Meaning orientation turns out to overlap substantially, with elaborative processing, as expected, but also with 'methodical study'. Our achieving orientation covers deep processing, methodical study, and fact retention, while our pathology scales are negatively related to deep processing and to a less extent to fact retention. Our 'styles' dimensions show little overall correspondence, although there is some link between comprehension learning and elaborative processing. These correlations imply a good deal of overlap between the two inventories in the domain that is being measured, but little conceptual agreement on the dimensions involved.

Table A5   ITEMS CONTAINED IN THE FINAL RESEARCH VERSION OF THE
COURSE PERCEPTIONS QUESTIONNAIRE

Corrected item-scale
correlation

Formal teaching methods (alpha = 0.70)

FT1	A great deal of my time is taken up by timetabled classes (lectures, practicals, tutorials, etc)	0.49
FT2	You can learn nearly everything you need to know from the classes and lectures; it isn't necessary to do much further reading	0.56
FT3	In this department you're expected to spend a lot of time studying on your own *	0.38
FT4	Lectures in this department are basically a guide to reading *	0.44
FT5	Lectures seem to be more important than tutorials or discussion groups in this department	0.43

Clear goals and standards (0.76)

CG1	You usually have a clear idea of where you're going and what's expected of you in this department	0.54
CG2	It's always easy here to know the standard of work expected of you	0.60
CG3	It's hard to know how well you're doing in the courses here *	0.42
CG4	Lecturers here usually tell students exactly what they are supposed to be learning	0.50
CG5	Lecturers here generally make it clear right from the start what will be required of students	0.58

Workload (0.80)

WL1	The workoad here is too heavy	0.54
WL2	It sometimes seems to me that the syllabus tries to cover too many topics	0.19
WL3	There is so much written work to be done that it is very difficult to get down to independent reading	0.29

* reversed scoring

238

Workload (0.80) (continued)

WL4   There seems to be too much work to get
through in the courses here   0.53

WL5   There's a lot of pressure on you as a
student here   0.39

Vocational Relevance (0.78)

VR1   The courses in this department are geared to
students' future employment   0.50

VR2   Lecturers in this department are keen to
point out that they are giving us a pro-
fessional training   0.34

VR3   The courses here seem to be pretty well
determined by vocational requirements   0.50

VR4   The work I do here will definitely improve
my future employment prospects   0.19

VR5   There seems to be considerable emphasis
here on inculcating the 'right' pro-
fessional attitudes   0.27

Good teaching (0.67)

GT1   Lecturers here frequently give the
impression that they haven't anything to
learn from students *   0.32

GT2   Most of the staff here seem to prepare
their teaching very thoroughly   0.40

GT3   Lecturers in this department seem to be
good at pitching their teaching at the
right level for us   0.42

GT4   Staff here make a real effort to understand
difficulties students may be having with
their work   0.49

GT5   The lecturers in this department always seem
ready to give help and advice on approaches
to studying   0.47

Freedom in learning (0.72)

FL1   There is a real opportunity in this department for students to choose the particular
areas they want to study   0.48

---

* reversed scoring

Freedom in Learning (0.72) (continued)

FL2 The department really seems to encourage us to develop our own academic interests as far as possible   0.38

FL3 We seem to be given a lot of choice here in the work we have to do   0.55

FL4 This department gives you a chance to use methods of study which suit your own way of learning   0.45

FL5 Students have a great deal of choice over how they are going to learn in this department   0.53

Openness to students (0.70)

OS1 Most of the staff here are receptive to suggestions from students for changes to their teaching methods   0.43

OS2 Staff generally consult students before making decisions about how the courses are organized   0.36

OS3 Most of the lecturers here really try hard to get to know students   0.53

OS4 Lecturers in this department seem to go out of their way to be friendly towards students   0.51

OS5 Lecturers in this department generally take students' ideas and interests seriously   0.47

Social climate (0.65)

SC1 A lot of the students in this department are friends of mine   0.40

SC2 Students from this department often get together socially   0.49

SC3 This department seems to foster a friendly climate which helps students to get to know each other   0.53

SC4 This department organizes meetings and talks which are usually well attended   0.25

SC5 Students in this department frequently discuss their work with each other   0.36

Table A6   MEANS OF SUBSCALES AND RANGES OF DEPARTMENTAL MEAN
SCORES, BY DISCIPLINE

Subscale	ENGLISH		HISTORY	
	Mean	Range	Mean	Range
Approaches to studying				
Deep approach	11.2	10.2 - 12.7	11.3	10.4 - 12.0
Relating ideas	10.5	8.6 - 11.5	10.1	9.6 - 11.2
Use of evidence	9.4	9.1 - 9.6	9.5	8.9 - 10.6
Intrinsic motivation	9.5	8.1 - 10.3	8.5	7.3 - 9.6
Surface approach	12.9	11.0 - 14.7	12.4	11.2 - 14.0
Syllabus-boundness	7.0	5.4 - 8.1	7.6	6.4 - 8.7
Fear of failure	5.8	4.5 - 6.9	5.7	5.0 - 6.4
Extrinisic motivation	2.8	1.5 - 5.1	3.3	2.0 - 4.4
Strategic approach	9.8	8.3 - 10.6	9.8	8.9 - 11.1
Disorganized study methods	9.2	7.8 - 11.4	8.2	7.1 - 10.6
Negative attitudes	4.5	4.4 - 6.3	5.9	5.0 - 6.4
Achievement motivation	9.0	8.0 - 10.0	9.0	8.0 - 10.0
Comprehension learning	11.0	10.0 - 11.7	8.7	7.8 - 10.0
Globetrotting	7.8	6.8 - 8.9	7.2	6.3 - 8.5
Operation learning	8.6	7.5 - 9.4	9.8	8.5 - 10.7
Improvidence	6.8	4.4 - 8.4	7.1	6.3 - 8.0
Perceptions of course				
Formal teaching methods	3.3	2.5 - 5.3	2.7	2.1 - 3.6
Clear goals and standards	6.7	3.6 - 9.5	8.0	6.2 - 10.2
Workload	10.0	5.6 - 12.3	11.2	7.5 - 14.8
Vocational relevance	3.9	3.1 - 4.7	4.8	3.5 - 5.6
Good teaching	11.4	8.1 - 13.8	11.8	9.8 - 14.0
Freedom in learning	11.7	7.4 - 15.8	11.2	5.0 - 13.2
Openness to students	8.5	5.9 - 13.5	7.7	4.2 - 9.8
Social climate	9.0	6.9 - 13.6	9.2	6.9 - 10.3

(Continued)

Table A6   MEANS OF SUBSCALES AND RANGES OF DEPARTMENTAL MEAN
SCORES, BY DISCIPLINE (continued)

Subscale	PSYCHOLOGY		ECONOMICS	
	Mean	Range	Mean	Range

Approaches to Studying

Subscale	Mean	Range	Mean	Range
Deep approach	10.8	9.9 – 12.4	10.2	8.4 – 12.1
Relating ideas	10.9	10.1 – 12.0	10.1	8.9 – 11.8
Use of evidence	9.6	8.5 – 11.0	9.4	8.7 – 10.4
Intrinsic motivation	9.3	7.3 – 10.5	7.0	4.9 – 9.6
Surface approach	12.8	11.7 – 14.1	13.8	12.8 – 15.0
Syllabus-boundness	7.7	6.4 – 8.6	8.8	7.5 – 9.5
Fear of failure	5.9	4.8 – 7.0	6.0	4.6 – 7.5
Extrinsic motivation	4.5	2.8 – 5.6	7.9	5.1 – 9.4
Strategic approach	10.2	8.8 – 11.2	10.3	9.5 – 10.8
Disorganized study methods	9.9	8.7 – 13.0	9.4	8.1 – 11.0
Negative attitudes	5.3	4.2 – 8.6	5.6	4.3 – 6.7
Achievement motivation	8.8	7.3 – 9.9	10.0	9.2 – 11.0
Comprehension learning	9.0	7.9 – 10.1	7.7	6.2 – 9.2
Globetrotting	8.2	7.4 – 9.3	7.8	6.9 – 8.5
Operation learning	9.2	8.2 – 10.2	10.8	10.1 – 12.0
Improvidence	7.4	6.2 – 8.7	8.4	7.6 – 9.0

Perceptions of courses

Subscale	Mean	Range	Mean	Range
Formal teaching methods	6.7	3.8 – 9.1	6.7	5.5 – 7.8
Clear goals and standards	8.6	5.6 – 11.9	11.0	8.4 – 12.7
Workload	9.0	5.3 – 12.6	9.0	5.6 – 13.5
Vocational relevance	6.5	4.7 – 8.4	8.2	6.2 – 9.0
Good teaching	11.8	9.2 – 14.0	11.8	8.0 – 14.1
Freedom in learning	9.7	7.9 – 12.6	10.4	7.4 – 12.6
Openness to students	9.9	7.4 – 12.8	8.7	6.2 – 11.8
Social climate	11.5	10.2 – 13.5	9.9	7.8 – 12.0

(Continued)

Table A6   MEANS OF SUBSCALES AND RANGES OF DEPARTMENTAL MEAN
            SCORES, BY DISCPLINE (continued)

Subscale	PHYSICS		ENGINEERING	
	Mean	Range	Mean	Range
Approaches to Studying				
Deep approach	10.1	8.5 - 11.9	10.4	8.4 - 12.0
Relating ideas	9.3	8.2 - 10.9	9.6	8.2 - 11.8
Use of evidence	9.8	8.6 - 10.3	9.9	9.0 - 11.0
Intrinsic motivation	8.8	7.9 - 9.9	7.3	5.3 - 10.1
Surface approach	13.2	10.9 - 14.7	13.2	10.8 - 16.1
Syllabus-boundness	8.6	7.6 - 9.9	9.2	8.5 - 10.1
Fear of failure	5.5	4.9 - 6.2	6.2	5.0 - 7.4
Extrinsic motivation	5.7	4.0 - 8.6	8.0	6.5 - 10.0
Strategic approach	10.6	9.2 - 11.5	10.5	8.5 - 11.5
Disorganized study methods	9.6	8.1 - 10.9	9.8	8.0 - 11.7
Negative attitudes	5.8	4.6 - 6.9	5.4	4.5 - 6.9
Achievement motivation	9.8	8.5 - 11.5	10.7	9.4 - 11.4
Comprehension learning	8.2	6.3 - 9.9	8.0	6.4 - 10.3
Globetrotting	7.4	6.3 - 8.2	7.5	6.6 - 8.6
Operation learning	10.1	9.2 - 11.8	11.1	9.7 - 12.8
Improvidence	7.4	4.9 - 8.4	7.8	6.7 - 9.3
Perceptions of courses				
Formal teaching methods	12.0	9.6 - 13.5	12.1	10.0 - 16.2
Clear goals and standards	11.4	10.0 - 13.3	12.2	11.5 - 13.8
Workload	9.9	8.4 - 12.1	12.9	5.5 - 14.3
Vocational relevance	8.9	5.3 - 12.6	13.4	9.0 - 15.1
Good teaching	11.8	10.7 - 12.8	11.4	9.1 - 13.2
Freedom in learning	8.2	6.3 - 11.3	8.1	5.8 - 11.7
Openness to students	9.2	6.4 - 12.1	8.6	6.7 - 11.1
Social climate	11.2	9.0 - 12.7	11.0	8.3 - 13.9